Basic Vowels	"I" Diphthongs (vowel #6 added to basic vowels)	(added to basic vowels)	various vowels)
1. 아 a (f<u>a</u>ther)	1a. 애 ae (h<u>a</u>t)	1b. 야 ya	와 wa (w<u>a</u>ter)
2. 어 ŏ (h<u>u</u>t)	2a. 에 e (s<u>e</u>t)	2b. 여 yŏ	왜 wae (w<u>e</u>t)
3. 오 o (h<u>o</u>me)	3a. 외 oe (w<u>e</u>t)	3b. 요 yo	워 wŏ (w<u>o</u>n)
4. 우 u (pl<u>u</u>me)	4a. 위 ui (w<u>e</u>)	4b. 유 yu	
5. 으 ŭ (s<u>oo</u>t)*	5a. 의 ŭi (w<u>e</u>)*		
6. 이 i (b<u>ee</u>t)			

*Pronounce without pursing the lips.

The "o" written with each vowel is an unvoiced consonant which functions to indicate where an initial consonant may be affixed to the vowel when writing a syllable. See the inside back cover for information on forming syllables.

A Guide to
KOREAN CHARACTERS

A Guide to
KOREAN
CHARACTERS

Reading and Writing
Hangŭl and *Hanja*

SECOND REVISED EDITION

by
BRUCE K. GRANT

HOLLYM

Copyright ©1982, 1979
by Bruce K. Grant

Second revised edition, 1982
Fourteenth printing, 1996
by Hollym International Corp.
18 Donald Place
Elizabeth, New Jersey 07208 U.S.A.
Phone: (908)353-1655   Fax: (908)353-0255

Published simultaneously in Korea
by Hollym Corporation; Publishers
14-5 Kwanchol-dong, Chongno-gu
Seoul 110-111, Korea
Phone: (02)735-7554   Fax: (02)730-5149

ISBN: 0-930878-13-2

Printed in Korea

For Audrey
    Michele
    Denise
    Mirae
    Bruce
    Maynard
    Monique
and Taylor

PREFACE

This book was designed as a guide for those who wish to learn written Korean. It presents for the first time in English the information necessary to read and write *hangŭl*, the Korean alphabet, and the 1,800 Chinese characters taught in Korean schools. *A Guide to Korean Characters* contains simplified charts explaining *hangŭl* and models showing exactly how to write each of the 1,800 Basic Characters. Sample vocabulary words, selected on the basis of frequency of use, are included for each character. This handbook also functions as a character dictionary since its entries are arranged in stroke-count order and it contains both a radical and a phonetic index.

I am very grateful to those who have helped in the preparation of *A Guide to Korean Characters*. Mr. Cho Pyŏng-ha was indefatiguable, and the writing models in the text are examples of his graceful calligraphy. Dr. Chŏn Yŏng-ch'ŏl and Mr. Yi Pang-hŏn kindly read the entire manuscript and made many useful suggestions. I am indebted to Mr. Chu Shin-wŏn, Chief Editor at Hollym Corporation: Publishers, for his patient guidance. I alone, of course, am responsible for errors.

Seoul, Korea

Bruce K. Grant
July 1979

CONTENTS

INTRODUCTION

THE KOREAN WRITING SYSTEM

Korean is a member of the Altaic family of languages and is very similar to Japanese. It has been spoken on the Korean peninsula for more than 2,000 years but has enjoyed an indigenous writing system since only the fifteenth century. Chinese exerted an early influence on Korean, and loan words from the Chinese now comprise about sixty percent of the Korean vocabulary.

Chinese is essentially uninflected, while Korean is polysynthetic. So different, in fact, are the two languages that Chinese and English have more in common than do Chinese and Korean. Ancient Koreans found Chinese ideographs unsuited to phonetically represent their richly inflected language, so they adopted written Chinese itself. Literate Koreans wrote one language, classical Chinese, and spoke another, Korean, until the dawn of the twentieth century, a period in excess of 1,500 years.

In 1440, King Sejong of the Yi Dynasty set a group of scholars to the task of inventing a means of writing the Korean language. The resulting phonetic alphabet was promulgated in 1446 but did not enjoy widespread use. *Hangŭl*, as it is now called, is perhaps the most scientific alphabet in general use in the world.

In 1972, the Ministry of Education of the Republic of Korea directed that 1,800 Sino-Korean characters, *hanja*, be taught in all middle and high schools in the nation. These are commonly called the Basic Characters, and each is treated in this book. Modern Korean is written in a mixed script in which *hanja* is used for Chinese loan words and *hangŭl* for purely Korean items.

HINTS ON LEARNING *HANGŬL*

The Korean alphabet is so simple that its sixteen totally

11

distinct letters can be learned in minutes with the aid of the *hangŭl*-in-a-hurry charts at the inside front cover of this book. Use these charts to decode *hangŭl* appearing in the book and elsewhere until it becomes entirely familiar to you. The charts at the inside back cover illustrate how to write each *hangŭl* letter and how to combine the letters into syllables.

Korean consonants are pronounced much as they are in English, though they annoyingly assume different shades of sound when they appear as initials, medials, or finals. The five stressed consonants are pronounced with greatest possible stress but with no expulsion of air. For example, "tt" (ㄸ) is pronounced akin to the d of don't in "Don't do that!" The aspirated consonants are pronounced with a heavy expulsion of air. The "k'" (ㅋ) is similar, for example, to the k of kill in "Kill that rattlesnake!" Vowels are pronounced essentially as noted on the inside front cover. Access to a native speaker is recommended for refined pronunciation.

HISTORY OF CHINESE CHARACTERS

In ancient China, pieces of bone and shell were incised with characters and then heated. The resulting cracks among the characters were used by oracles to foretell the future. Thousands of such "oracle bones" have been unearthed. The characters on them, the oldest extant, date from about 1,400 B.C. Virtually all principles for the formation of ideographs are evident on the oracle bones, suggesting a long period of development prior to 1,400 B.C. After that time, characters underwent a continuing evolution of form that ended about 2,000 years ago with the development of the "square characters" still used today. The following chart traces four characters through this evolution and illustrates character styles which a modern reader is likely to encounter. Dates are very approximate.

Forms of Chinese Characters

TYPE	Up	Sun	Moon	Horse
Oracle Bone Characters (circa 1,400 B.C.)				
Bronze Inscription Characters (Chou Dynasty, circa 900 B.C.)				
Greater Seal Characters (Chou Dynasty, circa 600 B.C.)				
Lesser Seal Characters (Ch'in Dynasty, circa 221 B.C.)				
Abbreviated Characters (Ch'in Dynasty, circa 206 B.C.)				
Square Characters (Han Dynasty, circa 100 B.C.)				
Modern Brush Style (virtually identical to the Square Characters)				
Modern Pen Style (style used for the writing models in this book)				
Modern Typeface (used for the main entries in this book)				
Semi-cursive Style (fluent style common in handwriting)				
Grass Writing (an art form fully legible only to connoisseurs)				

13

THE SIX CATEGORIES OF CHINESE CHARACTERS

Characters traditionally have been classified into Six Categories according to how they were originally fabricated or how they later accrued meaning. An understanding of these categories can bring a sense of order to the beginning reader who is likely to be bewildered by a forest of seemingly unrelated graphs. Moreover, the characteristics of the different types of *hanja* suggest varying learning strategies for their mastery. The Sung Dynasty scholar, Chêng Ch'iao, apportioned 24,235 characters to the Six Categories, and his results provide an indication of the relative size of each category. (Kwŏn, page 2. See Bibliography.)

Category One: Simple Pictographs

Simple Pictographs were the first type of character fabricated by the ancient Chinese. They picture objects, such as tree, 木. The trunk, branches and roots of a tree can be seen even in this modern form of the character. Another Simple Pictograph is 日 (sun). This stylized character was originally round, and the line in its center represented rays of sunshine. Only 608 of the characters classified by Chêng Ch'iao are Simple Pictographs, but they are important because many of them are the building blocks from which other *hanja* are made.

A Simple Pictograph is easily learned by associating its shape and meaning.

Category Two: Simple Diagrams

Simple Diagrams were among the earliest characters made and depict relationships for which no picture can readily be drawn. Two common examples are 上 (up) and 下 (down). The diagrammatic nature of this pair is readily apparent. Simple Diagrams are best learned by associating shape and meaning. Chêng Ch'iao allotted 107 of his characters to this category.

Category Three: Simple Compounds

A subsequent development in the history of characters, Simple Compounds are truly ideographic. They were made from two or more existing characters whose combined meanings provide a clue to the denotation of the compound. The Simple Compound resulting from the union of 日 (sun) and 木 (tree) is 東. The new character is pronounced 동 (tong), and signifies "east," taking its meaning from the "sun" rising from behind a "tree" in the "east." A Simple Compound is best learned by relating its meaning to that of its constituent elements. Of the graphs classified by Chêng Ch'iao, 740 were Simple Compounds.

Category Four: Phonetic Compounds

About ninety percent of the characters of Chêng Ch'iao, 21,811 *hanja*, are Phonetic Compounds. These graphs can be characterized as semi-ideographic and semi-phonetic since each is composed of a semantic element which furnishes a hint to the general meaning of the compound and a phonetic element which provides a direct clue to its pronunciation.

The phonetic clue in the vast majority of Sino-Korean characters is a significant potential mnemonic aid but is widely regarded as of limited value. Chinese lexicography obscures the phonetic relationships among characters, and some Phonetic Compounds which share an identical phonetic element have differing readings either because they were not originally homophonous or because their pronunciations diverged during centuries of phonetic and dialectic evolution. Nevertheless, it is likely that the phonetic clue is underexploited rather than overexploited by students of *hanja*.

Category Five: Derived Meanings

Derived Meanings originally belonged to one of the first four categories of characters. The evolution of Chinese generated a need to assign abstract meanings to characters with concrete denotations. Graphs of this type took on abstract meanings but maintained their original denotation as well. An example is 交, originally a Simple Pictograph of a man sitting with crossed legs. Its derived meanings are "exchange, communicate, intercourse, mix, join." This leap in meaning is comprehensible to anyone who has watched old Korean gentlemen sit cross legged by the hour and "communicate" with cronies. Chêng Ch'iao assigned 372 of his characters to this category. Its characters are best learned by relating their original and derived meanings.

Category Six: Arbitrary Meanings

Characters of this type also belonged to one of the first four categories and took on additional denotations, but they surrendered their original meanings altogether. An example is 來 , a Simple Pictograph of a growing stalk of grain. Other characters possessed the same meaning, but there was no character for "to come," which was pronounced the same as 來 . As a homophone, 來 was pressed into service to denote "to come" and has maintained only that meaning for millenia. Graphs of this category account for 598 of the characters of Chêng Ch'iao. They are best learned arbitrarily.

HINTS ON LEARNING *HANJA*

There is no royal road to learning characters, but the task is not as difficult as it may appear, either. The sheer number of *hanja* is daunting; large character dictionaries may run to 50,000 entries. But no one need learn anything like this ridiculous number, and fewer than 300 discrete graphs compose all others. A study in Taiwan showed that the most common 400 characters in use there comprised fully seventy-three percent of all written material. (DeFrancis, page xix.)

The learning of Chinese characters will unavoidably entail some memorization. Homemade flash cards and repeated writing of characters can be valuable memorization aids. Anything, including *hanja*, is easier to learn when approached as part of a meaningful context. Those already participating in a Korean language program can easily meld specific information about the 1,800 Basic Characters into their language materials. Those undertaking independent study can meld characters into available selections of written Korean . The vocabulary words accompanying each character in this book can also supply a measure of meaningful context. The 900 middle school characters in the appendix can be useful because the most common and frequently used characters appear in this list in the order they are first learned by Korean pupils.

Early attention to radicals, the 214 characters under which all others are listed in *hanja* dictionaries, is recommended for all. Familiarity with the radicals is requisite to the full use of a dictionary, and many radicals are numbered among the discrete graphs which comprise all others. The radicals can be found in the radical index of this handbook.

A student of *hanja* will find it valuable to develop the habit of estimating to which of the Six Categories a target character belongs since this will enable him to choose an appropriate learning strategy for it. Consult the preceding section of the Introduction for suggestions on learning strategies for each of the Six Categories of Chinese characters.

The vast majority of characters, perhaps ninety percent of all *hanja*, belong to the Phonetic Compound category. Each graph of this type contains an internal clue to its own pro-nunciation. One beginning student schooled himself to look for this internal phonetic clue, and, on a quiz, successfully matched readings to eleven of thirteen Phonetic Compounds he had not previously encountered. The student will be well advised to make it a practice to estimate the reading of a target character, whether newly-encountered or unrecalled, by assigning to it the pronunciation of its major component elements.

A forthcoming handbook by the present editor will contain some 2,000 characters arranged in sets. Each graph in a set contains the same phonetic element and shares an identical or similar reading as well. The mnemonic value of a set of characters which both look and sound alike can be appreciated by perusing the following chart.

Phonetic Compound Set

Character	Reading	Meaning	Semantic Element	Meaning	Phonetic Element	Reading
東	동(tong)	east	(This base character is a Simple Compound.)			
凍	동(tong)	icy	冫	ice	東	동 (tong)
棟	동(tong)	ridgepole	木	wood, tree	東	동 (tong)

EXPLANATION OF A SAMPLE CHARACTER ENTRY

The character entry below is typical of the 1,800 in *A Guide to Korean Characters.*

Sample Entry

字 子 3 238	丶	丿	宀	글자 character, letter 자
	宀	宁	字	文字 character, letter, writing 문자 漢字 Sino-Korean characters, Chinese characters 한자 字典 character dictionary 자전

The main character of the sample entry, 字, is one of the Basic *Hanja* taught in all Korean secondary schools. It appears first in a large-type, slightly-abbreviated form common in published material. In the box beneath the main character is listed the radical under which it can be found in a character dictionary. This radical is given in its unabbreviated form, while it may appear in the main character in its common, abbreviated form. (A chart of abbreviated radicals appears on page 348.) The number to the right of the radical indicates the number of strokes in the non-radical portion of the main character, datum that is vital when using a *hanja* dictionary.

The 1,800 main entries are numbered consecutively. For 字, this number is 238. These character numbers are used in cross references and indices.

To the right of the main character are nine squares in which its proper stroke order is progressively illustrated. The complete pen-written form of the main character occurs as the final entry in these squares. It is important to compare and contrast the written and printed forms of the main character since both will be encountered in reading materials.

The formal definition, or *hun*, of the main character occurs in the upper left corner of the area following the writing models. The *hun* for the sample character is 글자. This is followed to the right by English definitions of the main character and by its reading, or *ŭm*, in boldface *hangŭl*. In the sample entry, this *ŭm* is 자. The *hun* and *ŭm* are ordinarily said together as a verbal means of identifying a character.

Sample vocabulary words comprise the remainder of the entry. These were selected on the basis of frequency of use in the language. Usually, three such words are included in an entry. The *hanja* typeface used for sample words is the stylized variation increasingly common in published material. Compare and contrast these with the main character typeface in an entry.

A Guide to Korean Characters is designed to aid in learning *hangŭl* and *hanja*. As a mini-dictionary, its English definitions are not exhaustive. For the convenience of the reader and to exploit limited space, many English definitions appear in verbal, adjectival or adverbial form even though Korean referents may occur only as nouns.

English definitions were purposely inserted between *hanja* entries and their *hangŭl* readings in order to cause the eye of the reader to encounter first *hanja* and then its English meaning before coming to pronunciation. This arrangement may facilitate the learning process by obliging the reader to relate form and meaning for milliseconds before dealing with pronunciation.

WRITING CHARACTERS

A general rule of writing is to make the graphs of uniform size no matter how simple or complex they may be. *Hanja* are listed in character dictionaries in ways inextricably related to stroke count. (See How to Use a Character Dictionary, p.347.) A character must be written, therefore, with strokes of constant shape set down in unvarying order. Details regarding stroke type and stroke order are provided below, but the reader will doubtless find the writing models accompanying each character in the text to be a more practical calligraphic guide.

Types of Strokes

The following chart illustrates eighteen types of strokes used in writing characters. The samples are done in brush style, but the principles also apply to pen calligraphy. Generally, perpendicular strokes are made from top to bottom, while horizontal strokes are made from left to right. Even when it includes an angle, a stroke is written without lifting pen from paper.

Types of Strokes

﹀	永	丶	室	丶	示	﹀	烈
一	三	丨	目	丨	中	㇄	民
亅	事	亅	手	丿	人	丶	木
﹀	道	㇟	成	㇄	心	乙	風
㇆	力	㇄	元				

The Rules of Stroke Order

Two basic rules govern stroke order.

    1. Top to bottom.

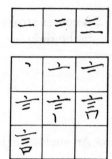

    2. Left to right.

Seven auxiliary rules also control the order of strokes.

    3. Horizontal strokes usually are written first when they cross perpendicular ones.

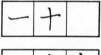

    4. Sometimes the reverse is true.

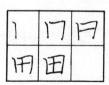

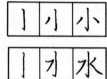

5. A center stroke is written first, then the left and finally the right.

6. An enclosure precedes its contents.

7. Diagonals running to the left precede diagonals flowing to the right.

8. A piercing perpendicular stroke is written last.

9. A piercing horizontal stroke is written last.

GLOSSARY

Basic Characters. Basic Characters are the 1,800 *hanja* taught by order of the Ministry of Education since 1972 in all Korean middle and high schools. Their formal name is "Basic Characters for Use in Classical Korean Instruction" (*hanmun kyoyukyong kich'o hanja*).

Basic *Hanja*. See Basic Characters.

Chinese Characters. See Six Categories of Chinese Characters.

Classical Korean. Classical Korean (*hanmun*) is classical Chinese used by Koreans as their written language for more than 1,500 years.

Hangŭl. *Hangŭl* is the modern name for the Korean alphabet promulgated in 1446 but not widely used until the present century.

Hanja. See Sino-Korean Characters.

Ideograph. An ideograph is a symbol representing an object or an idea but not the sound associated with that object or idea in spoken language.

Polysynthetic. Polysynthesism is the grammatical practice in Korean of combining word elements into a single word that can be the equivalent of phrases or even a sentence in English.

Phonetic Compound. One of the Six Categories of Chinese characters, Phonetic Compounds comprise some ninety percent of all characters. They are semi-ideographic and semi-phonetic.

Reading. The *ŭm*, or pronunciation, of a character is its reading.

Semantic Element. A semantic element is that part of a Phonetic Compound, usually one-half the total character, which provides a hint to the general meaning of the compound.

Simple Compounds.   One of the Six Categories of Chinese characters, Simple Compounds were formed from two elements whose combined meanings provide a clue to the denotation of the compound. They are ideographic.

Simple Diagrams.   One of the Six Categories of Chinese characters, Simple Diagrams depict relationships for which a picture cannot readily be drawn.

Simple Pictographs.   One of the Six Categories of Chinese characters, Simple Pictographs are drawings of objects. They were the first characters fabricated by the ancient Chinese.

Sino-Korean Characters.   Chinese characters as they are used in the Korean language.

Six Categories of Chinese Characters.   A traditional classification of Chinese characters into six types according to how they were originally fabricated or later accrued meaning. The Six Categories are Simple Pictographs, Simple Diagrams, Simple Compounds, Phonetic Compounds, Derived Meanings and Arbitrary Meanings.

THE 1,800 BASIC CHARACTERS

1 Stroke

一	一			한	one; unity; the same; the first, first	일
				一般	general, all, whole; alike	일반
一 0 1				一部	part, portion; a section	일부
				一切	all, the whole; wholly; absolutely	일체

乙	乙			새	2d of the 10 Heavenly Stems; the second	을
				甲論乙駁	the pros and cons	갑론을박
				乙種	class B; second grade	을종
乙 0 2				乙未	32d of the 60 binary terms of the sexagenary cycle	을미

2 Strokes

丁	一	丁		네째천간	4th of the 10 Heavenly Stems; person; T-shape	정
				壯丁	a strong young man, sturdy youth	장정
一 1 3				丁寧	surely, without fail	정녕

七	一	七		일곱	seven	칠
				七月	July	칠월
				七十	seventy	칠십
一 1 4				七旬	seventy days; seventy years	칠순

乃	ノ	乃		이에	also, and; but; then	내
				乃至	from… to…, between… and…; or	내지
ノ 1 5						

九	ノ	九		아홉	nine	구
				九月	September	구월
				九十	ninety	구십
				九死一生	a narrow escape from death	구사일생
乙 1 6						

了	フ	了		마칠	complete, finish; intelligent	료
				完了	complete, finish, conclude	완료
				修了	complete a course of study	수료
				終了	end, conclude, complete	종료
亅 1 7						

二	一	二		두	two	이
				二月	February	이월
				二種	two kinds, two classes; second class	이종
				二回	twice; two times; a second time	이회
二 0 8						

人	ノ	人		사람	man, mankind	인
				人物	person, man	인물
				人間	humans, a human being	인간
				人事	greeting; personal affairs	인사
人 0 9						

入	ノ	入		들	enter; put in	입
				入金	receive funds; pay on account	입금
				入學	matriculate; enter a school	입학
				收入	income, earnings	수입
入 0 10						

八 丿 八	여덟	eight	팔
	八月	August	팔월
	八道	the Eight Provinces of Korea	팔도
入 0 11	八方	the eight points of the compass; all directions; everywhere	팔방

刀 フ 刀	칼	knife, sword; razor	도
	短刀	short sword, dagger, stiletto	단도
	刀圭界	medical circles, the medical profession	도규계
刀 0 12	單刀直入	assault with one sword, get straight to the point	단도직입

力 フ 力	힘	strength, power	력
	努力	endeavor, exertion	노력
	武力	military force; armed, military	무력
力 0 13	力量	capability, capacity, ability	역량

十 一 十	열	ten	십 (시)
	十月	October	시월
	十二	twelve	십이
十 0 14	十字	a cross; a plus sign	십자

卜 丨 卜	점	divination; prognosticate; burden	복
	卜術	divination, fortune telling	복술
	問卜	have one's fortune told	문복
卜 0 15	卜師	fortune teller	복사

又 フ 又	또	and, also, again; in addition to, moreover, further	우
又 0 16	又況	much more, much less, still more, still less	우황

3 Strokes

三	一	二	三	석	three	**삼**
一 2 17				三角 三十 三寸	triangle; three-cornered thirty a paternal uncle	삼각 삼십 삼촌

上	一	卜	上	위	above; first, rise	**상**
一 2 18				上監 上流社會 上官	His Royal Majesty high society senior official	상감 상류사회 상관

丈	一	丈	丈	장부	ten feet; a senior	**장**
一 2 19				丈人 丈夫	father-in-law, a wife's father man, gentleman; full-grown man	장인 장부

下	一	丁	下	아래	below, down, low, under	**하**
一 2 20				下人 下流 下宿	servant downstream; lower social classes boarding, staying at a rooming house	하인 하류 하숙

丸	丿	九	丸	둥글	a pill; a bullet	**환**
丶 2 21				丸藥 丸劑 彈丸	pill, pellet pill, pellet bullet; projectile; shell	환약 환제 탄환

久	ノ	ク	久	오랠	a long time, finally	구
				長久	a long time, permanence	장구
				永久	permanence; perpetuity, eternity	영구
ノ 2 22				持久力	endurance, tenacity	지구력

也	フ	力	也	어조사	it is; also	야
				是也非也	right or wrong, true or false	시야비야
乙 2 23				或也	sometimes; maybe	혹야

于	一	于		어조사	on; to; with; from	우
				于今	till now, up to the present	우금
二 1 24				于先	first of all, before everything	우선

亡	丶	亠	亡	망할	die, perish; be lost; absent	망
				逃亡	flee, run away, escape	도망
				滅亡	be destroyed, collapse, fall	멸망
亠 1 25				亡命	defect, seek foreign refuge	망명

凡	)	几	凡	무릇	all; common; general; secular, earthly	범
				平凡	common, ordinary	평범
				大凡	in general, as a rule	대범
几 1 26				凡常	mediocre; common, ordinary	범상

刃	フ	刀	刃	칼날	knife blade, knife edge	인
				兵刃	bladed weapons; bayonets; weapons	병인
刀 1 27				自刃	kill oneself with a dagger	자인

千	ノ	二	千	일천	one thousand	천
				千萬	ten million	천만
				千秋	a thousand years	천추
				千字	a thousand characters	천자
十 1 28						

口	丨	冂	口	입	mouth, opening	구
				口實	excuse, pretext	구실
				口味	appetite	구미
				人口	population; inhabitants	인구
口 0 29						

土	一	十	土	흙	earth; local	토
				土地	land, real estate	토지
				土質	nature of the soil	토질
				土木	civil engineering	토목
土 0 30						

士	一	十	士	선비	scholar; gentleman; officer; soldier	사
				紳士	gentleman, man of honor	신사
				辯護士	lawyer, attorney	변호사
				勇士	brave man, man of courage	용사
士 0 31						

夕	ノ	夕	夕	저녁	evening, dusk	석
				夕陽	the setting sun, the evening sun	석양
				夕刊	evening edition	석간
				朝夕	morning and evening; breakfast and dinner	조석
夕 0 32						

大	一	ナ	大	큰	big, great	대
				大端히	very, very much, greatly	대단
				大部分	major portion, large part	대부분
				大學	college, university	대학
大 0 33						

女	ㄑ	ㄨ	女	계집	woman, girl	녀
				女性	women, womankind; feminity	여성
				男女	male and female, man and woman	남녀
女 0 34				女學生	female student, schoolgirl	여학생

子	ㄱ	了	子	아들	son, child	자
				子息	one's own child; a guy, a fellow	자식
				子孫	**descendants , sons and grandsons**	자손
子 0 35				子音	a consonant	자음

寸	一	寸	寸	마디	inch; degree of kinship	촌
				四寸	cousin	사촌
				寸數	degree of kinship	촌수
寸 0 36				寸劇	short dramatical performance; skit	촌극

小	丿	丿	小	작을	small; mean; concubine	소
				小説	novel, story; fiction	소설
				小賣	retail selling	소매
小 0 37				大小	large and small; size, magnitude	대소

山	丨	山	山	메	mountain, hill	산
				山脈	mountain range	산맥
				山林	forest, woodland	산림
山 0 38				山野	fields and mountains	산야

川	丿	川	川	내	stream	천
				川邊	stream bank, riverside	천변
				山川	mountains and rivers	산천
巛 0 39				大川	large river	대천

工	㇀	㇑	工	장인	labor; workman	공
				工業	industry; manufacturing industry	공업
				工夫	study, pursue scholarly activities	공부
工 0 40				工作	construct, build, maneuver, operate	공작

己	㇆	㇆	己	몸	6th of the 10 Heavenly Stems; self; private	기
				利己	selfishness, egoism	이기
				克己	self-denial, self-abnegation	극기
己 0 41				自己	one's self, self	자기

已	㇆	㇆	已	이미	already; finished	이
				已往	already, now that; the past	이왕
				不得已	unavoidably, inevitably	부득이
已 0 42				已往之事	bygones	이왕지사

巳	㇆	㇆	巳	뱀	6th of the 12 Earth's Branches; snake	사
				乙巳	42d of the 60 binary terms of the sexagenary cycle	을사
巳 0 43				乙巳士禍	literati purge of 1545	을사사화

干	一	二	干	방패	a shield; oppose, interfere	간
				若干	some, a little, a few; somewhat	약간
				干涉	intervene, meddle in	간섭
干 0 44				干拓	reclaim land by drainage	간척

弓	㇆	㇆	弓	활	a bow	궁
				弓術	archery, bowmanship	궁술
				弓手	archer, bowman	궁수
弓 0 45						

才	一	十	才	재주	talent	재
				人才	person of talent or ability	인재
				才能	ability, talents	재능
手 0 46				才幹	gift, talent, ability	재간

4 Strokes

不	一	丆	丆	아닐	no, not; un-, in-, non-	불 (부)
	不			不自然	unnatural	부자연
				不安	anxiety, uneasiness	불안
一 3 47				不過	only, merely, does not exceed	불과

丑	了	刀	丑	소	2d of the 12 Earth's Branches; ox	축
	丑			丑年	Year of the Ox	축년
				丑日	Day of the Ox	축일
一 3 48				丑時	the Watch of the Ox, the period between 1 and 3 A.M.	축시

中	丶	口	口	가운데	middle, within; China; hit, attain	중
	中			中心	the center, middle; balance	중심
				中等	medium quality	중등
	3 49			中間	the middle, center, medium, in-between	중간

丹	丿	门	丹	붉을	red, cinnabar; pill	단
	丹			丹楓	autumnal tints, red and yellow	단풍
				丹青	colors; red and green	단청
丶 3 50				一片丹心	fidelity; a sincere heart	일편단심

之	丶	宀	之	갈 go; arrive; of; it, him, her	지
				竹馬之友 a friend of bamboo stilts, a childhood friend	죽마지우
ノ 3 51				螢雪之功 success of glowworms and snow, success by diligent study	형설지공

云	一	二	云	이를 speak, say	운
	云			云云 et cetera; thus and thus, so and so	운운
二 2 52					

互	一	匸	互	서로 mutual	호
	互			互惠 mutual benefits, reciprocity	호혜
				互讓 mutual concession, compromise	호양
二 2 53				互選 co-optation, election by a group	호선

五	一	丁	五	다섯 five	오
	五			五月 May	오월
				五十 fifty	오십
				五倫 the five Confucian human relationships	오륜
二 2 54					

井	一	二	丰	우물 a well	정
	井			天井 ceiling	천정
				市井 streets, a town	시정
				井水 well water	정수
二 2 55					

今	ノ	人	今	이제 now, the present	금
	今			今年 this year	금년
				今番 this time	금번
				只今 now, the present time	지금
人 2 56					

36

					어질	humaneness, humanity	인
仁	ノ	イ	仁		仁慈	mercy; beneficence	인자
	仁				仁德	benevolence, humanity	인덕
人 2					仁義	benevolence and righteousness; humanity and justice	인의
57							

					끼일	individual, alone; unit; be between; introduce	개
介	ノ	人	介				
	介				介在	interposition, intervention	개재
					介入	intervene; introduce	개입
人 2					仲介	mediation, intermediation	중개
58							

					으뜸	first, head, chief, eldest, principal; large, great; dynasty	원
元	一	二	元				
	元				元帳	a ledger	원장
儿 2					元素	an original element	원소
59					元氣	vigor, vitality; energy	원기

					안	inside, within; wife, woman	내
内	丶	冂	内				
	内				内容	the substance, details; contents	내용
入 2					内部	the interior, the inner part, inside	내부
60							

					공변될	impartial, fair; public	공
公	ノ	八	公				
	公				公主	royal princess	공주
					公務員	civil servant, government employee	공무원
八 2					公評	public opinion; fair criticism	공평
61							

					여섯	six	륙 (유)
六	丶	亠	宀		六月	June	유월
	六				六十	sixty	육십
八 2					六書	the Six Categories of Chinese Characters	육서
62							

兮	ノ	八	亠	어조사	an exclamatory particle in classical Korean	혜
	兮					
八 2 63						

凶	ノ	メ	凶	흉할	cruel; evil; unfortunate; ugly	흉
	凶			凶年	a year of famine	흉년
				凶惡	wicked, bad	흉악
凵 2 64				凶作	a poor crop	흉작

分	ノ	八	分	나눌	divide; separate; duty; distinguish; measure; part; minute	분
	分			分量	a quantity, a measure, an amount	분량
刀 2 65				分科	a department, a section	분과

切	一	土	切	끊을	slice, cut, mince; earnest, urge	절
	切			온통	all, entirely	체
				切實	be immediate, real	절실
				一切	all, the whole; wholly; absolutely	일체
刀 2 66				切斷	cut off, sever	절단

勿	ノ	勹	勿	말	do not	물
	勿			勿論	of course	물론
				勿忘草	a forget-me-not flower	물망초
				勿驚	surprise, surprisingly enough	물경
勹 2 67						

化	ノ	亻	亻	될	transform, change	화
	化			惡化	deteriorate, aggravate, worsen	악화
				化學	chemistry	화학
匕 2 68				感化	inspire, influence	감화

38

| 匹
匸 2
69 | 一　厂　兀
匹 | 짝 | a roll; one of a pair; a horse; a cow | 필 |
| | | 配匹
匹敵
匹夫匹婦 | a spouse, a mate
a rival, an equal
Dick and Jane, common men and women | 배필
필적
필부필부 |

| 升
十 2
70 | ノ　ニ　チ
升 | 되 | ascend, rise, advance in office; a quart | 승 |
| | | 三升布 | course hemp cloth, 60-strand warp | 삼승포 |

| 午
十 2
71 | ノ　一　二
午 | 낮 | 7th of the 12 Earth's Branches; horse | 오 |
| | | 午後
午前
午睡 | the afternoon, P.M.
the morning, A.M.
midday nap, siesta | 오후
오전
오수 |

| 厄
厂 2
72 | 一　厂　厃
厄 | 액운 | difficulty, distressed | 액 |
| | | 厄運
橫厄
災厄 | misfortune, bad luck
unexpected misfortune
calamity, disaster | 액운
횡액
재액 |

| 及
又 2
73 | ノ　ア　乃
及 | 미칠 | extend, reach to; and, also | 급 |
| | | 言及
普及
及第 | mention, say
propagate, disseminate
pass an examination; pass the state examination | 언급
보급
급제 |

| 反
又 2
74 | 一　厂　万
反 | 돌이킬 | against, anti-; contrary, but, instead of; rebel; retreat | 반 |
| | | 反對
反省
反逆 | opposition, resistance; opposite
reflection; meditation
revolt, rebellion | 반대
반성
반역 |

友	一	ナ	友	벗	friend	우
	友			友邦	a friendly nation, an ally	우방
				友愛	fraternity, brotherliness	우애
又 2 75				親友	an intimate friend, a close friend	친우
壬	ノ	二	千	아홉째천간	9th of the 10 Heavenly Stems	임
	壬			壬辰倭亂	Japanese invasion of Korea in 1592	임진왜란
士 1 76				壬午	19th of the 60 binary terms of the sexagenary cycle	임오
天	一	二	天	하늘	heaven, nature; Nature; God, divine; weather	천
	天			天下	the universe; the world; the realm	천하
大 1 77				天體	a heavenly body, a celestial sphere	천체
夫	一	二	夫	사내	husband; man; laborer, artisan; sage, philosopher	부
	夫			夫婦	husband and wife, a married couple	부부
大 1 78				農夫	farmer, peasant	농부
太	一	ナ	大	클	great, grand; excessive, extreme	태
	太			太陽	the sun	태양
大 1 79				太極旗	the Korean national flag, Flag of the Great Ultimate	태극기
孔	ㄱ	了	子	구멍	hole, opening; Confucius	공
	孔			孔雀	a peacock, a peafowl	공작
				孔子	Confucius	공자
子 1 80				孔孟	Confucius and Mencius	공맹

少	丿	小	小	젊을	young; small; scarce; seldom; briefly	소
	少			少年	youth, a youth, a boy	소년
				少將	a major general	소장
小 1 81				少量	small amount, small quantity	소량

尤	一	ナ	尤	더욱	more, moreover	우
	尤			尤甚	extreme, severe	우심
尤 1 82						

尺	ㄱ	ㄹ	尸	자	a Chinese foot, a *ch'ŏk* (30.3 centimeters, 11.9 inches)	척
	尺			咫尺	a very short distance	지척
				三尺童子	a mere child	삼척동자
尸 1 83				尺數	number of feet, length	척수

弔	ㄱ	ㄹ	弓	조상	condolence; mourn; hang, droop; demand, ask for	조
	弔			弔客	a visitor of condolence	조객
				弔詞	a letter of condolence, a message of condolence	조사
弓 1 84				弔喪	condolence	조상

引	ㄱ	ㄹ	弓	끌	lead, guide; introduce	인
	引			引上	rise, increase; pulling up	인상
				引力	attraction; affinity; magnetism	인력
弓 1 85				引繼	transfer of duties	인계

心	丶	心	心	마음	heart, moral, nature, mind, affections; intention; core; center	심
	心			心理	a mental state; psychology	심리
				心情	affection; one's feelings	심정
心 0 86				心臟	the heart	심장

41

4 strokes

戈	一	弋	戈	창	spear, lance	과
	戈			兵戈	conflict, war, crossing of lances; lance, spear	병 과
戈 0 87				戈鋒	spear tip	과 봉

戶	丶	宀	宀	지게	door; family	호
	户			戶籍	governmental vital statistics register, a family register	호 적
戶 0 88				戶口	houses and inhabitants, population	호 구

手	丿	二	三	손	hand	수
	手			手段	means, measure, method	수 단
				手數料	commission, fee, service charge	수수료
手 0 89				手足	hands and feet, limbs	수 족

支	一	十	古	지탱할	prop, support; pay, expend; branch	지
	支			支拂	pay, disburse	지 불
				支配	manage, control	지 배
支 0 90				支店	branch office	지 점

文	丶	亠	宁	글월	characters, letters, writing, literature; culture; civil officials	문
	文			文化	culture; civilization	문 화
				文明	civilization; culture	문 명
文 0 91				文人	a literatus, a man of letters	문 인

斗	丶	冫	三	말	a dry measure (18 liters, 3.97 gallons)	두
	斗			泰斗	an authority, a luminary, a star	태 두
斗 0 92				斗量	measuring by pecks (*mal*)	두 량

斤	ノ	′	⼌
	斤		

도끼 an ax; a *kŭn*, a catty (600 grams, 1.32 pounds) — 근

斤量 weight 근량
斤數 poundage, weight 근수
斤重 weight 근중

斤 0 93

方	、	亠	方
	方		

모 direction; square; region; plan; recipe; just now — 방

方法 method, way, means 방법
方針 objective, aim; a magnetic needle 방침
方面 direction; aspect, angle 방면

方 0 94

日	丨	冂	日
	日		

날 sun, day; daily; Japan — 일

日常 everyday, common 일상
日曜日 Sunday 일요일
日記 a diary; a journal 일기

日 0 95

曰	丨	冂	曰
	曰		

가로 speak; say, it is said — 왈

曰可曰否 argue pro and con 왈가왈부
孔子曰 Confucius said 공자왈
曰牌 a female ruffian; a rowdy 왈패

曰 0 96

月	丿	几	月
	月		

달 moon, month — 월

月給 monthly salary 월급
月刊 a monthly magazine, a monthly publication 월간
月末 the end of the month, end of a month 월말

月 0 97

木	一	十	才
	木		

나무 tree, wood, wooden — 목

木手 a carpenter 목수
木材 lumber, timber, wood 목재
木星 the planet Jupiter 목성

木 0 98

止	⌐	⌐	⌐	그칠	stop; desist; rest	지
	止			中止	discontinue, suspend, interrupt	중지
				止血	staunch bleeding	지혈
止 0 99				防止	preserve, protect; prevent, check	방지

比	一	上	上'	비할	compare	비
	比			比較	compare	비교
				比例	comparison; proportion, ratio	비례
比 0 100				比率	ratio, percentage	비율

毛	'	⌐	⌐	털	hair, fur, down, feathers	모
	毛			毛織物	woolen fabrics, woolen goods	모직물
				毛細管	a capillary	모세관
毛 0 101				毛筆	a hair brush for calligraphy	모필

氏	'	⌐	仁	성	clan name, surname; clan, family; Mr.; female; woman's maiden name	씨
	氏					
				氏族	a clan, a family	씨족
氏 0 102				氏名	surname and personal name, one's full name	씨명

水	]	기	水	물	water; fluid, liquid	수
	水			水素	hydrogen	수소
				水產	marine products	수산
水 0 103				水平	the water level; the horizon	수평

火	`	``	⌐	불	fire	화
	火			火山	volcano	화산
				火災	a fire, a conflagration	화재
火 0 104				火力	firepower; the force of a fire	화력

父 `丶` `八` `ぅ` `父` 父 0 105	아비	father	부
	父母	father and mother, parents	부모
	父親	father, one's father	부친
	學父兄	parents of students	학부형

片 `丿` `丿` `丿` `片` 片 0 106	조각	piece, strip, bit	편
	片紙	a letter	편지
	片肉	sliced boiled meat	편육
	片心	a one-sided mind, eccentricity	편심

牙 `一` `二` `乎` `牙` 牙 0 107	어금니	tooth; molars; tusk, ivory	아
	象牙	ivory	상아
	齒牙	teeth	치아
	牙城	citadel, inner stronghold	아성

牛 `丿` `丿` `二` `牛` 牛 0 108	소	cow, ox	우
	牛乳	cow's milk	우유
	牛耳讀經	"Read classics into a cow's ear", cast pearls to swine	우이독경
	牛馬	cattle and horses	우마

犬 `一` `ナ` `大` `犬` 犬 0 109	개	dog	견
	狂犬病	rabies, hydrophobia	광견병
	愛犬	a pet dog	애견
	犬猿之間	be at odds with each other	견원지간

王 `一` `二` `干` `王` 玉 0 110	임금	king; royal	왕
	王后	queen, queen consort	왕후
	王子	prince	왕자
	王室	royal family, a king's household	왕실

予	ㄱ	マ	予	나	I, me; same, similar	여
	予					
⌯ 3 111						

5 Strokes

且	丨	冂	月	또	moreover, further, also	차
	月	且		苟且	poor, destitute; ignoble, unworthy	구차
一 4 112						

世	一	十	卅	인간	a generation; a lifetime; an age; world, society	세
	丗	世		世界	the world, the earth	세계
				世上	the world; society; a lifetime	세상
一 4 113				世代	a generation	세대

丘	ノ	仃	仁	언덕	hill, hillock	구
	斤	丘		丘陵	a hill, a hillock	구릉
				比丘僧	a Buddhist monk	비구승
一 4 114						

丙	一	丆	丙	남녘	3d of the 10 Heavenly Stems ; the third	병
	丙	丙		丙寅	3d of the 60 binary terms of the sexagenary cycle	병인
				丙種	third class, third grade	병종
一 4 115						

46

主	`丶`	`二`	`亖`	주인	lord, master, ruler; chief, principal	주
	`主`	`主`		主人	a landlord; the head of a family; a host	주인
`丶` 4 116		`.`		主張	assert, maintain, claim, advocate	주장

乎	`丿`	`丷`	`丷`	온	exclamation; interrogative final particle	호
	`丷`	`乎`		斷乎	be firm, decisive, resolute	단호
`丿` 4 117						

他	`丿`	`亻`	`们`	다를	other	타
	`仂`	`他`		他人	another person; a stranger	타인
				自他	self and others	자타
人 3 118				其他	and so forth, and the others, et cetera	기타

仕	`丿`	`亻`	`仁`	벼슬	be a government official, fill an office	사
	`什`	`仕`		給仕	office boy; errand girl; page; bell hop; waiter, waitress	급사
人 3 119				奉仕	service; render service	봉사

付	`丿`	`亻`	`亻`	붙을	transfer, hand over; commit to; pay	부
	`付`	`付`		付託	ask, solicit, request; charge with, entrust with	부탁
				送付	remit, forward, send	송부
人 3 120				交付	transfer, hand over, pass along	교부

仙	`丿`	`亻`	`亻`	신선	Taoist immortal, fairy, genie	선
	`仙`	`仙`		仙女	fairy, nymph	선녀
				神仙	Taoist immortal; hermit, ascetic; a spirit	신선
人 3 121				仙人	hermit, ascetic; a spirit; Taoist immortal	선인

代	丿	亻	仁	대신할 substitute; generation	대
	代	代		代身 in place of, instead of	대신
				代表 represent; be exemplary	대표
人 3 122				代理 acting, acting in lieu of, proxy	대리

令	丿	人	仐	명령할 command, order; causes; good; term of respect	령
	今	令		命令 command, order	명령
				司令官 commanding officer	사령관
人 3 123				假令 if, supposing, suppose that; even if	가령

以	丶	乚	以	써 through; with; by; from; reason, since	이
	以	以		以上 more than; beyond; that is all	이상
				以北 north of; north Korea	이북
人 3 124				所以 reason, the reason, the reason why	소이

兄	丶	口	口	맏 elder brother; seniors	형
	尸	兄		兄弟 brothers, sisters, brethren	형제
				兄夫 husband of a girl's elder sister	형부
儿 3 125				妹兄 husband of a man's elder sister	매형

冊	丨	冂	冂	책 book, register	책
	冂	冊		冊床 desk, table	책상
				書冊 books, publications	서책
冂 3 126				冊子 pamphlet, booklet	책자

冬	丿	夂	夂	겨울 winter	동
	冬	冬		冬期 winter, the winter season	동기
				冬眠 hibernation	동면
冫 3 127				冬至 the winter solstice	동지

				날	exit, come out, go out; issue; beget, produce; be born, appear	출
出	丨	屮	屮			
	出	出		出發	depart, leave, set out	출발
				出身	affiliation, origin; a graduate; rise in the world	출신
山 3 128						

				책낼	publish; engrave, cut	간
刊	一	二	千	刊行	publish, bring out	간행
	刊	刊		朝刊	morning edition of a newspaper; a morning newspaper	조간
刀 3 129				出刊	publish, issue	출간

				더할	add; apply	가
加	フ	力	加	加工	process, work; manufacture; treat	가공
	加	加		增加	increase, grow, gain	증가
力 3 130				加入	join, enter; to add, put in	가입

				공	merit, achievement	공
功	一	丁	工	功勞	meritorious service, meritorious deeds	공로
	功	功		功德	merit and virtue; Buddhist charity	공덕
力 3 131				功臣	a meritorious retainer or subject	공신

				쌀	wrap	포
包	丿	勹	勹			
	勹	包		包含	be included, contained, embraced, covered	포함
				包裝	wrap, pack up	포장
勹 3 132				包攝	convince, win over; connote	포섭

				북녘	north	북
北	一	十	北	달아날	suffer defeat	배
	北	北		北部	the north, the northern part	북부
				北極	the north pole	북극
匕 3 133				敗北	defeat, reversal	패배

	、	丷	丷	반	half	반
半	半	半		半徑	radius	반경
				半球	hemisphere	반구
十 3 134				半數	half the number, half	반수

	l	⼘	丫	점 칠	prognosticate, foretell; seize, usurp	점
占	占	占		占領	occupy; seize, take, capture	점령
				占據	occupy, possess (territory)	점거
⼘ 3 135				占有	possess, occupy (property)	점유

	⼃	⼁	⼓	토 끼	4th of the 12 Earth's Branches; hare, rabbit	묘
卯	卯	卯		己卯	16th of the 60 binary terms of the sexagenary cycle	기묘
				己卯士禍	literati purge of 1519	기묘사화
卩 3 136				卯年	the Year of the Hare	묘년

	一	十	土	갈	go away; gone, past; abandon; throw away	거
去	去	去		去來	come and go; lending and borrowing; transactions	거래
				去年	last year	거년
厶 2 137				去勢	castrate, emasculate, geld	거세

	一	⼗	ナ	예	ancient, old	고
古	古	古		古代	antiquity, ancient times	고대
				古今	past and present, all times	고금
口 2 138				古木	an old tree	고목

	丶	冂	口	다만	merely, only, but	지
只	只	只		只今	now, the present	지금
				但只	merely, only; but, however, provided that, on condition that	단지
口 2 139						

句	ノ	ク	勺	글귀	phrase, sentence	귀(구)
	句	句		句節	a phrase; a paragraph	귀절
				文句	a passage, a clause	문귀
口 2 140				一言半句	a word, a single word	일언반구

叫	ヽ	冂	口	부르짖을	call; animal cry	규
	叫	叫		絶叫	exclaim, cry out	절규
				叫喚	a cry, shout, shriek	규환
口 2 141				叫彈	impeach, censure, denounce, arraign	규탄

召	フ	刀	刀	부를	call, summon; cite, give notice	소
	召	召		召集	call, call up; convene, convoke	소집
口 2 142				召喚	summon, call, cite, subpoena	소환

史	ヽ	冂	口	사기	history, annals, chronicle	사
	史	史		史學	history	사학
				史記	a chronicle, a history	사기
口 2 143				史上	in history, in the pages of history	사상

可	一	丁	冂	옳을	able, may, can; right, proper	가
	可	可		可能	be possible	가능
				可憐	pitiful, pathetic	가련
口 2 144				可否	right or wrong; proper or improper	가부

右	一	ナ	ナ	오른	right; right side; honor	우
	右	右		右邊	right edge, right side	우변
				右翼	right wing; the right flank	우익
口 2 145				右側	the right side, the right	우측

司	丁	刁	司	맡을	control, manage, preside; officer; subdivision of a district	사
	司	司		司令部	a military headquarters	사령부
				司會	chair, preside, conduct	사회
口 2 146				上司	a higher officer, one's superior	상사

四	丶	冂	四	넉	four	사
	四	四		四十	forty	사십
				四方	the four directions; everywhere	사방
口 2 147				四寸	cousin	사촌

囚	丨	冂	囗	가둘	prisoner; imprison; criminal case	수
	囚	囚		罪囚	a prisoner, a jailbird	죄수
				死刑囚	a criminal condemned to death	사형수
口 2 148				脫獄囚	an escaped prisoner	탈옥수

外	丿	夕	夕	바깥	outside; foreign; extraordinary	외
	列	外		外國	a foreign state	외국
				內外	inside and outside; husband and wife	내외
夕 2 149				外交	diplomacy	외교

央	丶	冂	卩	가운데	center; finish, conclude	앙
	央	央		中央	central; the center, the middle	중앙
				中央廳	the Capitol Building in Seoul	중앙청
大 2 150				中央政府	the central government	중앙정부

失	丿	一	二	잃을	lose, neglect, miss, err; ommission	실
	失	失		失敗	fail, blunder, miscarry	실패
				失望	be disappointed; despair	실망
大 2 151				失手	make a mistake, err, blunder	실수

| 奴
 女 2
 152 | く | 女 | 女 |
| | 奴 | 奴 | |

노예 slave, servant; term of depreciation 노
奴隷 a slave 노예
奴婢 male and female servants (slaves) 노비
守錢奴 a miser, a skinflint 수전노

| 左
 工 2
 153 | 一 | ナ | 左 |
| | 左 | 左 | |

왼 left; inferior 좌
左右 right and left; influence, control 좌우
左側 the left side, the left 좌측
左遷 demotion, downgrading 좌천

| 巧
 工 2
 154 | 一 | 丁 | 工 |
| | 工 | 巧 | |

공교로울 skill, cleverness; opportune 교
巧妙 be skillful, deft 교묘
精巧 be exquisite, ingenious 정교
巧言 flattery, honeyed words 교언

| 巨
 工 2
 155 | 一 | 厂 | 尸 |
| | 巨 | 巨 | |

클 huge; chief; numerous 거
巨大 huge, colossal 거대
巨物 an enormous object; a prominent person 거물
巨星 a great man; a huge star 거성

| 市
 巾 2
 156 | 丶 | 亠 | 亠 |
| | 市 | 市 | |

저자 market, fair; trade; execution ground; city 시
市場 a market 시장
市民 citizens; townsmen; the populace 시민
市長 a mayor 시장

| 布
 巾 2
 157 | 一 | ナ | 才 |
| | 布 | 布 | |

베 linen; notify; display 포
布教 propagate, proselyte 포교
宣布 proclaim, declare, promulgate 선포
布木 linen and cotton 포목

平	一	二	二	평평할 level; ordinary; peaceful; weigh	평
	포	平		平和 peace, tranquility, harmony	평화
干 2 158				平均 average, mean	평균
				平等 equal, even, impartial	평등

幼	乙	幺	幺	어릴 young, immature, weak, delicate	유
	幻	幼		幼稚園 kindergarten	유치원
幺 2 159				幼兒 an infant, a baby	유아
				老幼 the young and the old	노유

弘	ㄱ	ㄹ	弓	클 broad, extensive, large	홍
	弘	弘		弘益 great profit, public benefit	홍익
弓 2 160				弘報 public information; widely known	홍보

弗	ㄱ	ㄹ	弓	아닐 not, no; un-, in-, non-; dollar	불
	弗	弗		弗素 fluorine	불소
弓 2 161				美弗 the U.S. dollar	미불
				弗貨 dollars, American money	불화

必	ㆍ	心	心	반드시 necessarily, for sure	필
	心	必		必要 be necessary, required	필요
心 1 162				必是 certainly, surely	필시
				必勝 certain victory	필승

戊	ノ	厂	六	다섯째천간 5th of the 10 Heavenly Stems	무
	戊	戊		戊種 Class E, 5th rank	무종
戈 1 163				戊辰 5th of the 60 binary terms of the sexagenary cycle	무진
				戊午 55th of the 60 binary terms of the sexagenary cycle	무오

打	一	十	扌	칠	hit, beat	타
	打	打		打擊	hit, strike; a blow	타 격
				打破	destroy, break down	타 파
手 2 164				打算	calculate, reckon	타 산

斥	′	⼂	⼓	물리칠	dismiss, reject, drive away; scold	척
	斥	斥		斥候	scout, reconnoiter	척 후
				排斥	reject, expel, exclude; boycott	배 척
斤 1 165						

旦	⼁	⼌	日	아침	morning; female impersonator	단
	日	旦		元旦	New Year's Day	원 단
				旦夕	morning and evening; on the brink of death	단 석
日 1 166						

未	一	二	丰	아닐	not, not yet, not being	미
	丰	未		未拂	be outstanding, in arrears, unpaid	미 불
				未明	early dawn	미 명
木 1 167				未開	unopened; uncivilized	미 개

末	一	二	于	끝	end, finally; powder, dust	말
	才	末		末葉	the end of an age	말 엽
				末日	the last day, the end	말 일
				末世	the end of the world; a degenerate age	말 세
木 1 168						

本	一	十	才	밑	root, source, origin, native; main; that, this, the; me; essential	본
	木	本				
				本國	one's native country, homeland	본국
木 1 169				本部	headquarters, home office	본부

5 strokes

正	一	丁	下	바를	upright; true; right, correct, straight; just at; adjust; principal, chief; January; whole	정
	圧	正		正確	be precise, correct, exact	정확
止 1 170				正式	proper (regular) form	정식
				正當	just, right, proper	정당

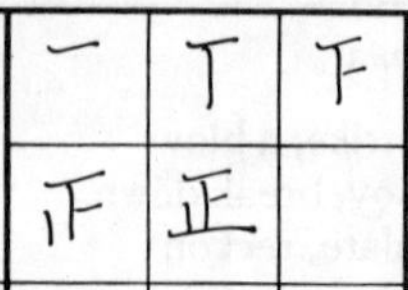

母	ㄴ	�13	日	어미	mother; female	모
	吕	母		母親	mother	모친
				母女	mother and daughter	모녀
毋 1 171				母國	homeland, mother country	모국

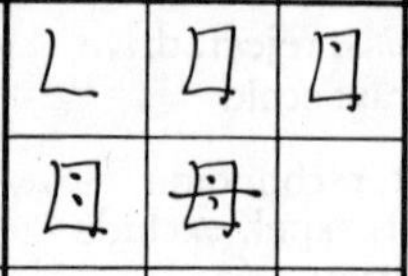

民	ㄱ	ㄱ	尸	백성	people, mankind	민
	尸	民		民間	the people, the folk; nongovernmental	민간
				民衆	the people, the masses, the populace	민중
氏 1 172				民主主義	democracy	민주주의

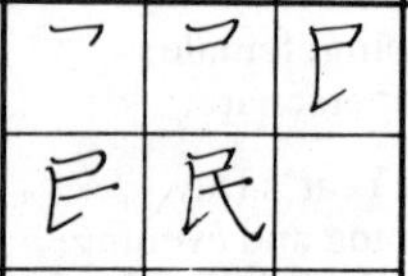

氷	丿	冫	汀	얼음	ice; cold; crystallized; frozen	빙
	汏	氷		氷點	the freezing point	빙점
				氷山	an iceberg	빙산
水 1 173				氷河	a glacier; an icebound river	빙하

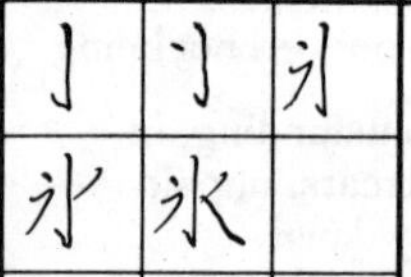

永	丶	刁	刃	길	perpetual, eternal, long	영
	永	永		永遠	perpetual, eternal	영원
				永久	permanence; perpetuity, eternity	영구
水 1 174				永訣	final farewell, part forever	영결

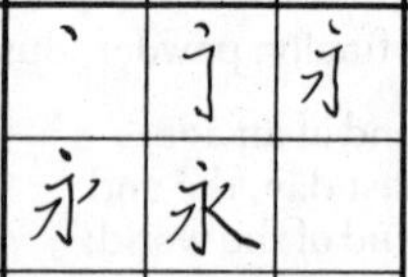

犯	丿	犭	犭	범할	transgress, violate; offend; invade	범
	犭	犯		犯罪者	an offender, a criminal, a convict	범죄자
				犯行	commit a crime	범행
犬 2 175				犯法	break the law, violate the law	범법

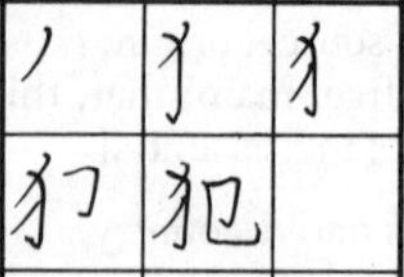

56

玄	、	二	亠	검을	dark; subtle; abstruse	현
	玄	玄		玄關	entrance hall	현관
玄 0				玄米	unpolished rice	현미
176				玄琴	a kind of harp	현금

玉	一	二	干	구슬	gem, precious stone, jade; valuable; your	옥
	王	玉		玉色	jade green	옥색
玉 0				玉水	clear water (as brook or spring water)	옥수
177				玉石	jade, precious stones; jade and stone	옥석

瓜	丿	厂	爪	참외	melon, gourd, cucumber	과
	瓜	瓜		瓜年	final year of term of service; a girl 15 or 16 years old	과년
瓜 0						
178				西瓜	a watermelon	서과

瓦	一	厂	工	기와	tile, earthenware, pottery; roof	와
	瓦	瓦		瓦解	disintegrate, fall to pieces; break up, collapse	와해
瓦 0				瓦家	a tile-roofed house	와가
179				瓦器	earthenware	와기

甘	一	十	廿	달	sweet; pleasant, voluntary	감
	甘	甘		甘草	licorice root	감초
				甘受	be willing to suffer, submit willingly	감수
甘 0						
180				甘味	sweetness, a sweet taste	감미

生	丿	仁	仁	날	be born; produce; life; student; raw, fresh; arbitrary, forced	생
	牛	生				
				生活	living, existence	생활
生 0				生命	life	생명
181				生存	survival, survive	생존

用 用 0 182	丿	冂	月	쓸	use, employ; consume; apply; practical	용
	月	用		使用	use, employ	사용
				用紙	forms; stationery	용지
				用務	business, matters to be taken care of	용무

田 田 0 183	丶	冂	日	밭	field	전
	冊	田		田畓	dry fields and paddy fields	전답
				田土	cultivated land, fields	전토
				田園	fields and gardens; rural areas	전원

由 田 0 184	丶	冂	日	말미암을	from, because of, according to; cause, instrument, means; source; permit	유
	申	由		經由	pass through	경유
				理由	reason, grounds, cause	이유
				由來	originate in, derive from	유래

甲 田 0 185	丶	冂	日	갑옷	1st of the 10 Heavenly Stems; first; armor	갑
	日	甲		甲板	the deck	갑판
				甲富	a millionaire, a magnate	갑부
				六甲	the sexagenary cycle	육갑

申 田 0 186	丶	冂	日	납	9th of the 12 Earth's Branches; monkey; state to a superior, report, notify; give orders	신
	日	申		申告	a report, declaration, statement	신고
				申請書	an application form	신청서

白 白 0 187	丿	亻	亇	흰	white	백
	白	白		白人	Caucasian, white man	백인
				白紙	blank paper; white paper	백지
				白衣	white clothes	백의

皮	ノ	厂	广	가죽	skin; fur; leather; bark	피
	皮	皮		皮膚	skin, the skin	피부
				皮相的	superficial, shallow	피상적
皮 0 188				皮帶	a conveyor belt	피대

目	｜	冂	月	눈	eye; regard, look on; chief; item	목
	月	目		目的	purpose, object, goal	목적
				目下	now, at present	목하
目 0 189				目標	target, goal	목표

矛	フ	マ	矛	창	lance, spear	모
	予	矛		矛盾	contradiction	모순
				矛盾名辭	contradictory terms	모순명사
矛 0 190						

矢	ノ	一	二	화살	arrow, dart; aim at; oath; marshal; display, set forth	시
	矢	矢		矢石	arrows and stones (in ancient warfare)	시석
				毒矢	a poisoned arrow	독시
矢 0 191				弓矢	bow and arrow	궁시

石	一	厂	石	돌	stone, rock, mineral	석
	石	石		石炭	coal	석탄
				石油	petroleum, kerosene	석유
石 0 192				石器	stone implement	석기

示	一	二	亍	보일	manifest, proclaim, exhibit; omen; see	시
	示	示		表示	indicate, show, express, manifest	표시
				示威	demonstrate; display; show off	시위
示 0 193				告示	announce, proclaim	고시

禾	丿 二 千	벼	growing grain, growing rice	화
	禾 禾	禾穀類	edible grains, cereals	화곡류

禾 0
194

穴	丶 ⼍ 宀	구멍	cave, hole	혈
	宀 穴	穴居	dwell in a cave	혈거
		穴深	depth of a grave	혈심
		墓穴	a grave	묘혈

穴 0
195

立	丶 亠 六	설	establish, set up; stand up; immediately	립
	立 立	立體	a solid body	입체
		立脚	be based on, rest on the basis of	입각
		立憲	establish a constitution	입헌

立 0
196

6 Strokes

交	丶 亠 六	사귈	exchange, communicate, intercourse, mix, join	교
	六 亥 交	交換	exchange, interchange	교환
		交涉	negotiate, bargain	교섭
		交流	alternating current; interchange	교류

亠 4
197

亥	丶 亠 亡	돼지	12th of the 12 Earth's Branches; boar, pig	해
	亥 亥 亥	亥時	Watch of the Boar, the period between 9 and 11 P.M.	해시
		亥年	Year of the Boar	해년
		亥日	Day of the Boar	해일

亠 4
198

亦 亠 4 199	丶	亠	广	또	and, also, moreover, likewise	역
	市	亦	亦	亦是	too, also, as well	역시
				亦然	be also the same	역연
				其亦	that too is, that also/ likewise is	기역
仰 人 4 200	丿	亻	亻	우러를	look up; face upwards; command	앙
	化	们	仰	仰慕	look up to with respect; adore	앙모
				仰望	look up to with hope; expect, wish	앙망
				信仰	faith, belief	신앙
仲 人 4 201	丿	亻	亻	버금	second in order, second-born; personal relations	중
	们	㣽	仲	仲介	mediation	중개
				仲媒	a go-between, a matchmaker	중매
				仲裁	mediation, arbitration	중재
件 人 4 202	丿	亻	亻	사건	an affair; article, thing, object	건
	仁	仁	件	事件	incident, affair, matter	사건
				條件	condition, stipulation	조건
				件數	number of cases, number of incidents	건수
企 人 4 203	丿	人	介	꾀할	stand on tiptoe and look for; anxious	기
	仐	企	企	企業	go into business, undertake an enterprise	기업
				企劃	plans; make a plan	기획
				企圖	intend; contemplate; undertake	기도
伏 人 4 204	丿	亻	亻	엎드릴	prostrate; yield; humble; hide, lie in ambush; suppress; secret	복
	伏	伏	伏	降伏	surrender, capitulate	항복
				三伏	three "dog days" of summer	삼복
				潛伏	hide, conceal oneself; dormant, latent	잠복

任	ノ イ イ´ イ´ イ仁 任	맡길	entrust; put in office; official position; allow; bear, burden	임
		任意	voluntary	임의
人 4 205		任員	officer, official; board, staff	임원
		任官	be commissioned	임관

伐	ノ イ イ´ 代 伐 伐	칠	attack; quell rebellion, chastise rebels	벌
		征伐	subjugate	정벌
		伐採	fell trees, cut timber	벌채
人 4 206		殺伐	attack and slaughter; brutality, savageness, fierceness	살벌

休	ノ イ イ´ 付 付 休	쉴	rest; cease; desist; inactive; blessings, good luck	휴
		休養	rest, relaxation, recreation	휴양
		休暇	vacation, leave	휴가
人 4 207		休戰	armistice, truce	휴전

充	丶 亠 亡 云 亢 充	가득할	fill up; satisfy; act as	충
		充分	be sufficient, adequate	충분
		充當	meet a demand; make up a deficiency; allocate, appropriate	충당
儿 4 208		充足	be adequate, sufficient	충족

兆	ノ ノ ノ 扎 兆 兆	억조	a trillion; omen, sign	조
		徵兆	indication, sign; omen	징조
		兆朕	sign, indication, omen	조짐
儿 4 209		億兆	a hundred million and a trillion ;myriads	억조

先	ノ 一 ナ 生 失 先	먼저	first, front, foremost	선
		先生	a teacher; gentleman; Mister (honorific)	선생
		先輩	a senior, an elder	선배
儿 4 210		先驅者	a forerunner; the vanguard	선구자

光	丨	丷	少	빛	light, brightness	광
	业	严	光	光線	light ray, beam of light	광선
				光明	brightness, brilliancy	광명
儿 4 211				光復	restore national independence; Korean liberation from Japan in 1945	광복

全	丿	人	人	온전할	entire, whole, complete, perfect	전
	仝	全	全	全體	the whole, all	전체
				全國	pan-national, nation-wide, the whole country	전국
入 4 212				全然	completely, entirely	전연

共	一	十	卄	한가지	together, collectively, all-sharing; cooperate; communism	공
	世	共	共	共同	combined, joint	공동
				共産主義	communism	공산주의
八 4 213				共通	be common, be common to	공통

再	一	冂	冎	두	again, repeated	재
	冃	再	再	再建	reconstruction	재건
				再次	a second time, twice	재차
冂 4 214				再昨年	year before last	재작년

刑	一	二	于	형벌	punishment	형
	开	荆	刑	刑事	a criminal case; detective, police investigator	형사
				刑法	criminal law	형법
刀 4 215				刑場	place of execution	형장

列	一	㇒	歹	벌일	arrange in order; enumerate, classify; each one; file, rank; series	렬
	歹	列	列	列車	a train	열차
				列強	the Great Powers	열강
刀 4 216				列島	archipelago	열도

劣	丿	小	小	용렬할	vile, degraded, bad; inferior	렬
	少	岁	劣	劣性	genetic recessiveness; inferiority	열성
				劣等	be inferior, poor	열등
力 4 217				劣勢	be inferior in numbers/ strength	열세

危	丿	ク	ク	위태할	dangerous, perilous; lofty	위
	尸	危	危	危險	dangerous; risky, hazardous	위험
				危機	crisis, emergency, critical situation	위기
卩 4 218				危急	urgent, critical	위급

印	丿	亻	亻	도장	official seal, mark; print, stamp	인
	𠂢	𠂤	印	印刷	print; put into print	인쇄
				印象	an impression	인상
卩 4 219				印鑑	a seal impression	인감

各	丿	ク	夂	각각	each, every; all	각
	冬	各	各	各各	each, every; all; respectively, individually	각각
				各國	each country; all countries	각국
口 3 220				各處	each place, every place	각처

合	丿	人	合	합할	join	합
	合	合	合	合計	sum total; add up, total	합계
				合同	combine, unite	합동
				合唱	chorus, choir; sing in unison	합창
口 3 221						

吉	一	十	士	길할	lucky, happy	길
	吉	吉	吉	吉夢	a lucky dream, dream containing a good omen	길몽
				吉日	a propitious day	길일
口 3 222				吉凶	fortune and misfortune, ups and downs	길흉

同	丨	冂	冋	한가지	together, identical, share in	동
	同	同	同	同時	simultaneous, at the same time	동시
				同胞	overseas Koreans	동포
口 3 223				同窓	an alumnus, alumni; former schoolmate	동창

名	丿	夕	夕	이름	name; fame; counter for persons	명
	夕	名	名	名譽	glory, honor; fame, reputation	명예
				名節	holiday, festive day	명절
口 3 224				名色	name, title, designation	명색

吏	一	一	丏	관리	officer, deputy; government servant	리
	弓	吏	吏	汚吏	corrupt official	오리
				税吏	tax official	세리
口 3 225				官吏	government official, public servant, bureaucrat	관리

吐	丨	冂	口	토할	vomit, spit	토
	口一	吐	吐	吐露	bare one's heart, speak one's mind; voice, express, utter	토로
				吐說	confess, own up to; tell the truth	토설
口 3 226				嘔吐	vomiting	구토

向	丿	亻	勹	향할	face towards	향
	向	向	向	向上	betterment, progress, advancement	향상
				向發	leave for, depart	향발
口 3 227				傾向	tendency, trend; inclination	경향

因	丨	冂	冋	인할	in consequence of, due to; cause; origin; follow, rely on	인
	用	厌	因	因緣	ties; karma; fate	인연
				因果	cause and effect; Buddhist retribution	인과
口 3 228				因子	a factor	인자

65

回	丨	冂	冂	돌아올 return; Mohammedan; time, occasion	회
	回	回	回	回附 return, send back	회부
				回轉 turn, rotate, revolve; a turn	회전
口 3 229				回答 reply, answer	회답

在	一	ナ	ナ	있을 exist, be at, be present	재
	右	存	在	現在 the present, now; at present; this world; present tense	현재
				存在 exist, be extant	존재
土 3 230				所在 site, position, location; whereabouts	소재

地	一	十	土	땅 earth, soil; place; cloth	지
	圵	地	地	地方 a district, a locality; a neighborhood	지방
				地球 the earth	지구
土 3 231				地形 terrain features, the terrain, topography	지형

多	ノ	ク	夕	많을 much, many, mostly	다
	夕	多	多	多少 many and few; some; quantity, amount	다소
				多幸 good fortune, good luck	다행
夕 3 232				多情 kindness, humaneness	다정

夷	一	弓	弖	오랑캐 barbarians; eastern barbarians; squat	이
	弓	夷	夷	夷俗 strange custom	이속
				東夷 the eastern barbarians	동이
大 3 233					

妃	く	ㄑ	女	왕비 queen; royal concubine; wife; lady	비
	女ㄱ	女ㄱ	妃	大妃 queen dowager	대비
				王妃 queen consort	왕비
女 3 234				妃嬪 queen and royal concubine	비빈

如 女 3 235	く	女	女	같을	like, as; equal to; supposing	여
	女	如	如	如前	as before, as ever	여전
				如何間	at any rate, in any event	여하간
				如實	realistic; vivid	여실

妄 女 3 236	丶	亠	亡	망령될	false, absurd, foolish; wild, disorderly	망
	亡	妄	妄	妄想	wild fancy, daydream	망상
				妄發	make an absurd remark, speak ignominiously	망발
				老妄	senility, dotage	노망

好 女 3 237	く	女	女	좋을	good, nice; like, love	호
	女	好	好	好奇心	curiosity, inquisitiveness	호기심
				好意	friendliness, amity	호의
				好感	favorable impression, good will	호감

字 子 3 238	丶	八	宀	글자	character, letter	자
	宀	字	字	文字	character, letter, writing	문자
				漢字	Sino-Korean characters, Chinese characters	한자
				字典	character dictionary	자전

存 子 3 239	一	ナ	右	있을	exist; keep, preserve	존
	存	存	存	存立	existence; support	존립
				存續	continue, continue to exist	존속
				存亡	life and death; existence	존망

宅 宀 3 240	丶	丶	宀	집	private dwelling, house, home	택
	宀	宅	宅	댁	spouse; wife of	댁
				自宅	a private residence; home	자택
				私宅	a private residence	사택
				宅内	your/his esteemed family	댁내

守	丶	丷	宀	지킬	guard, protect; observe, keep; hold on to, maintain	수
	宀	守	守	守舊	be conservative, hold to traditions	수구
'' 3 241				守備	defend, guard	수비
				守衛	a guard; guarding	수위

宇	丶	丷	宀	집	space, universe, canopy of heaven; cover, shelter	우
	宀	宀	宇	宇宙	the universe, the cosmos	우주
'' 3 242				宇宙船	space ship	우주선
				宇宙論	cosmology	우주론

安	丶	丷	宀	편안	peace; quiet; soothe; arrange	안
	宀	安	安	安全	safety, security	안전
'' 3 243				安寧	peaceful	안녕
				安否	well-being; regards, tidings	안부

寺	一	十	土	절	Buddhist temple; hall	사
	士	寺	寺	寺院	a monastery, a Buddhist temple	사원
小 3 244				寺刹	Buddhist temple	사찰
				佛國寺	famous Buddhist temple in Kyŏngju dating from 691 A.D.	불국사

尖	丿	丿丨	小	뾰죽할	pointed, sharp	첨
	尐	尖	尖	尖端	fine point, pointed tip; vanguard	첨단
小 3 245				尖銳	be sharp, acute; be radical	첨예
				尖兵	military spearhead	첨병

州	丶	丿	丷	고을	region, state, province	주
	州	州	州	州郡	provinces and counties	주군
巛 3 246				九州	the nine provinces of Silla	구주
				州知事	state governor	주지사

年 丨 于 3 247	ノ 仁	⌐一 彡	仁 年	해 每年 年代 年齡	year; age; harvest annually, each year years and generations; a period attained age	년 매 년 연 대 연 령

式 弋 3 248	一 工	二 式	〒 式	법
				
				式場
				儀式
				式順
					form, fashion, rule, pattern,
					  model; formality; formula;
					  employ; reverence
					
					place of a ceremony
					a ceremony, a rite
					program of events
						식
						
						식장
						의식
						식순

忙 心 3 249	丨 忄	忄 忙	忄 忙	바쁠
				多忙
				
				忙中閑
				
				忙忙
					busy, hurried, in haste
					always busy,
					  pressed with work
					a break, a moment of
					  relief from work
					be very busy
						망
						다 망
						
						망중한
						
						망 망

戌 戈 2 250	ノ 戌	厂 戌	戶 戌	개
				
				戌時
				
				戌年
				庚戌
					11th of the 12 Earth's
					  Branches; dog
					Watch of the Dog,
					  between 7 and 9 P.M.
					Year of the Dog
					47th of the 60 binary terms
						술
						
						술시
						
						술년
						경술

托 手 3 251	一 扌	扌 扌	扌 托	밀칠 依托 托鉢	entrust; request depend on, rely on Buddhist mendicancy	탁 의탁 탁발

收 攴 2 252	ㄴ 丱	丩 收	丱 收	거둘
				
				收入
				收容
				收穫
					harvest; collect; receive what
					  is due, gather together;
					  bind; bring to an end
					income, earnings
					to house, accommodate
					harvest, gather in
						수
						
						수 입
						수 용
						수 확

早	丶	冂	日	일찍	early	조
	日	旦	早	早速히	promptly	조속
				早朝	early morning	조조
日 2 253				早婚	early marriage	조혼

旬	丿	勹	勹	열흘	period of ten days; one-third of a month	순
	句	旬	旬	下旬	the final ten days of a month	하순
				中旬	the middle ten days of a month	중순
日 2 254				旬朔	first and tenth of a month	순삭

曲	丶	冂	曰	굽을	crooked, bent, false, wrong; tune	곡
	冉	曲	曲	曲線	a curved line, curves	곡선
				曲調	a tune, a melody	곡조
日 2 255				曲折	meandering; circumstances	곡절

有	一	ナ	ナ	있을	exist, be; have, possess	유
	冇	有	有	有名	be famous, well-known	유명
				有力	be influential; convincing; powerful	유력
月 2 256				有望	full of promise, hopeful	유망

朴	一	十	才	순박할	sincere, plain, simple; surname: Pak	박
	才	利	朴	淳朴	simple, unsophisticated, unspoiled	순박
				素朴	naive, simple, artless	소박
木 2 257				儉朴	frugal, thrifty, careful	검박

朱	丿	一	二	붉을	red, vermilion	주
	牛	牜	朱	朱錫	tin	주석
				朱紅	scarlet	주홍
木 2 258				朱黃	orange color	주황

次 欠 2 259	、 ; 冫 冫 次 次	다음
		
		次次
		
		次例
		次期
			next; sequence, series;
			  occasion; place
			gradually, step by step;
			  later, eventually,
			  in due course
			order, turn
			next term, following period
				차
				
				차차
				
				차례
				차기

此 止 2 260	丨 卜 止 止 此 此	이 彼此 此際 此後	this this and that; you and I, both this time hereafter, in the future	차 피차 차제 차후

死 歹 2 261	一 厂 歹 歹 死 死	죽을
		
		死刑
		
		死亡
		死後
			die; death; dead;
			  inanimate; inert
			death penalty, capital
			  punishment
			death
			after death, posthumous
				사
				
				사형
				
				사망
				사후

汎 水 3 262	、 冫 氵 汎 汎 汎	뜰
		汎溢
		
		汎濫
		
		汎論
			float; drift; careless
			overflow, run over, flood,
			  innundate
			overflow, flood;
			  be forward, presumptive
			summary, outline;
			  a vague remark
				범
				범일
				
				범람
				
				범론

汗 水 3 263	、 冫 氵 汗 汗 汗	땀 不汗黨 汗蒸 虛汗	perspiration, sweat a gang of thieves, noodlums steam bath, Turkish bath cold sweat	한 불한당 한증 허한

江 水 3 264	、 冫 氵 江 江 江	물
		江山
		
		江邊
		江湖
			river
			rivers and mountains,
			  scenary
			riverside
			rivers and lakes,
			  scenary, retreat
				강
				강산
				
				강변
				강호

汚 水 3 265	﹅	﹅	﹅	더러울	impure, filthy, vile; mean; defile	오
	氵	汀	汚	汚點	stain, flaw, blemish, blot	오점
				汚物	filth, feculence; muck; sewage; garbage	오물
				汚染	pollution	오염

汝 水 3 266	﹅	﹅	氵	너	you; your	여
	汃	汝	汝	汝等	you, you all	여등
				汝矣島	Yŏŭi Island in Seoul	여의도

池 水 3 267	﹅	﹅	氵	못	pond	지
	汭	池	池	電池	battery, electric cell	전지
				蓮池	lotus pond; pond	연지

灰 火 2 268	一	厂	灰	재	ashes; gray; lime	회
	灰	灰	灰	灰色	gray; ash color, drab color	회색
				灰白色	light gray	회백색
				生灰	limestone, quicklime	생회
				洋灰	cement	양회

百 白 1 269	一	丆	丆	일백	one hundred	백
	百	百	百	百姓	the people; the common people	백성
				百貨店	department store	백화점
				百日	one-hundred days	백일

竹 竹 0 270	丿	亻	产	대	bamboo	죽
	竹	竹	竹	竹林	bamboo grove	죽림
				竹馬	stilts	죽마
				竹筍	bamboo shoots	죽순

| 米 | 丶 | 丷 | 半 | 쌀 | hulled rice; grain | 미 |
| 米 0 271 | 半 | 米 | 米 | 米穀 玄米 米穀商 | rice
brown rice, unpolished rice
rice/grain dealer | 미곡
현미
미곡상 |

| 羊 | 丶 | 丷 | 丷 | 양 | sheep, goat | 양 |
| 羊 0 272 | 兰 | 兰 | 羊 | 羊毛 山羊 羊乳 | wool
goat; antelope
goat's milk | 양모
산양
양유 |

| 羽 | ㄱ | 刁 | 羽 | 깃 | feathers, plumes, wings | 우 |
| 羽 0 273 | 羽 | 羽 | 羽 | 羽毛 羽翼 羽緞 | feathers, plumes
wings of birds; assistance
velvet | 우모
우익
우단 |

| 老 | 一 | 十 | 土 | 늙을 | old; venerable; term of respect; well-cooked; experienced | 로 |
| 老 0 274 | 耂 | 耂 | 老 | 老人 老婆 老少 | old person, senior citizen
old woman
the old and the young | 노인
노파
노소 |

| 考 | 一 | 十 | 土 | 상고할 | examine, consider | 고 |
| 老 0 275 | 耂 | 耂 | 考 | 考查 考慮 考察 | examination, test
deliberate, consider
examine, inquire into | 고사
고려
고찰 |

| 而 | 一 | 丆 | 丆 | 말이을 | and; but; like; nevertheless | 이 |
| 而 0 276 | 丙 | 而 | 而 | 然而나
形而上學 | however, be that as it may
metaphysics | 연이
형이상학 |

耳	一	厂	下	귀	ear; handle; that which is at the side	이
	下	巨	耳	耳目	eye and ear	이목
耳 0 277				耳目口鼻	eye, ear, nose and mouth	이목구비

肉	丶	冂	内	고기	flesh, meat; pulp of fruit	육
	内	肉	肉	肉體	the body, the flesh	육체
				肉類	meats	육류
肉 0 278				肉感的	voluptuous, sensual, fleshly	육감적

臣	一	厂	臣	신하	government official, statesman; subject	신
	臣	臣	臣	臣下	minister; government official; subject	신하
				忠臣	loyal subject, faithful retainer	충신
臣 0 279				君臣	lord and subject	군신

自	丿	亻	竹	스스로	self; from	자
	竹	自	自	自己	self, oneself; himself, herself	자기
				自由	freedom, liberty	자유
自 0 280				自然	nature; natural; spontaneity	자연

至	一	工	云	이를	reach, arrive at; extreme	지
	云	至	至	至極	extreme, exceeding	지극
				至上	the supreme, the highest	지상
至 0 281				至誠	utmost sincerity	지성

舌	丿	二	千	혀	tongue	설
	千	舌	舌	舌禍	unfortunate slip of the tongue	설화
舌 0 282				舌戰	argument, battle of tongues	설전

					배	boat	주
舟 0 283					舟遊	boating; a boat ride	주유
					扁舟	skiff, small boat	편주
					舟橋	pontoon bridge	주교

					빛	color; beauty; appearance; lust, sex; sort, kind, quality	색
色 0 284					色彩	color, hue; coloring	색채
					色盲	color blindness	색맹
					赤色	red	적색

					피	blood	혈
血 0 285					血管	blood vessel	혈관
					血液	blood	혈액
					血肉	flesh and blood; offspring	혈육

					갈	walk; do; action, behavior	행
行 0 286					行動	behavior, conduct; action, movement	행동
					行事	conduct, actions; a function, an event	행사
					行方	whereabouts	행방

					옷	clothing	의
衣 0 287					衣服	clothing, a set of clothes	의복
					衣類	garments, clothing	의류
					衣食住	clothing, food and shelter	의식주

					서녘	west	서
西 0 288					西洋	the West, the Occident	서양
					西紀	Christian era, A.D.	서기
					西方	the west	서방

7 Strokes

亨	丶	亠	宀	형통할 pervade; successful	형
	宀	亨	亨	亨通 be realized, fulfilled, go well	형통
亠 5 289	亨			萬事亨通 be prosperous in everything	만사형통

伯	丿	亻	亻	맏 senior, elder; esteemed; uncle, father's elder brother	백
	伫	伯	伯	伯爵 count, earl	백작
				伯氏 esteemed elder brother	백씨
人 5 290	伯			伯父 uncle, father's elder brother	백부

伸	丿	亻	亻	펼 stretch out, extend; redress; report to	신
	们	伷	伸	伸長 stretch, expand, elongate	신장
				伸縮 expand and contract; be elastic	신축
人 5 291	伸			屈伸 extend and contract; be elastic	굴신

似	丿	亻	亻	같을 resemble; like, as if; continue by inheritance	사
	亻	似	似	似而非 false, sham, spurious; pseudo, quasi	사이비
				近似 closely resemble	근사
人 5 292	似			類似 similar, resembles	유사

位	丿	亻	亻	벼슬 rank; esteemed; seat; position	위
	亻	位	位	位置 place, location; position; situation	위치
				品位 dignity; nobility	품위
人 5 293	位			諸位 gentlemen	제위

但 人 5 294	ノ 仃 但	イ 佀	仁 但	다만 非但 但只 但書	only, but, yet, still merely; only only, just proviso, condition, provision	단 비단 단지 단서
佐 人 5 295	ノ 什 佐	イ 佐	仁 佐	도울 補佐 補佐官	assist, aid; subordinate official help, assist; advise a superior assistant, helper, aide	좌 보좌 보좌관
低 人 5 296	ノ 化 低	イ 低	亻 低	낮을 低氣壓 低廉 低俗	low low atmospheric pressure inexpensive, cheap vulgar, base, low	저 저기압 저렴 저속
住 人 5 297	ノ 亻 住	イ 亻	亻 住	머무를 住民 住所 住宅	dwell, stop residents, inhabitants address, place of residence residence, home, house	주 주민 주소 주택
余 人 5 298	ノ 今 余	入 全	入 余	나 余等	I, me we, us	여 여등
何 人 5 299	ノ 仃 何	イ 何	仁 佰	어찌 何如間 何必 何等	what, how in any event, anyway Why necessarily? Why must? slightest, any, little	하 하여간 하필 하등

					부처	Buddha; France	불
佛	ノ	イ	仁		佛教	Buddhism	불교
	仁	仴	佛		佛像	statue of the Buddha	불상
人 5 300	佛				佛經	Buddhist scriptures	불경

					지을	compose, write, make; work; do, act	작
作	ノ	イ	仁				
	仁	竹	作		作用	function, work, act	작용
					作品	a creation, a work of art	작품
人 5 301	作				作者	an author	작자

					이길	subdue	극
克	一	十	古		克服	conquer, overcome, subjugate	극복
	古	古	克		超克	conquer	초극
儿 5 302	克				克己	self-denial, self-abnegation	극기

					면할	avoid, escape; remit, excuse	면
免	ノ	ク	ク		免稅	tax exemption, customs exemption	면세
	夕	台	免		免除	exemption	면제
儿 5 303	免				免役	exemption from conscription	면역

					군사	soldier, troops; arms, weapons	병
兵	ノ	イ	仁				
	斤	立	丘		兵役	military service	병역
					兵力	military strength	병력
八 5 304	兵				兵事	military affairs	병사

					찰	cold; indifferent; solitary, quiet	랭
冷	、	ニ	ン		冷水	cold water, water with a meal	냉수
	入	冷	冷		冷靜	calm, composed	냉정
冫 5 305	冷				冷却	cool, refrigerate; be cooled	냉각

	丶	亠	齐	처음	first, the beginning	초
初	齐	齐	初	初期	an early age; beginning of a period	초기
				初級	primary grade, beginning class; low class	초급
刀 5 306	初			初旬	the first ten days of a month	초순

	丶	丷	亼	판단할	judge, discriminate; divide	판
判	亼	半	半	判決	judgment, decision	판결
				判斷	form a judgment, decide	판단
刀 5 307	判			判明	become clear, be ascertained	판명

	丶	口	口	다를	separate; a part; distinguish; other, another	별
別	号	另	別	別途	separate way; separate use; separately	별도
				別名	pseudonym, nickname	별명
刀 5 308	別			區別	discriminate, make a distinction	구별

	丿	二	千	이로울	profit, gain, advantage; interest on money; sharp, cutting; witty	리
利	才	禾	利	利用	utilize, use profitably; exploit	이용
				利益	profit, gain	이익
刀 5 309	利			便利	convenient, handy	편리

	丨	冂	目	도울	help, assist, aid	조
助	月	且	助	助手	helper, assistant	조수
				援助	aid, assist; help, support	원조
力 5 310	助			救助	rescue, save	구조

	乀	夕	女	힘쓸	exert, strive	노
努	如	奴	努	努力	strive, endeavor	노력
力 5 311	努					

79

却	一	十	去	물리칠 reject, decline, withdraw	각
	去	去	却	退却 retreat, withdraw; decline, reject	퇴각
				却説 "once upon a time", "to get back to the story"	각설
卩 5 312	却			却下 reject, decline; dismiss	각하

卵	ノ	ι	ㄅ	알 egg	란
	白	卯	卵	鷄卵 chicken egg	계란
				卵形 oval, egg-shaped	난형
卩 5 313	卵			卵巢 ovary	난소

吟	ヽ	口	口	읊을 hum, intone; moan; sigh; stutter	음
	口`	口人	吟	呻吟 groan, moan	신음
				吟味 savor; scrutinize	음미
口 4 314	吟			吟風弄月 "sing in the breeze and enjoy the moon", compose poetry	음풍농월

君	ㄱ	ㄱ	ㅋ	임금 ruler; gentleman; you	군
	尹	尹	君	君臣 lord and subject	군신
				君子 superior man, the Confucian gentleman	군자
口 4 315	君			君主 king, monarch, ruler	군주

否	一	フ	不	아닐 no, not; if not, whether or not; on the contrary; deny	부
	不	不	否	否認 deny, repudiate	부인
				否定 deny, refuse	부정
口 4 316	否			否決 vote down, reject	부결

吹	ヽ	口	口	불 blow, puff	취
	口'	口ハ	吹	鼓吹 play drums and flutes; inspire; advocate	고취
				吹込 record, cut a record	취입
口 4 317	吹			吹奏樂 music of wind instruments	취주악

吸 口 4 318	丶	口	口	마실	suck in, inhale	흡
	叻	叨	吸	吸收	absorb, assimilate, suck in	흡수
	吸			吸引	absorb, suck up	흡인
				吸煙	smoke tobacco	흡연

吾 口 4 319	一	厂	丙	나	I, me; resist, impede, defend	오
	五	吾	吾	吾等	we, us	오등
	吾			吾兄	my dear friend	오형
				吾人	I, me; we, us; mankind	오인

告 口 4 320	丿	一	牛	알릴	tell, inform, announce	고
	生	告	告	告祀	offering sacrifice to spirits	고사
	告			告白	confess, admit	고백
				報告	report, inform, give account of	보고

困 口 4 321	丨	冂	冂	곤할	difficulty, distress; weary, tired	곤
	用	困	困	困難	be difficult; troublesome	곤란
	困			困境	awkward situation, dilemma	곤경
				疲困	tired, exhausted	피곤

均 土 4 322	一	十	土	고를	equal, fairly	균
	圴	均	均	均衡	balance, equilibrium	균형
	均			均等	equal, uniform, even	균등
				平均	average; on the average	평균

坐 土 4 323	丿	人	从	앉을	sit; seat; assign	좌
	从	坐	坐	坐席	a seat	좌석
	坐			坐視	sit and watch unconcernedly	좌시
				連坐	complicity, implication, involvement	연좌

81

壯	ㄴ	ㄴ	기	씩씩할 robust, strong	**장**
	거	거ー	거	壯元 highest mark in old civil service examinations, examinee who scored it	장원
士 4 324	壯			壯丁 strong young man, sturdy youth	장정
				壯談 assert, assure, guarantee	장담

妙	く	女	女	묘할 wonderful, mysterious; young, subtle	**묘**
	회	회	회	巧妙 skillful, adroit, ingenious	교묘
				妙技 wonderful performance, exquisite skill	묘기
女 4 325	회			妙味 charm, beauty; fine point, nicety	묘미

妨	く	女	女	방해할 hinder, oppose, interfere with	**방**
	女	女	妨	妨害 obstruct, hamper, prevent	방해
				無妨 it is no hindrance, it is of no consequence	무방
女 4 326	妨			妨止 check, stave off, prevent	방지

妥	ノ	へ	へ	온당할 secure, safe; satisfactory; ready	**타**
	受	受	妥	妥協 compromise, come to terms with	타협
				妥當 reasonable, appropriate	타당
女 4 327	妥			妥結 compromise	타결

孝	一	十	土	효도 filial piety	**효**
	耂	考	考	孝女 filial daughter	효녀
				孝誠 filial piety	효성
				孝子 filial son	효자
子 4 328	孝				

完	丶	丷	宀	완전할 complete; finish; whole, unbroken; pay, settle	**완**
	宀	宁	宇	完全 perfect, complete, entire	완전
				完遂 accomplish, bring to successful conclusion	완수
宀 4 329	完			完了 complete, finish	완료

局	ㄱ	ㄱ	尸	판	office, bureau; position, circumstances; chess situation	국
	月	弓	局			
尸 4 330	局			局長	bureau director	국장
				局限	limited, localized	국한
				局部	part, section	국부

尾	ㄱ	ㄱ	尸	꼬리	tail; follow; end	미
	尸	屄	屄	尾行	follow; surveil	미행
尸 4 331	尾			交尾	copulate	교미
				末尾	end, tip	말미

巡	〈	《	巛	돌	go on circuit, cruise, patrol	순
	巛	巡	巡	巡檢	make one's rounds; inspection tour	순검
巛 4 332				巡警	patrolman, policeman; patrol	순경
				巡察	patrol	순찰

希	ノ	メ	ㄨ	바랄	hope for; Greece	희
	乑	矛	希	希望	hope; aspiration; prospect	희망
巾 4 333	希			希求	desire, want, aspire to	희구
				希願	hope, desire	희원

床	、	亠	广	평상	bed, couch; framework; table, desk	상
	广	庁	庁	冊床	desk	책상
广 4 334	床			病床	hospital bed	병상
				平床	a wooden bed	평상

序	、	亠	广	차례	preface; precedence, order	서
	户	庐	序	序文	preface, foreword	서문
广 4 335	序			序論	an introduction, introductory remarks	서론
				順序	program of events; order, sequence	순서

廷	ノ	ニ	千	조정	the court, the government	정
	壬	千	廷	朝廷	the court, the government	조정
				法廷	court of law, tribunal	법정
				宮廷	the Royal Court	궁정
廴 4 336	廷					

延	ノ	イ	千	연기할	postpone, prolong, delay; invite, engage; receive	연
	正	征	延	延期	postpone, put off	연기
				延長	prolong, lengthen	연장
廴 4 337	延			延滯	delay; overdue	연체

弄	一	二	干	희롱할	do, make, act; play with, handle	롱
	王	丟	弄	弄談	joke, jest	농담
				弄奸	intrigue, scheme	농간
廾 4 338	弄			嘲弄	ridicule, derision, mockery	조롱

弟	丶	丷	当	아우	younger brother	제
	当	弟	弟	弟子	disciple, follower, pupil, apprentice	제자
				師弟	teacher and pupil; master and disciple	사제
弓 4 339	弟			兄弟	brothers; sisters; brethren	형제

形	一	二	于	형상	shape, form	형
	开	开'	形	形便	situation, circumstances	형편
				形式	form; formal	형식
彡 4 340	形			形態	form, shape, appearance	형태

役	ノ	ク	イ	부릴	serve, work; military service, conscription; role, duty, function	역
	彳	伇	役			
				役割	role, function, part	역할
彳 4 341	役			役事	do construction work	역사
				役軍	laborer; construction worker	역군

忌	ㄱ	ㄱ	己	꺼릴	taboo; loathe; shun; abstain	기
	己	忌	忌	忌憚	shun, avoid	기탄
				忌避	evade, shun, shirk; take exception, make exception	기피
心 3 342	忌			忌中	in mourning	기중

忍	ㄱ	刀	刃	참을	endure, bear; repress, hold back	인
	刃	忍	忍	忍耐	patience; perseverance	인내
心 3 343	忍					

志	一	十	士	뜻	purpose, will, determination	지
	士	志	志	志士	a patriot	지사
				志願	aspire to; volunteer for	지원
心 3 344	志			志望	desire, ambition	지망

忘	、	亠	亡	잊을	forget, neglect	망
				忘年會	a year-end party	망년회
	亡	忘	忘	忘却	forget, be oblivious to	망각
心 3 345	忘			備忘録	a memo, a memo book	비망록

快	丨	忄	小	쾌할	quick, fast; sharp, keen; cheerful, happy	쾌
	忙	忙	快	快感	pleasant feeling, agreeable sensation	쾌감
				快活	cheerful; animated, light-hearted	쾌활
心 4 346	快			快男兒	jolly fellow, cheerful fellow	쾌남아

成	)	厂	厂	이룰	complete, perfect; succeed; finish, become; whole	성
	斤	成	成	成分	ingredient, component, element	성분
				成功	succeed, achieve	성공
戈 3 347	成			成長	growth	성장

我 戈 3 348	ノ 二 千 千 我 我 我	나 我軍 我國 我田引水	I, me; us, our our army, friendly forces our country draw water to one's own field, promote one's own interests	아 아군 아국 아전인수
戒 戈 3 349	一 二 テ 开 戒 戒 戒	경계할 破戒 戒嚴 警戒	warn, caution; precepts transgress, violate Buddhist law exercise vigilance; martial law warning; precaution; vigilance	계 파계 계엄 경계
扶 手 4 350	一 十 才 扌 扌 扶 扶	도울 扶助 扶養 相扶相助	help; support; prop up sustain, give relief; aid, help support, maintain mutual assistance, interdependence	부 부조 부양 상부상조
批 手 4 351	一 十 才 扌 扎 批 批	비평할 批判 批准 批評家	criticize, comment on; pass on, act on; endorse a petition; authorized criticize, comment on, judge ratification critic, reviewer	비 비판 비준 비평가
抄 手 4 352	一 十 才 扌 扩 抄 抄	뽑을 抄本 抄録 抄譯	seize; copy out; voucher; wholesale extract; abstract; abridged copy to extract, abstract selective translation, excerpt translation	초 초본 초록 초역
投 手 4 353	一 十 才 扌 扠 投 投	던질 投票 投資 投書	throw, cast, hand over; fit in; submit; go toward cast a ballot, vote invest, put up money anonymous note; contribute to, write for	투 투표 투자 투서

				누를	press down, repress; restrain, curb; or, or else	억
抑	一	寸	扌			
	扌	扣	抑	抑制	restrain, control	억제
				抑壓	oppress, repress	억압
手 4 354	抑			抑留	detain, intern	억류

				대항할	oppose, resist	항
抗	一	寸	扌			
	扌	扩	扩	抗拒	resist; rebel against	항거
				抗議	protest, remonstrate	항의
手 4 355	抗			抗爭	dispute, contend; resist	항쟁

				재주	talent, skill, ingenuity	기
技	一	寸	扌			
	扌	扩	technical 技	技術	skill, technical knowhow	기술
				技能	capability, talent	기능
手 4 356	技			技巧	craftsmanship, mechanical skill	기교

				꺾을	snap, break off; reduce, diminish; humble oneself, bow down; barter, sell; fold down	절
折	一	寸	扌			
	扌	扩	折	折半	half; divide in half	절반
手 4 357	折			折衷	make a compromise	절충
				挫折	collapse; be frustrated	좌절

				고칠	renew, revise, change	개
改	フ	コ	己			
	己	改	改	改革	reform	개혁
				改善	improve	개선
支 3 358	改			改良	improve, better	개량

				칠	attack	공
攻	一	丁	工			
	工	攻	攻	攻擊	attack, assault; verbally attack, denounce	공격
				攻防	offensive and defensive	공방
支 3 359	攻			專攻	field of specialization, major	전공

旱	丶	冂	曰	가물	drought	한
	日	旦	旦	旱災	drought, drought damage	한재
				旱魃	dry weather, lack of rain, drought	한발
日 3 360	旱			旱害	drought damage	한해

更	一	丆	冂	다시	**anew, again, newly**	갱
	冋	曰	更	고칠	change, alter; time	경
				更生	revival, rebirth, resuscitation	갱생
				更迭	change, replace, reshuffle	경질
日 3 361	更			更新	renewal, renovation, innovation	갱신

李	一	十	才	오얏	plum; surname: Yi	리
	木	杢	李	行李	baggage, luggage	행리
				李花	plum blossom	이화
木 3 362	李					

材	一	十	才	재목	material, stuff	재
	才	杧	村	材料	materials	재료
				材木	lumber, timber	재목
				資材	resources, material	자재
木 3 363	材					

束	一	冂	戸	묶을	bind; control, restrain, keep in order	속
	冟	束	束	約束	promise, give one's word	약속
				束縛	bind, put under the yoke, shackle	속박
木 3 364	束			束手無策	helpless, one's hands are tied	속수무책

村	一	十	才	마을	village	촌
	才	杧	村	農村	farm village, rural community	농촌
				村落	village, hamlet	촌락
木 3 365	村			村家	village house, country house	촌가

| 步 | ⼁ | ⼘ | ⽌ | 걸음 | step, pace | 보 |
| 止 3 366 | ⽌ | ⾙ | ⾭ | 步兵 步哨 步行 | infantry
sentry, guard
walk, go afoot | 보병
보초
보행 |
| 步 |

| 每 | ⼃ | ⼂ | ⼏ | 매양 | each, every | 매 |
| 毋 3 367 | ⼅ | 句 | 每 | 每日 每年 每回 | every day, each day
each year, yearly
each time; every round/inning | 매일
매년
매회 |
| 每 |

| 決 | ⼂ | ⼆ | ⼼ | 정할 | decide | 결 |
| 水 4 368 | 沪 | 沪 | 決 | 決定 決議 決心 | decide, determine
resolve; resolution
decide, resolve | 결정
결의
결심 |
| 決 |

| 求 | ⼀ | ⼗ | 求 | 구할 | demand, implore, beg, seek, search; buy | 구 |
| 水 2 369 | 求 | 求 | 求 | 求景 求愛 求刑 | inspect; sight-see
woo; court; make love to
demand penalty, prosecute | 구경
구애
구형 |
| 求 |

| 沈 | ⼂ | ⼆ | ⼼ | 잠길 | sink; perish; heavy | 침(심) |
| 水 4 370 | 沙 | 沪 | 沙 | 沈黙 沈鬱 沈沒 | silent, reticent, taciturn
gloomy, melancholy
go to the bottom, sink | 침묵
침울
침몰 |
| 沈 |

| 沐 | ⼂ | ⼆ | ⼼ | 머리감을 | wash, bathe, cleanse | 목 |
| 水 4 371 | 沪 | 沐 | 沐 | 沐浴 沐浴湯 沐浴桶 | bathe, wash oneself
public bathhouse
bathtub | 목욕
목욕탕
목욕통 |
| 沐 |

				빠질	sink; drown; die, dead; no, not	몰
沒	⼂	⼂	氵	沒落	collapse, go to ruin	몰락
	氵	汐	汐	沒頭	absorbed in, engrossed in; give oneself up to, be devoted to	몰두
水 4 372	沒			沒收	confiscate, seize	몰수
	⼂	⼂	氵	모래	sand, gravel, pebbles; granulated	사
沙	氵	沙	氺	沙漠	a desert	사막
				沙汰	landslide; avalanche; mass lay off	사태
水 4 373	沙			沙工	a boatman	사공
	⼂	⺌	⼮	재앙	calamity	재
災	巛	災	災	災難	disaster, calamity	재난
				災害	disaster	재해
火 3 374	災			災民	disaster victims	재민
	⼂	冂	曰	사내	man, male	남
男	田	田	男	男子	a man, a male	남자
				男女	man and woman, male and female	남녀
田 2 375	男			男妹	one's own children; brother and sister	남매
	⼂	厶	乞	어조사	simply, only (as a final particle)	의
矣	台	乞	矢	萬事休矣	All is lost! All hope is gone!	만사휴의
矢 2 376	矣					
	丿	二	千	빼어날	accomplished, refined, elegant	수
秀	禾	禾	禾	秀麗	graceful; handsome	수려
				秀才	a prodigy, a genius	수재
禾 2 377	秀			優秀	superior; predominant	우수

私	ノ	ニ	チ	사정	private, personal; illicit	사
	矛	禾	私	私立	private establishment institution	사립
禾 2 378	私			私有	private ownership	사유
				私利	self-interest, private gain	사리

究	、	ハ	宀	궁구할	examine, research	구
	宀	穴	灾	講究	deliberate, study, consider	강구
				探究	investigate, inquire, research	탐구
穴 2 379	究			研究	study, research	연구

系	一	ノ	歪	혈통	connection; lineage; related	계
	玊	乑	系	系統	lineage; source, origin; network, system	계통
糸 1 380	系			系列	an order; faction; party	계열
				系譜	genealogy; lineage	계보

肖	l	⺀	小	같을	like, likeness, imitate	초
	心	肖	肖	肖像	a portrait, likeness	초상
				肖似	resemblance	초사
肉 3 381	肖			不肖	be unworthy of one's father, be unlike one's father	불초

肝	ノ	刀	月	간	liver	간
	月	肝	肝	肝油	liver oil, cod-liver oil	간유
				肝臟	the liver	간장
肉 3 382	肝			肝膽	liver and gall; one's innermost heart	간담

良	、	⺈	⺩	어질	good, excellent; peaceful; virtuous	량
	当	自	良	良心	conscience	양심
				良民	good citizens, respectable people	양민
艮 1 383	良			良好	good, fine, satisfactory	양호

見	丨	冂	目	볼 나타날	see, observe, perceive appear, get seen	견 현
	目	目	見	見地 見本 謁見	view, standpoint sample, specimen royal (presidential) audience	견지 견본 一알현
見 0 384	見					
角	丿	ク	ク	뿔	horn; corner, angle	각
	门	角	角	直角 角度 角膜	a right angle an angle; view, standpoint cornea	직각 각도 각막
角 0 385	角					
言	丶	亠	言	말씀	words, speech; talk, speak, express; mean	언
	言	言	言	言語 言及 言行	language, speech allude to, mention words and deeds, speech and action	언어 언급 언행
言 0 386	言					
谷	丿	八	公	골	valley, ravine	곡
	父	谷	谷	山谷 幽谷 峽谷	mountain valley dark valley, deep valley gorge, canyon, ravine	산곡 유곡 협곡
谷 0 387	谷					
豆	一	一	口	콩	beans; peas	두
	口	戸	豆	大豆 豆腐 綠豆	soy beans bean curd green peas	대두 두부 녹두
豆 0 388	豆					
貝	丨	冂	目	조개	shells; treasure	패
	目	目	貝	貝類 貝物 貝殼	shellfish shellware, shell goods a shell	패류 패물 패각
貝 0 389	貝					

赤 赤 0 390	一 赤	十	土 赤	붉을 red; naked 赤道 the equator 赤十字 the Red Cross 赤化 communize, sovietize	적 적도 적십자 적화
走 走 0 391	一 走	十 卡	土 赤	달아날 run, walk, go, travel 逃走 run away, flee, escape 競走 a foot race, a sprint 走馬看山 view cursorily, snatch a look from a running horse	주 도주 경주 주마간산
足 足 0 392	丶 尸 足	口 足	口 足	발 foot; enough, complete, full 豐足 abundant, plentiful 不足 insufficient, short, wanting 滿足 satisfied, contented	족 풍족 부족 만족
身 身 0 393	丿 勺 身	亻 自	勹 身	몸 body, person; hull; oneself, I, me; lifetime 身體 the body 身分 social position; identity 身長 height; stature	신 신체 신분 신장
車 車 0 394	一 車	一 百	亓 亘	수레 carriage, chariot; vehicle 自轉車 bicycle 車輛 vehicles 自動車 automobile, car, truck	거 (차) 자전거 차량 자동차
辛 辛 0 395	丶 立 辛	亠 立	亠 立	쓸 bitter, acrid; distressing, toilsome, grievous 辛苦 suffer bitter experiences 辛辣 be sharp, biting, pungent 辛味 spicy hot taste	신 신고 신랄 신미

辰
 	
辰 0
396
	一
	尸
	辰
		厂
		辰
			尸
			辰
				별
				辰時
				
				日辰
				
				生辰
					5th of the 12 Earth's
					   Branches; star; dragon
					Watch of the Star, the period
					   between 7 and 9 A.M.
					the binary designation
					   of the day
					birthday
						진 (신)
						진시
						
						일진
						
						생신

邑
 	
邑 0
397
	丶
	弓
	邑
		口
		吕
			口
			吕
				고을
				邑内
				
				都邑
				
				邑長
					town, township
					town; in town; head
					   village of a township
					the capital;
					   set up a capital
					town mayor
						읍
						읍내
						
						도읍
						
						읍장

邪
 	
邑 4
398
	一
	牙
	邪
		二
		牙'
			于
			邪
				간사할
				
				妖邪
				
				邪道
				
				邪戀
					depraved, vicious, heretical;
					   evil, demoniacal
					capricious, fickle; vicious;
					   weird; crafty, cunning
					vice, an evil course;
					   heresy, heterodoxy
					illicit love, wicked love
						사
						
						요사
						
						사도
						
						사련

邦
 	
邑 4
399
	ノ
	丰
	邦
		二
		丰'
			三
			邦
				나라
				聯邦
				
				友邦
					state, country, nation
					commonwealth,
					   federal state,
					   confederation
					ally, friendly state
						방
						연방
						
						우방

那 邑 4 400	ノ 月 那	刀 那'	月 那	어찌 刹那 那落 那邊	that, there; what, where moment, instant hell, an inferno vicinity, neighborhood; where	나 찰나 나락 나변

酉
 	
酉 0
401
	一
	丙
	酉
		丆
		西
			丏
			西
				닭
				酉時
				
				酉年
				酉日
					10th of the 12 Earth's
					   Branches; cock, rooster
					Watch of the Cock,
					   the period between
					   5 and 7 P.M.
					Year of the Rooster
					Day of the Rooster
						유
						유시
						
						유년
						유일

里	丶	𠃌	曰	마을	village; street; a *li*, about one-third mile	리
	日	旦	甲	洞里	a village	동리
				里長	village chief	이장
里 0 402	里			萬里長城	Great Wall of China	만리장성

防	⁊	阝	阝	막을	embank; prevent, guard against, ward off	방
	阝	阝⁻	防	防衛	defense (as in ''defense industry'')	방위
阜 4 403	防			防備	fortify, defend	방비
				防空	air defense	방공

含	丿	人	스	머금을	hold in the mouth	함
	今	今	含	含水	hydrous, hydrate	함수
				包含	include, contain; embraces; covers	포함
口 4 404	含			含蓄	imply, suggest	함축

8 Strokes

乳	丿	⺊	乊	젖	milk; breast, nipple; suckle	유
	乊	糸	孚	乳母	a wet nurse	유모
				乳酸	lactic acid	유산
乙 7 405	乳	乳		乳房	the female breast	유방

事	一	二	冚	일	affair, matter; undertaking, business; serve	사
	口	写	写	事實	fact, reality; actuality; truth	사실
				事情	circumstances, the situation, state of things	사정
丨 7 406	写	事		事件	incident, affair, case	사건

亞	一	ㅜ	ㄷ	버금	secondary, inferior; ugly; Asia	아
	亞	亞	亞	亞麻	flax, hemp	아마
				亞熱帶	the subtropics; subtropical	아열대
二 6 407	亞	亞		亞細亞	Asia	아세아

享	丶	亠	亠	누릴	enjoy; receive	향
	市	言	亨	享樂	enjoy, seek pleasure in	향락
				享年	one's age at death	향년
亠 6 408	亨	享		享壽	enjoy longevity	향수

京	丶	亠	亠	서울	a capital; metropolis	경
	市	古	亨	上京	go to Seoul	상경
				京鄉	the capital and the country	경향
亠 6 409	京	京		京城	former name of Seoul	경성

使	丿	亻	仁	하여금	employ, use; send; cause; messenger	사
	仁	何	何	使用	use, employ, apply	사용
				使節	delegation, mission	사절
人 6 410	使	使		天使	angel, messenger from God	천사

佳	丿	亻	仁	아름다울	beautiful; fine, good	가
	什	件	佳	佳作	good piece of creative work	가작
				佳人	beautiful woman	가인
人 6 411	佳	佳		佳境	delightful spot; interesting part	가경

來	一	十	才	올	come, coming	래
	才	木	來	來日	tomorrow	내일
				將來	the future; prospects, possibilities	장래
人 6 412	來	來		來週	next week	내주

例 ロ ロ	ノ	イ	仁	법식	law, regulation; custom, precedent, usage, example	례
	仴	佀	佀	實例	concrete example	실례
				例事	common practice, custom; customary	예사
人 6 413	例	例		例年	average year	예년

供	ノ	イ	仁	이바지할	supply, contribute	공
	仕	供	供	供給	supply, furnish, provide	공급
				提供	furnish, provide	제공
人 6 414	供	供		供出	deliver produce to the government at the fixed official price	공출

侍	ノ	イ	仁	모실	serve, wait upon	시
	仕	仕	佳	侍女	lady-in-waiting, female attendant	시녀
				侍從	chamberlain, lord-in-waiting, male attendant	시종
人 6 415	侍	侍		侍生	I, me, your humble servant	시생

依	ノ	イ	亻	의지할	depend on, trust, comply with, follow; obey; according to	의
	仁	佂	仿	依支	depend upon	의지
				依賴	request; entrust; depend upon	의뢰
人 6 416	依	依		依存	rely on, depend on	의존

兔	コ	カ	尹	토끼	rabbit	토
	刕	刕	孕	兎糞	rabbit droppings	토분
				兎舍	hutch, rabbit box	토사
儿 6 417	兎	兎		兎皮	rabbit skin	토피

兒	´	仁	门	아이	son, child	아
	臼	臼	臼	兒童	child, children	아동
				孤兒	orphan	고아
儿 6 418	臾	兒		小兒	infant; young child	소아

兩 入 6 419	一 而 兩	一 而 兩	一 而 兩	두 兩班 兩親 兩得	two, a pair, both; a tael aristocrats, two classes of Korean noblemen parents a double gain, kill two birds with one stone	량 양반 양친 양득
其 八 6 420	一 廿 其	十 甘 其	廿 苴	그 其他 及其也 各其	its; his; that the others, the rest; et cetera at last, in the end each, individually	기 기타 급기야 각기
具 八 6 421	丶 目 具	冂 目 具	目 且	갖출 具體的 具備 器具	prepare; tool, implement concrete, tangible, definite possess, be equipped with implements; fixtures; tools	구 구체적 구비 기구
典 八 6 422	丶 用 典	冂 曲 典	曰 曲	법 辭典 古典 典型的	law; documents; control; mortgage dictionary, lexicon a classic, the classics, old books typical, model	전 사전 고전 전형적
到 刀 6 423	一 죠 到	乙 至 到	五 至	이를 到着 到處 到來	arrive at, reach arrive at a destination everywhere, everyplace arrival, advent; visitation	도 도착 도처 도래
制 刀 6 424	丿 仒 制	仨 片 制	二 牛	법 制限 制定 制服	laws; regulate, govern; determine, decide, fix; prepare restrict, limit establish, enact, institute regulation dress, uniform	제 제한 제정 제복

刷

刀 6
425

박을	brush; scrub, cleanse; print	쇄
印刷	printing	인쇄
刷新	reform, renovate, clean up	쇄신
縮刷版	pocket edition	축쇄판

券

刀 6
426

문서	contract, bond, deed, chit, bank note	권
證券	certificate, bond, security	증권
旅券	a passport	여권
入場券	admission ticket	입장권

刺

刀 6
427

찌를	stab; thorn; card	자 (척)
刺戟	stimulate, incite, irritate	자극
刺繡	embroider; embroidery	자수
刺客	assassin	자객

刻

刀 6
428

새길	engrave	각
刻苦	work laboriously; apply oneself	각고
刻薄	severe, harsh, hardhearted; miserly, stingy	각박
刻木	woodcarving	각목

卑

十 6
429

낮을	low, inferior, humble; I, me, my	비
卑怯	cowardly, craven	비겁
卑屈	obsequious, sneaking, craven	비굴
卑賤	lowly, obscure, humble	비천

卒

十 6
430

군졸	soldier; underling; to die, finish; finally, completely; suddenly, urgently	졸
卒業	graduate, complete a course of study	졸업
卒兵	enlisted man	졸병

協	一	十	十
	十力	十劦	协
十 6 431	協	協	

화할 harmonize; agree; unite　　협

協定 agreement, pact　　협정
協力 cooperate, work together　　협력
協同 collaborate; join forces with　　협동

卷	丶	丷	丷
	丷	半	关
卩 6 432	券	卷	

책권 book, volume, scroll　　권

卷頭言 foreword, preface　　권두언
上卷 volume one, book one　　상권
席卷 overwhelm, overrun　　석권

取	一	厂	厂
	耳	耳	耳
又 6 433	取	取	

가질 take　　취

取扱 handle, deal with, treat　　취급
取得 acquire, purchase　　취득
取調 examine, investigate　　취조

叔	一	卜	上
	上	赤	赤
又 6 434	叔	叔	

아재비 younger brother of one's father　　숙

叔父 uncle, younger brother of one's father　　숙부
叔母 wife of the younger brother of one's father　　숙모

受	丷	丷	丷
	爫	爫	爫
又 6 435	受	受	

받을 receive; endure, suffer　　수

受信 receive a message, receive　　수신
受難 suffer, face hardships　　수난
引受 take over, assume　　인수

周	丿	门	门
	用	周	周
口 5 436	周	周	

두루 encircle; all around; complete, entire; relieve; assist　　주

周圍 circumference; environs, vicinity　　주위
周邊 circumference; environs　　주변
周旋 arrange; aid, assist　　주선

味	﹀	﹁﹁	口	맛	taste, flavor, scent	미
	口一	口二	吐	意味	meaning, significance, import	의미
				趣味	hobby; taste, interest	취미
口 5 437	吽	味		興味	interesting, attracting, amusing	흥미

呼	﹀	﹁	口	부를	cry out, call; exhale	호
	口′	口′	吖	呼吸	respiration, breath; time, rhythm	호흡
				呼應	call to; act in concert	호응
口 5 438	吁	呼		呼名	call roll; call a person by name	호명

命	﹀	人	合	목숨	life; command	명
	令	合	合	命令	order, command	명령
				天命	will of Heaven, God's will	천명
口 5 439	命	命		生命	life	생명

和	′	二	千	화할	harmony, peace	화
	禾	禾	和	和睦	be at harmony, be at peace	화목
				和親	amity, friendly relations	화친
口 5 440	和	和		和平	peace, harmony	화평

固	﹀	冂	冃	굳을	firm, strong	고
	冃	用	周	固體	a solid	고체
				固執	stubborn; persistent	고집
口 5 441	固	固		堅固	firm, solid, strong	견고

坤	一	十	土	땅	the earth; last of the 8 trigrams	곤
	圠	圳	坦	坤殿	queen	곤전
				坤道	womanhood, the duty of women	곤도
土 5 442	坦	坤		坤方	southwest	곤방

夜 夕 5 443	、 广 广 夜 夜	亠 疒 疒 夜	广 疒 夜	밤 night, nighttime; the dark 야 夜間 nighttime, night 야간 夜警 night guard 야경 夜勤 night duty, night shift work 야근
奇 大 5 444	一 太 呑 奇	ナ 杏 奇	大 吞	기이할 strange, rare, wonderful 기 奇異 curious, extraordinary 기이 奇妙 strange, odd; exquisite, wonderful 기묘 奇談 a strange story 기담
奈 大 5 445	一 太 奈	ナ 夵 奈	大 杢	어찌 but, how; endure 내(나) 奈何 how 내하 奈落 hell, hades, the inferno 나락
奉 大 5 446	一 丰 表	二 夫 奉	三 奏	받들 receive with both hands; offer; serve; respectfully 봉 奉仕 service, serve 봉사 奉職 serve in government, hold official office 봉직 奉養 support one's parents, serve parents 봉양
奔 大 5 447	一 本 牵	ナ 本 奔	大 奉	분주할 be in a hurry; urgent; run away 분 奔走 be busy; distracting 분주 奔忙 be very busy, rushed, pressed for time 분망 狂奔 be busy; run madly about, run amuck 광분
妾 女 5 448	、 六 妾	亠 立 妾	亠 亥	첩 concubine 첩 妾 concubine, mistress 첩 蓄妾 keep a mistress 축첩 愛妾 favorite concubine, beloved mistress 애첩

姉	く	么	女	누이	elder sister	자
	女'	女宀	女宀	姉妹	sisters	자매
				姉兄	an older sister's husband	자형
女 5 449	姉宁	姉		長姉	the eldest sister	장자
				(Originally 姊 .)		

妹	く	么	女	손아래누이 younger sister		매
	女一	女二	女丰	男妹	brother and sister	남매
				妹夫	brother-in-law, husband of one's sister	매부
女 5 450	妹	妹		妹兄	an older sister's husband	매형

妻	一	丁	三	아내	wife	처
	圭	妻	妻	妻子	one's wife and children	처자
				妻男	brother-in-law, brother of one's wife	처남
女 5 451	妻	妻		妻家	home/family of one's wife	처가

始	く	么	女	비로소 begin, start; first		시
	女'	女ム	女ム	始作	begin, start	시작
				始初	the beginning, inception	시초
女 5 452	始	始		始動	start (as a vehicle)	시동

姓	く	么	女	성	surname; clan; people	성
	女'	女宀	女七	百姓	the people, citizens of a nation	백성
				姓名	surname and given name, full name	성명
女 5 453	女牛	姓		同姓	the same surname	동성

姑	く	么	女	시어머니 husband's mother; husband's sister; father's sister		고
	女一	女宀	女古			
				姑母	paternal aunt	고모
女 5 454	姑古	姑		姑婦	mother-in-law and daughter-in-law	고부

103

委 女 5 455	'	二	千
	禾	禾	禾
	委	委	

맡길 put in charge of, commission; give up; petty **위**

委員 committee member 위원
委任 entrust, authorize 위임
委託 entrust, commission 위탁

孟 子 5 456	'	了	子
	子	舌	舌
	孟	孟	

맏 great, senior, eldest, first, chief; Mencius **맹**

孟浪 false; untrue; incredible; unbelievable 맹랑
孟子 Mencius 맹자
孟春 early spring 맹춘

季 子 5 457	'	二	千
	禾	禾	季
	季	季	

끝 last of a series; young and tender; season, seasonal **계**

季節 a season 계절
季刊 a quarterly publication 계간
季氏 your/his esteemed younger brother 계씨

孤 子 5 458	'	了	子
	孑	孔	孤
	孤	孤	

외로울 lonely, alone; orphan **고**

孤兒 orphan 고아
孤獨 friendless, lonesome, lonely 고독
孤立 stand alone, be isolated, helpless 고립

官 宀 5 459	'	'	宀
	宀	官	官
	官	官	

벼슬 government official **관**

官廳 government office 관청
官吏 government official 관리
警官 police officer; the police 경관

宜 宀 5 460	'	'	宀
	宀	宀	宜
	宜	宜	

마땅할 right, fitting; ought, should; suitable **의**

便宜 convenient; advantageous 편의
宜當 natural, matter of course; right, proper 의당

宗	、	丶	宀	마루	class, sect; ancestral; clan; distinguished	종
	宀	空	宀	宗教	religion, a religion	종교
				宗廟	Royal Ancestral Tablet Hall	종묘
宀 5 461	宗	宗		宗派	religious sect	종파

宙	、	宀	宀	집	universe; eternity	주
	宀	宀	宀	宇宙	the universe, the cosmos	우주
				宇宙旅行	space travel	우주여행
宀 5 462	宙	宙				

定	、	宀	宀	정할	fix, settle, decide	정
	宀	宀	宀	定期	regular, scheduled, periodic; a fixed period	정기
				定價	fixed price	정가
宀 5 463	定	定		定量	set amount, fixed quantity	정량

尚	丨	小	小	오히려	still, yet, and besides; add; esteem; surpass; in charge of	상
	小	尚	尚	高尚	noble, elegant; high-minded	고상
小 5 464	尚	尚		尚今	still, as yet, even up till now	상금

居	一	一	尸	살	dwell, remain, occupy, be in	거
	尸	尸	居	居處	dwell at, live in	거처
				居住	dwell, reside, inhabit	거주
尸 5 465	居	居		居室	a living room	거실

屈	一	一	尸	굽힐	bend it down; wrong, injustice	굴
	尸	屈	屈	屈辱	humiliation, disgrace	굴욕
				屈曲	bent, winding	굴곡
尸 5 466	屈	屈		屈服	surrender, yield	굴복

岸	ノ	山	山	언덕	shore, bank, beach	안
	屵	屵	屵	沿岸	coast, shore	연안
				海岸	seashore, seacoast	해안
山 5	岸	岸		彼岸	the other shore;	피안
467					the other world,	
					the promised land	

岳	ノ	⺊	⺊	큰산	mountain peak	악
	仟	丘	乓	山岳	mountain peaks	산악
				山岳人	alpinist	산악인
山 5	岳	岳		雪岳山	Mt. Sŏrak	설악산
468						

幸	一	十	土	다 행	fortunate, lucky	행
	𡈼	去	击	不幸	unfortunate, unhappy	불행
				幸福	happy, blissful, fortunate	행복
干 5	垚	幸		幸運	good fortune, good luck	행운
469						

底	丶	亠	广	밑	bottom, base	저
	广	庀	庄	徹底히	thoroughly, exhaustively	철저
				底意	intention	저의
广 5	底	底		底邊	base line	저변
470						

府	丶	亠	广	마을	prefecture; treasury;	부
	广	疒	疘		palace; mansion;	
					storehouse	
				政府	the government,	정부
广 5	府	府			the administration	
471				府院君	queen's father's title	부원군
					(Great Lord)	

庚	丶	亠	广	일곱째천간	7th of the 10 Heavenly	경
	庁	庚	庚		Stems; evening star	
				庚戌	47th of the 60 binary	경술
广 5	庚	庚			terms of the	
472					sexagenary cycle	

店	丶	亠	广	가게	shop, inn, tavern	점
	广	庐	店	本店	head office, main store	본점
广 5 473	店	店		店員	clerk, salesperson	점원
				閉店	close a store; go out of business	폐점

弦	¬	ㄱ	弓	활시위	bowstring	현
	引	引	弦	上弦	a young (waxing) moon	상현
弓 5 474	弦	弦		弦月	a crescent moon, new moon	현월
				弦樂	string music	현악

往	丿	彳	彳	갈	go towards, depart; gone; formerly, past	왕
	彳	行	行	往來	comings and goings, coming and going	왕래
彳 5 475	往	往		往復	go and come, go and return; round trip	왕복
				往往	often, time and again	왕왕

彼	丿	彳	彳	저	that, those; he, them; the other one, the other ones	피
	初	彷	彼	彼此	this and that; you and I; both	피차
彳 5 476	彼	彼		彼我	we and they, both parties, both sides	피아

征	丿	彳	彳	정벌할	subdue; attack; levy taxes, raise troops; go, pass time	정
	彳	彳	征	征服	conquer, subjugate, master	정복
彳 5 477	征	征		征伐	conquer, subjugate	정벌
				遠征	go on expedition	원정

忠	丶	口	口	충성	loyal, devoted	충
	中	中	忠	忠臣	loyal subject, faithful retainer	충신
心 4 478	忠	忠		忠告	advice, counsel; warning	충고
				忠義	loyalty, fidelity	충의

107

	ノ	ク	勺	문득	suddenly; despise, snub, be inconsiderate	홀
忽	勿	勿	忽	忽地	suddenly, unexpectedly	홀지
				忽然히	suddenly, in an instant	홀연시
心 4 479	忽	忽		忽視	slight, snub, be inconsiderate of	홀시
	ノ	入	스	생각할	think of, recall; chant, repeat from memory	념
念	今	今	念	念慮	worry, be uneasy	염려
				概念	concept	개념
心 4 480	念	念		雜念	distracting thoughts; worldy thoughts	잡념
	｜	｜	忄	성품	nature; anger; property, quality; sex	성
性	忄	忄	忄	性質	nature; property; character	성질
				性格	personality, character	성격
心 5 481	忄	性		性別	sex (whether male or female)	성별
	｜	｜	忄	괴상할	weird, strange, uncanny	괴
怪	忄	怪	怪	怪常	odd, strange, monstrous	괴상
				怪物	monster, creature; mysterious figure	괴물
心 5 482	怪	怪		怪漢	strange character, suspicious-looking fellow	괴한
	一	一	戸	혹	perhaps; some	혹
或	戸	豆	或	或時	by chance; sometimes	혹시
				間或	occasionally; at times; rarely	간혹
戈 4 483	或	或		或者	someone, some person	혹자
	丶	亠	彐	방	room; house, building, shop; concubine; wife	방
房	戸	戸	庐	房門	door of a room	방문
				茶房	tearoom	다방
戸 4 484	房	房		冷房	a cool room; cooling a room, air conditioning	냉방

					바	place; office, bureau; actually; that which; him who; what, whatsoever; whereby	소
所謂	so-called, what is called	소위
所聞	rumor, gossip	소문
戶 4 485		所得	income, earnings	소득

所

이을	receive, inherit; support; hold, contain; contract for; continue; acknowledge; flatter; meet
承認	consent, approve, recognize	승인
承諾	approve, accept, consent	승낙
手 4 486	傳承	hand down	전승

承

안을	embrace, take in the arms	포
抱負	ambition, aspiration	포부
抱擁	embrace, hug	포옹
手 5 487	懷抱	innermost thoughts	회포

抱

밀칠	resist, oppose; substitute	저
抵抗	resist, stand against; defy, oppose	저항
抵當	a mortgage	저당
手 5 488	抵觸	conflict with, contravene	저촉

抵

뽑을	pull out, take out; levy	추
抽籤	lottery; draw lots	추첨
抽象的	abstract, metaphysical	추상적

抽 手 5 489

털	shake off, brush away; expel	불
支拂	pay; payment	지불
拂下	sell, transfer	불하
手 5 490	拂拭	clean, wipe out, sweep off	불식

拂

109

				막을	resist, oppose	거
拒	一	扌	扌	拒否	reject, deny, veto	거부
	扌	扩	拒	拒絶	refuse, rebuff, reject	거절
手 5 491	拒	拒		抗拒	disobey, rebel	항거

				손뼉칠	strike with the hand, pat, clap	박
拍	一	扌	扌			
	扌	扩	拍	拍手	applause, clapping	박수
手 5 492	拍	拍		拍子	musical beat, time, rhythm	박자

				열	open up	척
拓	一	扌	扌	박을	take up, pick up; collect	탁
	扌	扩	拓	開拓	pioneer, bring under cultivation; exploit, develop	개척
手 5 493	拓	拓		拓本	rubbing, stone rubbing	탁본
				干拓	reclaim land by drainage	간척

				뽑을	root up, extract, pull out, pluck	발
拔	一	扌	扌			
	扌	扩	拔	拔萃	excel, be outstanding; abstract, select	발췌
				選拔	select, choose; draft	선발
手 5 494	拔	拔		奇拔	original, novel	기발

				잡을	grasp; adhere	구
拘	一	扌	扌	拘束	restrain; put under restraint	구속
	扌	扚	拘	拘留	detain, keep in custody	구류
手 5 495	拘	拘		不拘	not be hindered by; disregard obstacles	불구

				옹졸할	clumsy, unskillful, stupid; one's own	졸
拙	一	扌	扌	拙夫	your humble husband	졸부
	扌	扑	扯	拙劣	clumsy, awkward, inexpert	졸렬
手 5 496	拙	拙		拙作	poor work; my unworthy work	졸작

招	一 丨 扌		부를	call; beckon; proclaim; welcome, receive; cause; confess	초
	扌 扚 扚		招來	bring about, cause	초래
手 5 497	扨 招		招待	invite	초대
			招人鐘	doorbell, a call bell	초인종

放	丶 亠 亠		놓을	place in, place on; release, loosen, liberate; let go; drive away; indulge	방
	方 方 扩		放送	(radio) broadcasting	방송
攴 4 498	扴 放		放學	school vacation	방학
			放出	release, emit, discharge	방출

於	丶 亠 亠		어조사	in, on, at, to, by	어
			탄식소리	sigh, lament	오
	方 扩 扵		於焉間	so soon, before one is aware of the passage of time	어언간
方 4 499	扵 於		於是乎	thereupon, at this	어시호
			甚至於	what is more	심지어

明	丨 刂 日		밝을	bright; understand; chastity; explain	명
	日 明 明		明朗	bright, cheerful	명랑
日 4 500	明 明		明白	plain, obvious	명백
			明確	definite, clear	명확

易	丨 𠃌 日		바꿀	change, mutation	역
	日 旦 昜		쉬울	easy; lenient	이
			貿易	trade, commerce	무역
日 4 501	昜 易		容易	easy, simple	용이
			易學	fortune telling, divination	역학

昇	丶 𠃌 日		오를	ascend; peaceful	승
	日 貝 旦		昇降	ascend and descend; fluctuate	승강
日 4 502	㫕 昇		昇天	ascension to heaven	승천
			昇級	be promoted	승급

昌	丶	冂	曰	창성할 prosperous; glorious	창
	日	日	昌	繁昌 prosperous, thriving	번창
				昌盛 prosperous, flourishing	창성
日 4 503	昌	昌		隆昌 thriving, flourishing	융창

昏	丶	乇	氏	어두울 dark; confused; stupid	혼
	氏	氏	昏	黃昏 dusk, twilight	황혼
				昏倒 faint, fall unconscious	혼도
日 4 504	昏	昏		昏睡 lapse into a coma, become comatose	혼수

昔	一	卄	卄	예 ancient times; formerly; a long time	석
	共	苁	昔		
				今昔 past and present	금석
日 4 505	昔	昔		昔年 last year; ancient times	석년

朋	丿	几	月	벗 friend, companion; match, pair	붕
	月	刖	朋	朋友 friend, companion	붕우
				朋黨 faction, clique, coterie	붕당
月 4 506	朋	朋		朋友有信 "confidence between friends"	붕우유신

服	丿	八	月	옷 clothes; swallow; dose of medicine; serve, submit	복
	月	月	肝	克服 overcome, conquer	극복
				服從 obey; yield	복종
月 4 507	朋	服		服務 public service	복무

板	一	十	才	널 board, plank	판
	木	朾	朾	板子 a board, a plank	판자
				板本 woodblock-printed book	판본
木 4 508	板	板		板門店 P'anmunjŏm	판문점

杯 木 4 509	一 木 扛	十 朴 杯	才 扣	잔 苦杯 祝杯 巡杯	cup, tumbler, glass a bitter cup, hardships; be sadly defeated a toast, to toast pass around the wine cup	배 고배 축배 순배

東 木 4 510	一 司 東	一 百 東	一 東	동녘 東西 東洋 東邦	east
					east and west; the East
					  and the West
					the East, the Orient
					Korea; an eastern country;
					  an Oriental country
						동
						동서
						
						동양
						동방

松 木 4 511	一 木 松	十 杪 松	才 朴	소나무 松林 松蟲 松竹	pine tree; fir tree pine forest pine-eating caterpillar pine and bamboo	송 송림 송충 송죽
林 木 4 512	一 木 材	十 朷 林	才 村	수풀 林業 林產 農林	grove, forest; grave; collection of books forestry forest products agriculture and forestry	림 임업 임산 농림
析 木 4 513	一 木 析	十 朾 析	才 析	쪼갤 分析 解析	divide, split, break analyze; analysis analyze, study	석 분석 해석
枕 木 4 514	一 木 杪	十 朷 枕	才 朳	베개 枕木 木枕 枕席	a pillow a block; railroad crosstie wooden pillow pillow and bed; sleeping place	침 침목 목침 침석

8 strokes

果 木 4 515	丶 日 男	冂 旦 果	日 甲	과실 果實 果然 果樹園	fruit; results fruit as expected, sure enough orchard	과 과실 과연 과수원
枝 木 4 516	一 才 杧	十 村 枝	才 朴	가지 枝葉 枝幹 竹枝	branch branches and leaves; nonessentials, minor details trunk and branches bamboo branches	지 지엽 지간 죽지
武 止 4 517	一 ﾃ 武	二 疋 武	亍 正	건장할 武器 武裝 武術	military; warlike, fierce; firm; violent weapons, arms arm, bear arms, equip and arm military arts	무 무기 무장 무술
毒 毋 4 518	一 主 毒	二 夌 毒	丰 青	독 毒蛇 毒藥 毒感	poison; evil, hurtful a poisonous snake poison influenza, a bad cold	독 독사 독약 독감
河 水 5 519	丶 氵 沪	氵 汀 河	氵 河	물 河川 河馬 運河	river rivers; streams and rivers hippopotamus canal, waterway	하 하천 하마 운하
油 水 5 520	丶 沂 油	氵 汩 油	氵 沪	기름 石油 油田 原油	oil, fat, grease; paint, varnish petroleum; kerosene an oil field crude oil, petroleum	유 석유 유전 원유

114

					다스릴 govern; regulate; punish; cure, heal	치
治	`冫`	`氵`	`汁`			
	`汋`	`治`	`治`		自治 autonomy, self-government	자치
水 5 521	`治`	`治`			治安 public peace	치안
					治療 medical treatment	치료

					물따를 follow a course, go along; hand down, continue, conserve; along; riverside	연
沿	`冫`	`氵`	`氵`			
	`氿`	`沿`	`沿`		沿岸 seacoast	연안
水 5 522	`沿`	`沿`			沿革 history; development; changes	연혁
					沿道 area along a route/way	연도

					하물며 all the more, all the less	황
況	`冫`	`氵`	`氵`			
	`氿`	`沪`	`汩`		盛況 prosperity, success	성황
水 5 523	`沪`	`況`			近況 recent situation, recent conditions	근황
					戰況 battle situation, war situation	전황

					쉴 be at leisure, rest, spend the night	박
泊	`冫`	`氵`	`氵`			
	`氵`	`汋`	`泊`		外泊 lodge away from home	외박
水 5 524	`泊`	`泊`			宿泊 lodge, stay at, stop at	숙박
					碇泊 anchor, berth, moor	정박

					법 law, statute, rule; plan, method; example; doctrines of Buddha	법
法	`冫`	`氵`	`氵`			
	`汁`	`汁`	`法`		法律 a law; the law	법률
水 5 525	`法`	`法`			法院 court of law	법원
					法官 a judge	법관

					울 cry, weep	읍
泣	`冫`	`氵`	`氵`			
	`氵`	`汸`	`汸`		感泣 be moved to tears	감읍
水 5 526	`泣`	`泣`			泣諫 tearful remonstrance	읍간
					泣請 implore, request with tears	읍청

115

波	丶	氵	氵	물결	waves (on water)	파
	氵	氵	沪	波濤	waves, rough sea	파도
水 5				波動	wave-motion, undulation; fluctuation	파동
527	波	波		波紋	ripples	파문

泥	丶	氵	氵	진흙	mud, mire; plaster; paste	니
	氵	氵	泥	泥醉	get dead drunk	이취
水 5				泥土	mud; clay, potter's clay	이토
528	泥	泥		泥金	gilt paint	이금

注	丶	氵	氵	물댈	pour water; concentrate	주
	氵	汁	汁	注意	heed, pay attention, be cautious of	주의
水 5				注文	order (as a suit of clothes), commission	주문
529	注	注		注目	take notice, pay attention	주목

泳	丶	氵	氵	헤엄칠	swim, dive	영
	氵	氵	泳	水泳	swim	수영
水 5				背泳	the backstroke	배영
530	泳	泳		水泳場	swimming pool	수영장

炎	丶	丷	少	불꽃	flame; bright; brilliant; inflammation, … itis	염
	火	火	炒	炎熱	intense summer heat	염열
火 4				炎天	broiling weather; a blazing sun	염천
531	炎	炎		暴炎	intense heat	폭염

爭	丿	丷	爫	다툴	dispute, wrangle	쟁
	爫	爭	爭	競爭	contest, competition	경쟁
爪 4				鬪爭	struggle; strife; a campaign	투쟁
532	爭	爭		爭奪	compete, scramble, struggle	쟁탈

				조각	printing block	판
版	ノ	ゝ	广	版局	situation, state of affairs	판국
	片	片	片	組版	set type, compose type	조판
片 4 533	版	版		出版	publish, print, bring out	출판

				만물	things; matter; articles, goods	물
物	ノ	ゝ	牛			
	牛	牛	牞	物件	articles, goods	물건
				物體	an object; substance	물체
牛 4 534	物	物		物資	goods, commodities	물자

				칠	tend sheep; watch cattle; shepherd; pastor; rear, raise	목
牧	ノ	ゝ	牛			
	牛	牛	牜	牧師	pastor, clergyman, minister	목사
				牧場	ranch; pasture	목장
牛 4 535	牜	牧		牧童	herdboy, shepherd boy	목동

				형상	form, appearance, shape	상
狀	㇄	丬	爿	문서	document, certificate	장
	爿	狀	壯	形狀	shape, form	형상
				狀態	condition, state, situation	상태
犬 4 536	狀	狀		賞狀	certificate of merit	상장

				개	dog, term of contempt	구
狗	ノ	㇀	犭	走狗	running dog, puppet; hound	주구
	犭	犳	犵			
				海狗	a seal	해구
犬 5 537	狗	狗		狗肉	dog meat	구육

				과녁	target; object; adjectival particle	적
的	ノ	´	白			
	白	白	白	理想的	ideal	이상적
				標的	target	표적
白 3 538	的	的		目的	object, goal, purpose	목적

盲 目 3 539	、 亡 亡	亡 育 肓	亡 盲	소경 盲目的 盲信 盲啞	blind; deluded blindly, recklessly blind faith, blind belief the blind and the dumb	맹 맹목적 맹신 맹아
直 目 3 540	一 古 直	十 古 直	广 有	곧을 直線 直接 直前	straight, direct; honest straight line directly; personally immediately prior, right before	직 직선 직접 직전
知 矢 3 541	ノ 午 知	ト 矢 知	匕 矢	알 知識 知覺 知性	know knowledge, learning sense, judgment; perception intellect, mentality	지 지식 지각 지성

祀
 	
示 3
542
	一
	礻
	祀
		二
		利
		
			于
			祀
				제사
				
				祭祀
				
				奉祀
				墓祀
					sacrifice, offering; sacrifices
					    to the dead; a year
					sacrificial rite; ancestor
					    worship service
					sacrifice to one's ancestors
					memorial sacrifice held
					    at a grave
						사
						
						제사
						
						봉사
						묘사

社
 	
示 3
543
	一
	礻
	社
		二
		礻
		
			于
			社
				모일
				
				社會
				社用
				社告
					company, society; earth god,
					    altar to the earth god
					society, the public
					company use, business use
					public commercial
					    announcement;
					    advertisement
						사
						
						사회
						사용
						사고

空 穴 3 544	、 空 空	、 穴 空	宀 空	빌 空冊 空然히 空想	sky, air; empty; hollow; zero notebook vainly, fruitlessly vain dream, fantasy	공 공책 공연 공상

罔 网 3 545	丨 冂 冂 冂 冂 罔 罔		없을 罔測 罔極 罔民	not, without absurd, senseless immeasurable, infinite (as grief or favor) deceive the public	망 망측 망극 망민
育 肉 4 546	丶 亠 云 云 亠 育 育 育		기를 訓育 發育 育成	nurture, nourish, raise instruct, train grow, develop rear, raise	육 훈육 발육 육성
肥 肉 4 547	丿 月 月 月 月 月 肥 肥		살찔 肥料 肥沃 肥大	fat, plump; rich, fertile fertilizer; compost fertility obese, corpulent	비 비료 비옥 비대
肩 肉 4 548	丶 亠 ユ 户 户 肩 肩 肩		어깨 比肩 肩章 兩肩	shoulder be comparable to epaulette, shoulder piece both shoulders	견 비견 견장 양견
肯 肉 4 549	丨 卜 止 止 止 肯 肯 肯		즐길 肯定 首肯	willing, consent answer in the affirmative; affirm nod approval, consent; be convinced of, be persuaded of	긍 긍정 수긍
臥 臣 2 550	丨 厂 厄 臣 臣 臣 臥 臥		누울 臥病 臥席 臥食	lie down, rest lie sick in bed lie down with sickness sleep and eat, live an ideal life	와 와병 와석 와식

	ノ	人	스	집	cottage, shed; lodge, reside at; my younger relative; put away; omit	사
舍	스	全	余	舍廊	room for entertaining male guests	사랑
舌 2 551	舍	舍		寄宿舍	boarding house; dormitory	기숙사
				官舍	an official residence	관사

	ン	十	扩	꽃	flowers; vice; assorted	화
花	扩	芬	花	花郎	Silla youth excelling in beauty, bravery, and military arts	화랑
艸 4 552	花	花		花盆	flowerpot	화분
				花園	flower garden	화원

	ン	十	扑	움	sprout, shoot, germ	아
芽	艹	芒	芒	發芽	germinate, sprout	발아
				芽接	bud-grafting	아접
艸 4 553	芽	芽				

	ン	十	扑	꽃다울	fragrant; beautiful; pleasant; virtuous; excellent	방
芳	艹	芦	艹	芳名	your/his name	방명
				芳姿	a graceful figure	방자
艸 4 554	芳	芳		芳年	the sweet age of a young girl	방년

	ー	ト	上	범	tiger	호
虎	广	卢	虎	猛虎	fierce tiger	맹호
				虎列刺	cholera	호열자
虍 2 555	虎	虎		虎皮	tiger skin	호피

	一	二	丰	겉	surface, external; display; chart; gauge	표
表	主	丰	表	表示	show, express, manifest	표시
				表紙	a book cover	표지
衣 3 556	表	表		表明	show, manifest	표명

Character	Stroke order			
迎 辵 4 557		맞을	meet, welcome, receive	영
		歡迎	a welcome; to welcome	환영
		迎接	receive, meet, welcome	영접
		迎新	greet the new; greet the new year	영신
近 辵 4 558		가까울	near, near to, recent; approach	근
		近世	recent times, the modern age	근세
		近代	modern times, the modern age	근대
		近處	vicinity, neighborhood	근처
返 辵 4 559		돌이킬	revert to, return to	반
		返還	restore, replace; repay	반환
		返送	return, send back	반송
		返納	return, restore	반납
金 金 0 560	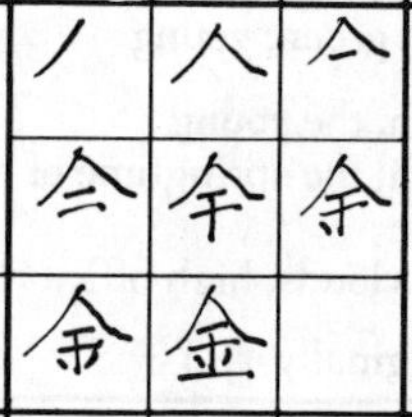	쇠	metal; gold; money	금
		성	surname: Kim	김
		金額	a sum, an amount of money	금액
		金融	finance, financing, banking, money circulation	금융
		金氏	Mr. Kim	김씨
長 長 0 561	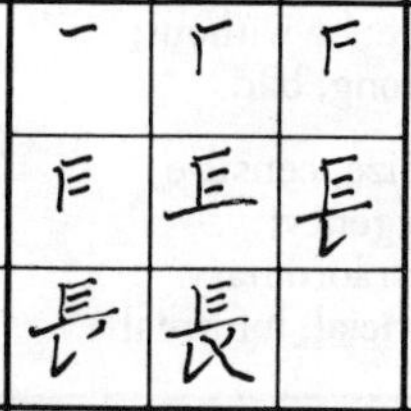	긴	long	장
		長官	cabinet minister	장관
		長短	long and short, length; merits and faults	장단
		社長	president of a company	사장
門 門 0 562	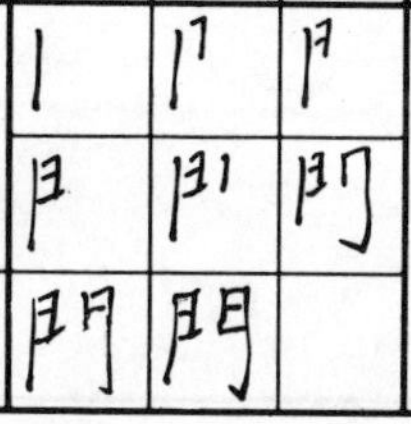	문	gate, door; family; school, sect	문
		家門	the family, the clan	가문
		門前	in front of the gate	문전
		正門	front gate, main entrance	정문

8 strokes

附	⁻	⁊	⻖	붙을	stick to, adhere; append, enclose; depend on; accessory; near to	부
	⻖	阝/	阶			
阜 5 563	附	附		附近	vicinity, environs	부근
				寄附	contribution, donation	기부
				附録	appendix; supplement	부록

阿	⁻	⁊	阝	언덕	river bank; flatter; pillars, beams; Africa	아
	阝⁻	阿	阿	阿片	opium	아편
阜 5 564	阿	阿		阿附	flattery, sycophancy	아부
				阿修羅	Asura, battling giant demon of Buddhism	아수라

雨	⁻	⁻	⼀	비	rain	우
	而	雨	雨	雨量	rainfall, amount of rainfall	우량
雨 0 565	雨	雨		雨期	rainy season	우기
				雨中	in the rain, while raining	우중

青	⁻	⁼	⼿	푸를	blue, green; young	청
	圭	青	青	青年	youth, the young	청년
青 0 566	青	青		青春	youth; the springtime of life	청춘
				青雲	blue clouds; high office	청운
				(Originally 青.)		

非	⁄	⁊	⺷	아닐	not be; be without; wrong, bad	비
	⺷	非	非	非難	criticize, censure	비난
非 0 567	非	非		非常	emergency; extraordinary	비상
				非公式	unofficial, informal	비공식

9 Strokes

亭	丶	亠	亠	정자	pavilion, kiosk, shed	정
	古	古	古	亭子	pavilion, summerhouse	정자
				亭閣	pavilion, summerhouse	정각
亠 7 568	高	高	亭			

侵	丿	亻	亻	침범할	usurp; encroach upon; raid; invade	침
	亻	伊	侵	侵略	invade	침략
				侵犯	intrude; violate, infringe	침범
人 7 569	侵	侵	侵	侵害	trespass, infringe, violate	침해

侯	丿	亻	亻	제후	feudal lord	후
	亻	仾	仾	侯爵	marquis, marquess	후작
				諸侯	feudal lords	제후
人 7 570	侯	侯	侯	王侯	king and peers; princes and lords	왕후

便	丿	亻	亻	편할	convenient	편
	亻	佰	佰	오줌	excretion, feces, urine	변
				便紙	letter, epistle	편지
				便所	toilet; restroom	변소
人 7 571	佰	便	便	便利	convenient, handy, useful	편리

係	丿	亻	亻	맬	belong to; consequences; person in charge; section	계
	亻	任	伍	關係	relations; relationship; take part in; affect, influence	관계
				係數	a coefficient; a factor	계수
人 7 572	係	係	係	係長	a section chief	계장

123

俊 人 7 573	ノ 仏 俊	亻 仲 俗	仁 伶 俊	준걸 俊秀 俊才 俊傑	superior, eminent, heroic, refined, handsome be talented and refined eminent ability, talent a great man, a hero	준 준수 준재 준걸
促 人 7 574	ノ 仰 伊	亻 伊 促	亻 伊	독촉할 urge 再促 促進 促迫	importune, press, urge promote, expedite urgent, imminent; acute	촉 재촉 촉진 촉박
俗 人 7 575	ノ 伶 俗	亻 伶 俗	仁 伏 俗	풍속 俗談 俗世 民俗	customs, practices; vulgar, common; worldly; unrefined; lay (not clerical) proverb, saying the mundane world, earthly existence folkways, folk customs	속 속담 속세 민속
保 人 7 576	ノ 伊 伊	亻 伊 保	亻 但	보호할 protect, guard; guarantee 保護 保管 保存	protect, safeguard take custody, watch over preserve, maintain	보 보호 보관 보존
信 人 7 577	ノ 仁 信	亻 信 信	亻 信	믿을 信用 信念 信義	believe in, trust; confidence; token; letter; news; envoy trust, rely on; credit belief, conviction fidelity, truthfulness; faithfulness	신 신용 신념 신의
冠 冖 7 578	ノ 冝 冠	冖 戸 冠	冖 完 冠	갓 冠婚 冠帶 冠禮	cap, crown ceremonies for coming of age and marriage ancient court costume; attire of a bridegroom "hat ceremony", coming of age ceremony	관 관혼 관대 관례

削	丶	小	少	깎을	pare, scrape; scrape away; delete; sharpen to a point; sloping, sheer	삭
	小	肖	肖			
				削減	cut, reduce, slash	삭감
				削除	strike out, delete, eliminate	삭제
刀 7 579	肖	肖	削	添削	correct, revise	첨삭

則	丨	冂	日	법칙 곧	rule; law; pattern; standard consequently, accordingly	칙 즉
	日	目	貝			
				原則	fundamental principle, general rule	원칙
				規則	law, rule	규칙
刀 7 580	貝	則	則	然則	therefore, so; in this case	연즉

前	丶	丷	丷	앞	front; before	전
	广	芹	肯	前後	before and after; about, approximately	전후
				前進	advance	전진
刀 7 581	肖	前	前	前例	precedent, previous example	전례

勇	一	マ	マ	날랠	brave, daring, plucky, heroic	용
	丙	禹	甬			
				勇氣	bravery, courage	용기
				勇士	brave man; warrior	용사
力 7 582	角	勇	勇	勇猛	intrepid; valiant	용맹

勉	丿	丶丶	夕	힘쓸	exert oneself; urge, constrain	면
	夕	台	免			
				勤勉	diligence, industry	근면
				勉學	pursuit of knowledge, diligent study	면학
力 7 583	免	免	勉	勉勵	exertion, endeavor	면려

南	一	十	广	남녘	south	남
	肖	南	南	南方	the South; southern districts	남방
				南極	the south pole	남극
十 7 584	南	商	南	南北	south and north; south Korea and north Korea	남북

卽	ノ	イ	勹	곧	immediately; now; then; even if; go, approach	즉
	勹	白	自	卽時	immediately, at once	즉시
				卽刻	instantly	즉각
卩 7 585	自	卽	卽	卽死	die instantly	즉사

厚	一	厂	厂	두터울 thick; generous		후
	厈	厚	后	濃厚	thick, heavy, dense, rich	농후
				厚待	hospitality	후대
厂 7 586	厚	厚	厚	厚意	kindness, hospitality	후의

叛	丶	丷	丷	배반할 rebel, revolt		반
	半	半	半	叛逆	revolt, mutiny	반역
				叛亂	rebel, revolt	반란
又 7 587	扝	叛	叛	謀叛	revolt; plot treason	모반

哀	丶	亠	亠	슬플	sadness; pity; sympathize with; wail; "alas!"	애
	产	宀	戸	哀願	implore, supplicate	애원
				哀愁	grief, sorrow	애수
口 6 588	戸	亨	哀	哀痛	be heart-stricken, grieve	애통

咸	ノ	厂	厂	다	all, togther	함
	斤	咸	咸	咸興差使 a lost messenger		함흥차사
				咸氏	esteemed nephew (honorific)	함씨
口 6 589	咸	咸	咸	咸鏡道 Hamkyŏng province		함경도

品	丶	口	口	물건	things, goods; quality; kind, class; conduct, deportment	품
	口	吕	吕	品種	kind, variety, species	품종
				品質	quality	품질
口 6 590	品	品	品	物品	articles, commodities, goods	물품

哉	一	十	士	어조사	exclamatory classical Korean particle	재
	士	吉	吉	快哉	delight, "wonderful", "great"	쾌재
口 6 591	武	哉	哉			

契	一	二	三	맺을	agreement, bond; mutual savings society	계
	丰	刧	刧	契約	contract, agreement	계약
				契機	chance, opportunity	계기
大 6 592	刧	契	契	黙契	tacit agreement, implicit understanding	묵계

姻	人	夕	女	혼인	marriage; marriage connections; bride	인
	妇	娴	妼	婚姻	marry; marriage	혼인
				姻戚	in-laws, relatives by marriage; maternal relatives	인척
女 6 593	姻	姻	姻	姻家	home of a son-in-law or daughter-in-law	인가

姦	乙	夕	女	간사할	adultery; rape	간
	女	女	女	强姦	rape	강간
				姦通	adultery, illicit intercourse	간통
女 6 594	姦	姦	姦	姦淫	adultery; fornication	간음

姿	、	ン	ソ	모양	manner, bearing; beauty	자
	ソ	次	次	姿勢	posture; a posture; a figure	자세
				姿態	personal appearance, one's figure	자태
女 6 595	姿	姿	姿	雄姿	majestic appearance, gallant figure	웅자

姪	人	夕	女	조카	nephew, niece	질
	妇	妊	妊	姪女	niece	질녀
				叔姪	one's uncle and nephews/nieces	숙질
女 6 596	姪	姪	姪	姪孫	grandnephew, grandson of one's brother	질손

威	ﻝ	厂	尸	위엄	severe, stern; **majestic**; pomp; overawe	위
	反	反	反	威脅	threaten, intimidate; threat	위협
女 6 597	威	威	威	威嚴	dignity, majesty	위엄
				威力	power; influence	위력
客	丶	丷	宀	손	guest, customer	객
	宀	少	灾	客觀的	objectively	객관적
				客地	strange land one is visiting	객지
宀 6 598	宓	客	客	觀光客	tourist	관광객
宣	丶	丷	宀	베풀	proclaim; display; spread; wide, comprehensive	선
	宀	宁	宦	宣言	declare, pronounce; declaration	선언
宀 6 599	盲	盲	宣	宣布	proclaim, promulgate	선포
				宣敎師	a missionary	선교사
室	丶	丷	宀	집	room, chamber, office; home, house, apartment; wife	실
	宀	宔	宏	室內	inside, indoors; interior of a room	실내
				室外	outside, outdoors	실외
宀 6 600	宐	室	室	溫室	hothouse, greenhouse; warm room, hot room	온실
封	一	十	土	봉할	seal, seal up; blockade; enfeoff; bestow honor, confer nobility	봉
	告	丰	圭			
寸 6 601	圭	封	封	封紙	a paper bag, a packet	봉지
				封套	an envelope	봉투
				封鎖	blockade; to block	봉쇄
屋	一	7	尸	집	house, room	옥
	尸	戸	层	家屋	house; building, structure	가옥
				屋外	outside, outdoors	옥외
尸 6 602	屋	屋	屋	洋屋	Western-style house	양옥

屏	一	二	尸	병풍	screen; protection; reject	병
				屏風	a folding screen; any screen against a draft	병풍
	尸	屈	屈	畫屏	pictured screen	화병
尸 6 603	屈	屏	屏			

巷	一	十	艹	골목	alley, street; hole	항
	艹	芒	共	巷間	on the street, about town	항간
				巷説	street gossip, town talk	항설
				巷談	town talk	항담
己 6 604	巷	巷	巷			

帝	、	亠	亠	임금	emperor, ruler; god	제
	亠	产	立	帝國	an empire	제국
				帝政	imperial government, rule by imperial government	제정
巾 6 605	帝	帝	帝	帝王	emperor	제왕

帥	丿	亻	亽	장수	commander, leader	수
				元帥	field marshal, fleet admiral	원수
	户	自	自	將帥	generalissimo, commander-in-chief	장수
巾 6 606	自	帥	帥	統帥	command, control, leadership	통수

幽	丨	幺	纠	깊을	dark, gloomy; arcane; subtle; retired, lonely	유
	幺	纠	幽	幽靈	spirit of the dead; ghost, specter; supernatural visitor	유령
幺 6 607	幽	幽	幽	幽閉	incarcerate, confine	유폐
				幽明	brightness and darkness	유명

度	、	广	广	법도	rule, law, limit, degree	도
				헤아릴	calculate, estimate	탁
	庐	庐	庄	制度	system	제도
				度數	frequency, number of times; percent alcohol in liquor	도수
广 6 608	庐	度		度地	survey land	탁지

129

建	フ	ヨ	ヨ	세울	establish, erect, build, found	건
	⺕	圭	圭	建物	building, structure	건물
				建築	construct, build; establish	건축
⻌ 6 609	聿	津	建	建意	recommend	건의

待	ノ	ク	彳	기다릴	wait for; entertain, treat	대
	彳	祉	往	待接	entertain, treat	대접
				期待	expect, count on; anticipate, hope for	기대
彳 6 610	往	待	待	待機	stand by, await call	대기

律	ノ	ク	彳	법	law; rhythm	률
	彳	律	律	音律	tones and rhythm, music	음률
				規律	rules, laws; discipline, order	규율
彳 6 611	律	律	律	律動	rhythm; rhythmic movement	율동

後	ノ	ク	彳	뒤	after, behind, later	후
	彳	祉	徟	後方	the rear, rear area	후방
				後悔	regret, be sorry for	후회
彳 6 612	移	徬	後	後退	military retreat; retreat	후퇴

怒	く	夕	女	성낼	anger, rage, passion	노
	奴	奴	奴	憤怒	become angry, fly into a rage	분노
				大怒	great anger	대노
心 5 613	怒	怒	怒	怒氣	anger, wrath, rage	노기

思	丶	冂	曰	생각	think, contemplate; thought; yearn, long for	사
	用	田	田			
				思想	idea; ideology	사상
				思慕	yearn for, long for	사모
心 5 614	思	思	思	思考	think, consider	사고

怠	ㄥ	ㄙ	台	게으를 lazy; remiss; disrespectful	태
	台	台	台	倦怠 fatigue, lassitude	권태
				怠業 deliberate idleness, a slowdown	태업
心 5 615	怠	怠	怠	怠慢 careless, negligent; remiss	태만

怨	ノ	ク	夕	원망할 hatred; resentment; find fault with; murmur against	원
	夘	夗	夗	怨讐 an enemy	원수
				怨痛 chagrined, resentful, indignant	원통
心 5 616	怨	怨	怨	怨聲 complain, murmur	원성

急	ノ	ク	勹	급할 urgent, hasty	급
	刍	刍	刍	急速히 rapidly, expeditiously	급속
				急性 quick temper, impetuous	급성
心 5 617	急	急	急	急激 sudden, precipitous	급격

恒	l	l	小	항상 constant, always	항
	忙	忙	恒	恒常 always, constantly	항상
				恒時 always; the usual time	항시
心 6 618	恒	恒	恒	恒久的 perpetually, permanently	항구적

恨	l	l	小	한할 grudge	한
	忙	忖	忖	怨恨 grudge, resentment, malice	원한
				恨歎 lament, deplore; sigh with regret	한탄
心 6 619	恨	恨	恨	餘恨 lingering spite, remaining malice	여한

拜	ノ	ニ	三	절 bow, salute, greet, obeisance; pay respects to; visit	배
	手	手	手	崇拜 worship; adore, admire	숭배
				禮拜 worship	예배
手 5 620	手三	手三	拜	參拜 worship at a temple; pay reverence at	참배

拾	一	寸	才	주울 열	pick up, tidy up ten (legal form)	습 십
	扌	扒	拎	拾得 拾遺 拾萬	learn, acquire, pick up supplement, addendum 100,000 (legal form)	습득 습유 십만
手 6 621	拎	拾	拾			

持	一	十	扌	가질	hold, grasp; restrain; support	지
	扌	扩	抺	維持 持續 所持	maintain, support sustain, maintain possess, bear, carry	유지 지속 소지
手 6 622	拤	持	持			

挑	一	寸	扌	돋을	pick out; raise; carry with a pole over the shoulder; provoke	도 (조)
	扎	扎	拊	挑戰	challenge; provoke battle; defiant, provocative	도전
手 6 623	挑	挑	挑	挑走 挑發	flee, run away provoke; provocation	도주 도발

指	一	十	才	손가락	finger; toe; to point	지
	扌	拃	拃	指導 指示	guide, lead, direct guidance, instruction, order	지도 지시
手 6 624	指	指	指	指名	nominate; designate	지명

政	一	丁	F	정사	govern, rule; government; politics	정
	正	正	正	政治 政策 政權	politics; government policy political power; regime	정치 정책 정권
支 4 625	政	政	政			

故	一	ナ	ナ	연고	reason, cause; die, the former	고
	古	古	刮	故鄉	native place, place of origin	고향
				事故	accident; reasons, circumstances	사고
支 5 626	故	故	故	故人	the departed, the deceased	고인

施	、	二	亠	베풀	bestow, grant; act, do; exhibit; extend to	시
	方	方	方	施設	equipment, facilities, plant; institution; establishment	시설
方 5 627	拖	施	施	施行 施賞	execute, carry out award a prize	시행 시상

星	丶	冂	曰	별	star	성
	日	月	旦	流星 火星 星座	meteor Mars constellation	유성 화성 성좌
日 5 628	旦	星	星			

映	丨	刂	日	비칠	shine, reflect, glare; cinema	영
	日	日	旳	映畫 映寫 映像	a movie project an image image, reflection	영화 영사 영상
日 5 629	映	映	映			

昭	丨	刂	刃	밝을	brightness of the sun; bright, luminous; show, display	소
	日	旫	旫	昭詳히 昭明 昭然히	clear and exact bright plain, obvious	소상 소명 소연
日 5 630	昭	昭	昭			

昨	丨	刂	日	어제	yesterday, just past	작
	日	旫	旷	昨年 昨今 昨日	last year recently, these days yesterday	작년 작금 작일
日 5 631	昨	昨	昨			

是	丶	冂	日	이	this, that; right, correct	시
	日	旦	早	是非 是認 是正	right and wrong approve, endorse correct, rectify	시비 시인 시정
日 5 632	早	昇	是			

春	一	二	三	봄	spring (season); youth; sex	춘
	夫	夫	表	春風	a spring breeze, a spring wind	춘풍
				春秋	spring and autumn; time, years	춘추
日 5 633	春	春	春	春夢	spring dreams; springtime fantasies	춘몽

枯	一	十	才	시들	dried, rotten	고
	才	朴	村	枯渴	run dry, dry up; be exhausted	고갈
				枯木	dead tree, withered tree	고목
木 5 634	村	枯	枯	枯葉	withered leaf	고엽

架	フ	力	加	시렁	frame, stand, rack	가
	加	加	架	書架	book shelf, book rack	서가
				架設	build, construct; install	가설
木 5 635	架	架	架	架橋	bridge-building	가교

某	一	十	廿	아무개	so-and-so, such-and-such	모
	甘	甘	甘	某某	somebody, something, so-and-so, such-and-such	모모
				某處	a certain place, someplace	모처
木 5 636	苴	某	某	某種	a certain kind, some kind of	모종

查	一	十	才	조사할	seek out, search into, survey, investigate	사
	木	杏	杏	查定	assess taxes; revise a budget	사정
				查頓	in-laws, relatives by marriage	사돈
木 5 637	杳	杳	查	查察	investigate, inspect	사찰

柔	フ	マ	子	부드러울	soft, pliant; gentle, yielding	유
	予	矛	圣	柔順	submissive, docile, gentle	유순
				柔軟	soft, pliable, flexible	유연
木 5 638	矛	柔	柔	柔道	judo, jujitsu	유도

				기둥	pillar, post; support	주
柱	一	十	才	電柱	telephone pole	전주
	才	术	术	支柱	a support, a prop	지주
木 5 639	柠	枠	柱	柱石	pillar and cornerstone; mainstay	주석

				물들	dye; apply color; infect; catch a disease	염
染	丶	冫	氵	染料	dye, dyes	염료
	氵	氿	迖	染色	to dye	염색
水 5 640	染	染	染	感染	contract, be infected; be contaminated	감염

				버들	willow tree; pleasure, dissipation	류
柳	一	十	才	花柳界	place of flowers and willows, prostitute areas	화류계
	木	札	札	細柳	a weeping willow	세류
木 5 641	柳	柳	柳	柳氏	Mr. Yu	류씨

				재앙	misfortune, calamity, retribution	앙
殃	一	丁	歹	災殃	calamity, disaster, evils	재앙
	歹	死	如	殃禍	divine wrath, misfortune from sin	앙화
歹 5 642	妸	殃	殃	天殃	divine retribution, the punishment of Heaven	천앙

				위태할	dangerous; almost	태
殆	一	丁	歹	危殆	risk, peril	위태
	歹	死	殆	殆半	about half, the greater part	태반
歹 5 643	殆	殆	殆	殆無	scarce, virtually nonexistent	태무

				층계	section, division, piece, paragraph	단
段	丿	亻	千	段階	stage, phase	단계
	乍	耳	耳	手段	means, measure; device	수단
殳 5 644	卧	段	段	階段	steps, stairs; stage, phase	계단

135

泉	ノ	イ	白	샘	spring, fountain; wealth	천
	白	白	白	溫泉	hot springs, medicinal springs	온천
水 5 645	身	泉	泉	冷泉	cold mineral springs	냉천
				黃泉	Hades, the "yellow spring" of Hades	황천
洋	丶	冫	氵	큰바다	ocean, sea; foreign; wide, vast; foreign items	양
	氵	氵	洋	洋服	suit, Western-style suit	양복
水 6 646	洋	洋	洋	洋式	Western style	양식
				大洋	ocean, sea	대양
洗	丶	冫	氵	씻을	wash, bathe; purify	세
	氵	氵	汼	洗手	wash up, wash the hands and face	세수
水 6 647	洪	洗	洗	洗鍊	polish, refine, finish	세련
				洗禮	baptism	세례
洛	丶	冫	氵	물이름	name of a river, name of a capital; falling drops of water	락
	氵	氵	汐			
水 6 648	洛	洛	洛	洛東江	the Naktong River	낙동강
洞	丶	冫	氵	고을	sub-ward; street, block; village; cave; grotto; see through	동
	沠	沠	洞	洞里	village	동리
水 6 649	洞	洞	洞	洞民	villagers	동민
				洞會	village council, block council	동회
洪	丶	冫	氵	넓을	vast; flood	홍
	氵	沜	沞	洪水	a flood	홍수
水 6 650	洪	洪	洪	洪恩	great favor, great kindness; indebtedness	홍은
				洪福	great happiness	홍복

洲	`、`	`氵`	`氵`	물가	islet, island; continent 주
	`氵`	`氵`卅	`氵`卅	歐洲	Europe 구주
				美洲	American continents 미주
水 6 651	洲	洲	洲	亞洲	Asian continent 아주
活	`、`	`冫`	`氵`	살	life, live; lively 활
	`氵`	`氵`二	`氵`千	活動	be active; move, work, take part in 활동
				活潑	lively, animated 활발
水 6 652	汗	活	活	活用	utilize, make practical use of 활용
派	`、`	`冫`	`氵`	나눌	branch, branch off; send 파
	`氵`	`氵`	`氵`	派遣	dispatch forces, send representatives 파견
				派閥	faction, clique 파벌
水 6 653	泒	泒	派	黨派	party faction; clique, junta 당파
炭	`l`	山	山	숯	charcoal 탄
	屵	尸	岸	炭酸	carbonic acid 탄산
				炭水	coal and water; carbon and hydrogen 탄수
火 5 654	岸	炭	炭	炭田	coalfield 탄전
珍	`一`	`二`	`王`	보배	precious, rare; delicious 진
	`王`	`王`	`玖`	珍奇	rare, curious, strange 진기
				珍味	delicate flavor; delicacy 진미
玉 5 655	珍	珍	珍	珍貴	rare and precious, priceless 진귀
甚	`一`	`十`	`廿`	심할	extreme, extremely 심
	甘	甘	苴	甚至於	on top of that, what is more 심지어
				深甚	profound, deep 심심
甘 4 656	其	其	甚	極甚	extreme, excessive; violent 극심

界	丶	丨┐	日	지경	world; region; limit, boundary	계
	甲	田	界	境界	boundary, border;	경계
					one's karma condition	
				政界	the political world,	정계
					political circles	
田 4 657	界	界	界	財界	the financial world,	재계
					financial circles	

畓	丿	刁	氺	논	paddy, wet field	답
	水	水	氺	田畓	dry fields and paddy	전답
				沃畓	fertile paddy	옥답
田 4 658	畓	畓	畓			

畏	丶	丨┐	日	두려워할	dread, fear; awe	외
	甲	田	田	敬畏	revere and fear	경외
				畏縮	flinch, wince; cower; recoil	외축
田 4 659	畏	畏	畏			

疫	丶	亠	广	전염병	epidemic, pestilence	역
	广	疒	疒	防疫	prevention of epidemics	방역
				免疫	immunity	면역
					(from a disease)	
广 4 660	疠	疫	疫	疫痢	dysentery	역리

癸	フ	ヲ	⅔	열째천간	last of the 10 Heavenly Stems	계
	⅔″	癶	癶	癸未字	type cast in 1403	계미자
				癸亥	60th of the 60 binary terms	계해
					of the sexagenary cycle	
癶 4 661	癶	癸	癸	癸丑	50th of the 60 binary terms	계축
					of the sexagenary cycle	

皆	一	上	比	다	all, every; entirely	개
	比	比	比	皆勤	perfect attendance	개근
				皆既蝕	total eclipse	개기식
				皆兵	universal conscription	개병
白 4 662	皆	皆	皆			

皇	′	⺊	宀	임금	emperor		황
	白	白	自	皇帝	emperor		황제
白 4 663	皁	皂	皇	皇室	imperial household		황실
盾	′	⺀	厂	방패	buckler, shield		순
	户	斤	盾	矛盾	spear and shield; contradiction; contradictory		모순
目 4 664	盾	盾	盾				
相	一	十	才	서로	mutual, reciprocal, each other; direction towards; assist; face; appearance, likeness; portrait; prime minister		상
	一	木	机	相當	considerable, much;suitable		상당
目 4 665	机	相	相	相關	relationship; mind,care about		상관
				相議	ask advice, consult		상의
看	′	⺥	⺫	볼	see, observe; examine, consider		간
	手	丰	看	看板	sign, billboard		간판
				看護員	a nurse		간호원
目 4 666	看	看	看	看做	regard as, consider as		간주
眉	⺆	⺕	⺕	눈썹	eyebrow		미
				眉間	space between the eyebrows, the brow		미간
	尸	尸	眉	白眉	one who excels, a gifted person		백미
目 4 667	眉	眉	眉	愁眉	knitted eyebrows, worried look		수미
省	⼁	⼩	小	살필	examine, watch		성
				덜	diminish; curtail; save, reduce; frugal; detailed, minute		생
	少	半	省	反省	reflect, meditate		반성
				省略	abbreviate, abridge		생략
目 4 668	省	省	省	歸省	return home, visit parents		귀성

139

研 石 6 669	一 石 石一	厂 石一 石一	丆 石一 研	갈	grind, rub fine; investigate thoroughly, study, research	연
				研究	study, research, inquire into	연구
				研修	study and train, take training	연수
					(Originally 研 .)	

祈 示 4 670	丶 示 祈	亠 礻 祈	才 礻	빌	pray	기
				祈禱	pray, offer prayer	기도
				祈願	pray, supplicate	기원
				祈雨祭	shamanist rite to pray for rain	기우제

秋 禾 4 671	丿 禾 秋	二 禾 秋	千 禾 秋	가을	autumn	추
				秋收	the harvest	추수
				秋夕	Autumn Moon Festival on the 15th day of the 8th moon	추석
				秋波	autumn waves, an amorous glance	추파

科 禾 4 672	丿 禾 禾	二 禾 科	千 禾 科	과목	class; order, series; department; science	과
				科學	science	과학
				科目	course of study, subject	과목
				科舉	traditional state examiniations, civil service examinations	과거

突 穴 4 673	丶 宀 突	丶 穴 突	宀 穴 突	부딪칠	abrupt, abruptly; rush out; suddenly protrude; offend; chimney	돌
				突然히	suddenly, without warning	돌연
				突入	rush in, dash in	돌입
				突擊	assault, rush at	돌격

紅 糸 3 674	乙 糸 糸一	幺 糸 紅丁	幺 糸 紅工	붉을	red	홍
				紅疫	measles	홍역
				紅茶	tea, black tea	홍차
				紅顏	ruddy face, pink cheeks	홍안

約	ㄥ	ㄠ	ㄠ	약속할 promise, covenant; treaty; bind; economical; concise; approximate; estimate	약
	糸	糸	糸	約束 promise	약속
糸 3 675	糸	約	約	約婚 be engaged to marry, engagement	약혼
				豫約 reserve, make a reservation	예약

紀	ㄥ	ㄠ	ㄠ	기록할 century; 12 years (anciently); regulate; discipline	기
	糸	糸	糸	紀念 commemorate	기념
糸 3 676	紀	紀	紀	紀律 order, discipline	기율
				風紀 discipline; public morals	풍기

美	丶	丷	䒑	아름다울 beautiful, fine, admirable; America, American	미
	丷	芉	羊	美人 beautiful woman	미인
羊 3 677	羊	美	美	美術 art; fine arts	미술
				美國 the United States of America	미국

者	一	十	土	놈 person, one; thing, he, it	자
	耂	耂	者	勞動者 laborer, worker	노동자
老 5 678	者	者	者	筆者 writer, author	필자
				使者 envoy, messenger; a mission	사자

耐	一	厂	厂	견딜 patient; bear, endure; enduring	내
	而	而	而	忍耐心 patience; perseverance	인내심
而 3 679	而	耐	耐	耐乏 self-denial; bearing poverty	내핍
				耐寒性 resistant to cold	내한성

耶	一	厂	F	어조사 classical Korean particle for rhetorical question	야
	F	巨	耳	耶蘇教 Christianity	야소교
耳 3 680	耳	耶	耶		

9 strokes

胃	、	冂	日	밥통 stomach	위
	用	田	田	胃腸 stomach and intestines	위장
肉 5 681	胃	胃	胃	胃潰瘍 stomach ulcer 胃痛 stomachache	위궤양 위통

胡	一	十	大	오랑캐 barbarian; foreign; Manchurian; Manchu; Chinese	호
	古	古	自	胡人 a Manchurian; a Chinese	호인
肉 5 682	胡	胡	胡	胡服 a Chinese garment 胡桃 walnut	호복 호도

背	ノ	キ	丬	등 back; behind; disavow, turn the back on	배
	⺆	北	北	背景 background; scenery, setting; behind the scenes backing	배경
肉 5 683	背	背	背	背信 betray confidence 背恩 forget a favor, be ungrateful	배신 배은

肺	ノ	月	月	허파 lungs	폐
	月	肝	肝	肺病 lung disease, lung trouble	폐병
肉 4 684	肝	肺	肺	肺結核 pulmonary tuberculosis 肺臟 lungs	폐결핵 폐장

胞	ノ	几	月	아기집 uterus, womb	포
	月	肝	肕	細胞 a cell 同胞 brothers; fellow countrymen; overseas Koreans	세포 동포
肉 5 685	胊	胊	胞	胞子 spore; cyst	포자

若	丶	十	⺯	만약 if, supposing; as, like	약
	艹	艹	芊	若干 a little, a few, some 明若觀火 as clear as light 萬若 if, supposing, by chance	약간 명약관화 만약
艸 5 686	若	若	若		

142

苗	丶	十	屮	싹 sprouts; growing corn		묘
	屮	屮	节	苗木 sapling		묘목
				種苗 plant a seedling; a seedling		종묘
艸 5 687	节	苗	苗	苗床 seedbed, seed-plot		묘상

苟	丶	十	屮	진실로 indeed; if, only		구
	屮	屮	芍	苟且 indigent; ignoble		구차
				苟安 ease temporarily		구안
艸 5 688	芍	苟	苟			

苦	丶	十	屮	괴로울 suffering; bitter		고
	屮	屮	艹	苦生 suffer; undergo difficulties		고생
				苦難 trouble, affliction		고난
艸 5 689	芒	苦	苦	苦楚 hardship, privation		고초

茂	丶	十	屮	성할 exuberant; flourishing; healthy		무
	屮	屮	艹	茂盛 closely-grown, dense		무성
				茂林 dense forest		무림
艸 5 690	茂	茂	茂			

英	丶	屮	屮	꽃부리 brave; eminent; flower; beauty		영
	屮	艹	芇	英特 wise, sagacious; exceptional		영특
				英斷 wise and prompt decision; a drastic measure		영단
艸 5 691	芇	苗	英	英國 England		영국

要	一	冖	冖	중요로울 important, necessary; must; summarize; demand; seek for; make an agreement		요
	襾	襾	西	要素 essential element; requisite		요소
				要求 demand; request; call for		요구
襾 3 692	要	要	要	要領 the main point, the general idea; outline, summary		요령

訂	、	亠	二	정정할 arrange, settle; edit	정
	言	言	言	改訂 revise	개정
				校訂 edit, correct	교정
言 2 693	言	言	訂	修訂 edit, retouch	수정

計	、	亠	二	꾀 calculate; plan, device	계
	言	言	言	計劃 plan; project	계획
				計算 compute, calculate	계산
言 2 694	言	計	計	計策 scheme, trick	계책

貞	丶	卜	卜	곧을 upright, correct; pure, chaste, virtuous; lucky	정
	占	占	貞		
				貞操 chastity, faithfulness	정조
貝 2 695	貞	貞	貞	貞淑 chaste, virtuous	정숙
				貞節 fidelity, faithfulness	정절

負	丿	夕	仔	질 suffer defeat, lose, fall; bear, carry on the back; trust to; negative; minus	부
	竹	肖	負	負擔 be responsible for, bear, assume	부담
貝 2 696	負	負	負	負債 incur debt	부채
				抱負 ambition, aspiration	포부

赴	一	十	土	갈 go to, go; attend	부
	キ	キ	走	赴任 go to a new post, assume a new position	부임
				赴役 mutual aid; go aid	부역
走 2 697	走	赴	赴	赴援 go for assistance	부원

軍	丿	冖	冃	군사 military, army	군
	冒	冐	罕	軍事 military, military affairs	군사
				軍隊 the army, military forces	군대
車 2 698	冒	軍	軍	軍人 soldier, military man	군인

迫	ノ	イ	白	핍박할 persecute, oppress; draw near, imminent	박
	白	白	白	迫害 oppress, persecute 迫頭 draw near; be imminent 迫力 impact, force, power	박해 박두 박력
辵 5 699	迫	迫			

述	一	十	オ	지을 narrate, tell the details, state; transmit	술
	朮	朮	沭	著述 write a book 陳述 state; a statement 述語 terms; technical terms; a predicate	저술 진술 술어
辵 5 700	述	述			

郊	丶	亠	广	들 waste land; open country	교
	六	亥	交	郊外 suburbs, outskirts 近郊 suburban districts, outskirts 遠郊 a place far from a city	교외 근교 원교
邑 6 701	交刀	交了	郊		

重	ノ	二	亡	무거울 heavy; important; severe	중
	台	台	旨	重要 be important, consequential 重大 be important, momentous 重點 emphasis; central point	중요 중대 중점
里 2 702	盲	重	重		

限	フ	了	阝	한정 bounds, limits, a limit	한
	阝ヿ	阝ヨ	阝ヨ	制限 restrict, limit 期限 term, period 限定 limit, qualify, restrict	제한 기한 한정
阜 6 703	阴	限	限		

面	一	二	币	낯 face, surface, front	면
	丙	而	而	面積 area, square measure 面目 aspects, features; face, countenance, honor 表面 the surface, the face, the outside; appearance	면적 면목 표면
面 0 704	而	面	面		

革	一	十	艹	가죽	leather; remove; revolt	혁
	世	芦	芑	革命	revolution	혁명
				改革	reform	개혁
革 0 705	苫	草	革	革帶	leather belt	혁대

音	`	亠	亠	소리	sound, tone, pronunciation	음
	立	立	立	音樂	music	음악
				音節	a syllable	음절
音 0 706	音	音	音	雜音	noise; static; dissenting voices	잡음

風	ノ	几	凡	바람	wind; custom; style; scenery; influence	풍
	凡	同	同	風俗	customs, manners	풍속
				風景	scenery, a scene	풍경
風 0 707	風	風	風	風波	wind and waves, a storm; hardships; trouble, disturbance	풍파

飛	乁	飞	飞	날	fly	비
	飞	飞	飛	飛行機	airplane, aircraft	비행기
				飛躍	leap, jump; rapid progress	비약
飛 0 708	飛	飛	飛	飛虎	"flying tiger"	비호

食	ノ	人	亼	밥	food; eat, drink	식
	今	今	會	飲食	food and drink; food	음식
				食糧	provisions, foodstuff	식량
食 0 709	食	食	食	食事	a meal; eat a meal (honorific)	식사

首	`	丷	丷	머리	head; chief, leader; first, beginning; stanza, poem	수
	丷	首	首	首相	prime minister, premier	수상
				元首	sovereign, head of state	원수
首 0 710	首	首	首	首位	head position, position of primacy	수위

146

香	ノ 二 千 ｜ 禾 禾 禾	향기	fragrance; incense	향
香 0 711	乔 香 香	香氣	perfume; fragrance	향기
		香料	perfume; perfume ingredients	향료
		香水	liquid perfume	향수

10 Strokes

乘	二 二 千 ｜ 一 亐 玉 ｜ 垂 乖 乘	탈	ride; mount, get on, ascend; avail oneself of; multiply; record	승
乘 9 712		乘客	passenger	승객
		乘務員	crew member, crewman	승무원
		乘車券	conveyance ticket	승차권

俱	イ イ 们 ｜ 们 俱 俱 ｜ 但 俱 俱	함께	all, altogether	구
人 8 713		俱樂部	a club, a social club	구락부
		俱存	have one's parents still living	구존
		俱現	embody, manifest	구현

修	イ イ イ ｜ 仁 仔 攸 ｜ 攸 修 修	닦을	pare, prune; repair; reform; self-improvement	수
人 8 714		修正	revise, amend	수정
		修理	fix, repair; remodel	수리
		修身	morals, ethics; moral training	수신

倉	人 入 今 ｜ 今 今 今 ｜ 倉 倉 倉	창고	granary; flustered	창
人 8 715		倉庫	storehouse, warehouse	창고
		倉皇히	hastily, in a rush	창황
		倉卒間	in the midst of a great hurry	창졸간

147

個	亻	𠆢	价	낱	individual, unit, one	개
	侗	侗	個	個性	individuality, individual traits	개성
				個別的	individually; separately	개별적
人 8 716	個	個	個	個人	an individual, a private person; privately	개인

倒	亻	亻	仁	넘어질	fall over, knock down	도
	佢	佢	侄	卒倒	faint; die; be stunned	졸도
				倒壞	demolish, tear down; collapse, fall down	도괴
人 8 717	侄	倒	倒	壓倒	overwhelm, crush; overwhelming	압도

倍	亻	亻	仁	곱	double, multiple, times, fold	배
	亻	仿	位	倍數	a multiple; a double number	배수
				倍加	double; be doubled	배가
人 8 718	倍	倍	倍	倍增	double	배증

借	亻	亻	仁	빌릴	borrow; lend	차
	仹	借	借	貸借	debt and credit; letting and hiring	대차
				借用	borrow	차용
人 8 719	借	借	借	借越	overdraw	차월

倣	亻	亻	仁	본받을	imitate; like, according to	방
	仿	倣	倣	模倣	imitate, follow an example	모방
				倣似	resemble, be similar to	방사
人 8 720	倣	倣	倣			

候	亻	亻	仁	기후	climate; wait, expect	후
	仁	侯	侯	氣候	climate	기후
				徵候	symptom of a disease; omen, sign	징후
人 8 721	侯	侯	候	候補	candidate, candidacy	후보

値 人 8 722	亻 亻 亻 亻 佇 佇 佇 佇 值 值	값	price, value; meet; happen; take in hand	치
		價值	value, worth, merit	가치
		數值	numerical value	수치
		價值判斷	estimate, judge value	가치판단

倫 人 8 723	亻 亻 亻 亻 伶 伶 伶 倫 倫	인륜	constant, ordinary; right principles; degrees	륜
		倫理	ethics; moral principles	윤리
		人倫	humaneness; human relations	인륜
		五倫	the Five Human Relationships of Confucianism	오륜

兼 八 8 724	丷 丷 丷 当 当 草 兼 兼 兼	겸할	jointly, concurrently, together; unite in one	겸
		兼床	table for two	겸상
		兼職	hold two positions concurrently	겸직

冥 冖 8 725	冖 冖 冖 冃 冃 冒 冥 冥	어두울	dark, obscure, deep; Hades	명
		冥王星	the planet Pluto	명왕성
		冥想	meditate, contemplate	명상
		冥福	happiness in the other world, heavenly bliss	명복

凍 冫 8 726	冫 冫 冫 泂 泂 泂 涷 涷 凍	얼	freeze; icy	동
		凍死	freeze to death	동사
		凍結	freeze	동결
		凍傷	be frostbitten	동상

涼 冫 8 727	冫 冫 冫 六 浐 泞 涼 涼 涼	서늘할	cool, cold	량
		凄涼	desolate; plaintive; sad; pensive	처량
		納涼	enjoy cool air, cool off (in summer)	납량
		清涼	clear and cool, refreshing	청량

剛	冂	冂	冋	군셀	hard, unyielding	강
	円	冊	岡	剛氣	firmness; fortitude; strength of character	강기
刀 8 728	岡	岡	剛	剛斷	decisive; determined; resolute	강단
				剛直	be upright, have integrity	강직

原	厂	厂	厈	근원	source, origin, beginning; natural; derivation; plateau, high plain; high level	원
	厉	后	盾			
厂 8 729	原	原	原	原因	the cause, cause; the origin	원인
				原料	raw materials	원료
				平原	plain, prairie	평원

哲	十	扌	扌	밝을	wise, knowing	철
	扚	扩	折	哲學	philosophy	철학
				哲理	philosophy of, philosophical principles of	철리
口 7 730	折	哲	哲	哲學者	philosopher	철학자

哭	冂	口	口	울	weep, cry, mourn for	곡
	吅	吅	哭	痛哭	lamentation	통곡
				號哭	wail, weep aloud	호곡
口 7 731	罚	哭	哭	泣哭	wailing	읍곡

員	冖	口	吕	인원	member; associate	원
	吊	肙	肙	人員	staff member, personnel	인원
				醫員	member of a medical staff	의원
口 7 732	員	員	員	議員	National Assemblyman	의원

唐	亠	广	庐	당나라	Tang Dynasty, China, Chinese	당
	庐	庙	唐	唐根	carrot	당근
				唐突	audaciously; presumptuously	당돌
口 7 733	唐	唐	唐	唐紙	Chinese rice paper	당지

	十	土	圵	재	a walled city, citadel; walls of a city; defense wall	성
城	圵	圹	坊			
土 7 734	城	城	城	山城 城壁 城主	mountain fortress castle walls lord of the castle	산성 성벽 성주

	十	土	圠	묻을	bury; lie in wait	매
埋	圳	坦	坦	埋葬 埋沒 埋伏	bury, entomb; ostracize bury lie in ambush, set an ambush	매장 매몰 매복
土 7 735	坦	埋	埋			

	一	了	丂	여름	summer	하
夏	百	百	百	夏期 夏至 夏服	summer, summer season the summer solstice summer clothes, summer uniform	하기 하지 하복
夂 7 736	頁	頁	夏			

	✓	✓✓	⋎⋎	어찌	how	해
奚	幺	幺	幺	奚琴	single-stringed fiddle	해금
大 7 737	奚	奚	奚			

	ㄑ	攵	女`	각시	girl, woman; wife	낭
娘	女ㄅ	女ㅋ	女ㅋ	娘子 娘子軍	maiden, maidens a mass of women, an army of women	낭자 낭자군
女 7 738	娘	娘	娘			

	ㄑ	攵	女`	즐길	rejoice; amuse; pleasure	오
娛	女ㅁ	女ㅁ	娱	娛樂 娛樂室	amusement; entertainment amusement room, arcade	오락 오락실
女 7 739	娛	娛	娛			

孫	了	孑	孖	손자	grandson, grandchild	손
	孖	拯	孫	孫子	grandson	손자
				孫女	granddaughter	손녀
子 7 740	孫	孫	孫	曾孫	great-grandson	증손

宮	ハ	宀	宀	집	palace; temple	궁
	宀	宮	宮	宮中	the court, in the court	궁중
				宮闕	court, palace	궁궐
宀 7 741	宮	宮	宮	宮女	court lady; maid of honor	궁녀

宴	ハ	宀	宀	잔치	feast, banquet; party; entertain; relaxation	연
	宀	宴	宴	宴會	dinner party, a social dinner	연회
宀 7 742	宴	宴	宴	酒宴	feast and wine, banquet	주연

害	ハ	宀	宀	해칠	hurt, harm, injury; loss, damage	해
	宔	宔	宔	妨害	hinder, prevent, obstruct	방해
				利害	gain and loss, advantage and disadvantage	이해
宀 7 743	害	害	害	殺害	murder, kill	살해

家	ハ	宀	宀	집	house; family; specialist, professional; class, school	가
	宀	宁	宇			
				家庭	family; home	가정
				家族	family, household	가족
宀 7 744	家	家	家	家具	furniture	가구

容	ハ	宀	宀	얼굴	appearance, manner; allow, accommodate; endure; forgive; contain; admit; capacity; easy	용
	宀	宀	突			
				容恕	forgive, pardon	용서
				容積	capacity; volume; bulk	용적
宀 7 745	突	容	容	容貌	looks, features, appearance	용모

射	イ	イ	白	쏠	shoot, fire, shoot out; project, aim at	사
	白	自	身	反射	reflect; reverberate	반사
				射擊	fire, shoot	사격
寸 7 746	身	射	射	發射	fire; launch; emit	발사

展	ュ	尸	尸	펼	open, unroll, spread out	전
	尸	屏	屈	展開	develop; unfold	전개
				展望	outlook, prospect	전망
尸 7 747	展	展	展	發展	make progress, develop; prosper	발전

峯	山	山	屮	봉-우리	peak, mountain top; hump	봉
	屮	灾	夆	山峯	peak, summit	산봉
				靈峯	sacred peak	영봉
山 7 748	夆	峯	峯	絶峯	sheer peak	절봉

島	イ	白	白	섬	island	도
	白	自	鳥	島國	an island state, island country	도국
				半島	peninsula	반도
山 7 749	鳥	島	島	無人島	uninhabited island	무인도

差	ゝ	ゝ	兰	어긋날	difference, discrepancy; send	차
	羊	羊	羊	差異	difference, disparity	차이
				差別	discriminate, differentiate	차별
工 7 750	差	差	差	差押	confiscate, seize	차압

師	イ	白	白	스승	teacher, instructor, master; army division	사
	白	自	自	師團	army division	사단
				技師	engineer, technician	기사
巾 7 751	師	師	師	師母 님	Madame, Mrs. (honorific form)	사모

10 strokes

席	亠	广	广	자리	seat, mat, place; feast, entertainment; a sail	석
	庐	庐	庐	出席	attend, be present	출석
巾 7 752	庐	庐	席	首席	the head seat; the president	수석
				席卷	overrun a place, overwhelm, conquer	석권

座	亠	广	广	자리	a seat; throne; base, stand; constellation	좌
	厐	座	座	座席	a seat; be seated, be present	좌석
广 7 753	座	座	座	座談	conversation, table talk	좌담
				座長	senior person seated	좌장

庫	亠	广	广	집	storehouse, treasury	고
	广	庐	庐	金庫	cash depository; "piggy bank"; cash box; bank	금고
广 7 754	庐	盲	庫	書庫	book depository	서고
				車庫	garage; train shed	차고

庭	亠	广	广	뜰	hall, court, courtyard	정
	庐	庐	庐	庭園	garden; park	정원
				庭球	tennis	정구
				校庭	playground; campus	교정
广 7 755	庭	庭	庭			

弱	丂	弓	弓	약할	weak, yielding; young; deficient	약
	弓	弱	弱	貧弱	poor; scanty, limited	빈약
				弱者	the weak, a weak person	약자
弓 7 756	弱	弱	弱	老弱	the old and the weak	노약

徐	彳	彳	彳	천천히	slow; grave, dignified	서
	彴	徐	徐	徐徐히	slowly	서서
				徐緩	slow, sluggish	서완
彳 7 757	徐	徐	徐	徐來	"Slow", "Reduce Speed"; go slowly	서래

154

徑	彳	彳	行	지름길 shortcut, byway; straight **경**
	行	徑	徑	直徑 diameter 직경 半徑 radius 반경 徑路 course, route; process, 경로 stage, step
彳 7 758	徑	徑	徑	

徒	彳	彳	行	무리 crowd; followers **도**
	什	往	徍	學徒 pupil, cadet 학도 徒黨 gang; cabal 도당 徒步 walk, go on foot 도보
彳 7 759	徏	徒	徒	

恕	女	女	女	용서할 forgive; show mercy, **서** absolve, excuse
	如	如	如	容恕 forgive, pardon 용서 寬恕 forbearance, leniency 관서
心 6 760	恕	恕	恕	

恣	ン	ン	次	방자할 impudent, impertinent, **자**
				  uppish; licentious;
				  dissipation

	次	次	次	放恣 impertinent, impudent 방자 恣行 willfulness, 자행 self-indulgence
心 6 761	恣	恣	恣	

恐	工	工	卫	두려울 fearful **공**
	巩	巩	巩	恐怖 fear, terror 공포 恐喝 intimidate, threaten, 공갈 blackmail
心 6 762	恐	恐	恐	恐妻家 henpecked husband 공처가

恥	丁	下	巨	부끄러울 ashamed; shame **치**
	巨	耳	耳	恥辱 shame, disgrace 치욕 國恥 national disgrace, 국치 national humiliation
心 6 763	恥	恥	恥	羞恥 dishonor, disgrace 수치

10 strokes

恩	口	日	田	은혜	grace, favor, kindness, mercy	은
	田	因	因	恩惠	grace, kindness; moral obligation	은혜
				恩師	teacher to whom one is indebted, honored teacher	은사
心 6 764	恩	恩	恩	恩人	benefactor; a person to whom one is beholden	은인

恭	十	卄	丗	공손할	reverence, respect	공
	尹	共	茶	恭遜	be respectful, deferential	공손
				恭敬	respect	공경
				不恭	disrespectful, irreverent, rude	불공
心 6 765	恭	恭	恭			

息	亻	亻	白	숨쉴	breath, vapor; sigh; rest; put a stop to, appease; grow; son, posterity; interest on money; news	식
	白	白	白			
				休息	a break, a rest	휴식
心 6 766	息	息	息	子息	one's children; "fellow"	자식
				消息	news, word, information	소식

悅	亻	忄	忙	기쁠	pleased, contented, glad, happy	열
	忙	忙	悄	法悅	rapture, ecstasy; religious exaltation	법열
心 7 767	悄	悅	悅	喜悅	glee, delight	희열

悔	亻	卜	忄	뉘우칠	repent, regret; reject	회
	忙	忙	恀	後悔	regret, feel sorry for	후회
				悔改	repent	회개
心 7 768	悔	悔	悔	悔心	remorse	회심

悟	亻	忄	忙	깨달을	become aware of, apprehend, awake	오
	忤	悟	伍	覺悟	understand; perceive; be ready to	각오
心 7 769	悟	悟	悟	悔悟	regret, feel remorse	회오

拳	`	``	```
	並	苎	关
手 6 770	耂	耄	拳

주먹 fist; clench, clasp **권**
拳銃 pistol 권총
拳鬪 boxing, box 권투
鐵拳 iron fist, strong fist 철권

捕	十	扌	打
	扝	折	捎
手 7 771	捎	捕	捕

잡을 seize **포**
捕虜 prisoner of war 포로
逮捕 arrest, apprehend 체포
捕縛 arrest and tie up, apprehend 포박

捉	十	扌	打
	扣	扣	捉
手 7 772	捉	捉	捉

잡을 seize, grasp **착**
捕捉 catch, capture; catch, understand 포착

振	十	扌	扩
	扩	护	护
手 7 773	振	振	振

떨칠 shake; move; flap **진**
振興 promote, encourage; be encouraged; be aroused 진흥
振動 oscillate, swing; vibrate 진동
不振 dull, stagnant, depressed 부진

效	亠	宀	六
	亣	交	岁
攴 6 774	欵	効	效

본받을 be like, imitate; efficacious; endeavor **효**
效果 efficacy; results, effect 효과
效率 efficiency, efficient 효율
失效 lose effect, be invalidated, be nullified 실효

料	`	亠	半
	半	米	米
斗 6 775	半	料	料

헤아릴 calculate, estimate, consider; arrange; materials, ingredients **료**
材料 materials 재료
料金 the fee, the cost 요금
無料 free of charge 무료

旅	丶	亠	方	나그네 guest; travel	려
	方	扩	扩	旅行 travel, take a trip	여행
方 6 776	斿	斿	旅	旅客 passenger, traveler 旅券 a passport	여객 여권

時	刂	月	日	때 time; hour, o'clock; season	시
	旷	旷	旷	時間 time; an hour 時期 time, season, period	시간 시기
日 6 777	旷	時	時	時刻 the hour and minute; the exact time	시각

書	刁	刁	刁	글 to write; writings, books	서
	圭	聿	聿	書類 documents 書店 bookstore	서류 서점
日 6 778	書	書	書	書記 secretary, clerk	서기

朔	丷	丷	丷	초하루 first day of a lunar month; new moon; north	삭
	屰	屰	朔	朔風 north wind of winter 朔料 monthly salary	삭풍 삭료
月 6 779	朔	朔	朔	朔月 the new moon	삭월

栢	十	才	木	측백나무 Chinese juniper tree; pine nut	백
	朾	朾	朾	栢子 pine nuts, pine seeds 側栢 Chinese juniper tree	백자 측백
木 6 780	栢	栢	栢		

栗	一	襾	襾	밤 chestnut tree; firm, durable; full (as when ripe); cold, chilly	률
	襾	西	西	栗木 chestnut tree 栗園 chestnut grove	율목 율원
木 6 781	栗	栗	栗		

校				학교	school; check, examine, revise	교
	十	才	木	校長	the principal, headmaster	교장
	木'	杧	杧	校庭	school playground, campus	교정
木 6 782	栌	栌	校	校訂	revise	교정

核				씨	kernel; investigate	핵
	十	才	才	結核	tuberculosis; tubercle	결핵
	木'	栌	杧	原子核	atomic nucleus	원자핵
木 6 783	核	核	核	核子	kernel; core	핵자

株				그루	tree trunk; stock	주
	十	才	木	株式	shares, stocks	주식
	木'	杧	杧	株主	stockholder	주주
木 6 784	枡	枡	株	株券	stock certificate	주권

栽				심을	to plant; sow	재
	十	土	吉	栽培	cultivate, raise, grow	재배
	寺	寺	寺	栽植	plant trees	재식
木 6 785	栽	栽	栽	盆栽	potted plant	분재

根				뿌리	root, beginning, cause	근
	十	才	木	根本	root, origin, source	근본
	杧	杓	杓	根源	origin, fountainhead, source	근원
木 6 786	柤	根	根	根據	basis, foundation; based on, founded on; authority	근거

桂				계수나무	cinnamon, cassia	계
	十	才	木	桂皮	cinnamon bark	계피
	木'	杧	杜	月桂	laurel tree; bay tree	월계
木 6 787	柱	桂	桂	桂樹	cinnamon tree; cassia tree	계수

159

格	十	才	木	법식	rule; limit; frame; form; ruled spaces; category	격
	朴	权	柊	人格	character, personality	인격
				格鬪	grapple, fight hand-to-hand	격투
木 6 788	柊	格	格	格式	rules, norms, form	격식

桃	十	才	木	복숭아	peach; profligacy	도(두)
	木	材	材	桃色	pink, rose (color of love); love	도색
				胡桃	walnut	호도
木 6 789	机	桃	桃	桃花	peach blossom	도화

桐	十	才	木	오동나무	paulownia tree	동
	桁	桁	桐	桐油	paulownia oil, tung oil	동유
				桐油紙	oiled paper	동유지
木 6 790	桐	桐	桐	梧桐	paulownia tree	오동

案	丶	宀	宀	책상	table; plan, idea	안
	安	安	安	案內	guide, show around, usher	안내
				改正案	a revised bill, a revision	개정안
木 6 791	宰	宰	案	起案	draft, draw up	기안

桑	又	叒	叒	뽕나무	mulberry tree	상
	叒	叒	叒	農桑	agriculture and sericulture	농상
				桑葉	mulberry leaves	상엽
木 6 792	桑	桑	桑			

殊	丆	歹	歹	다를	different, peculiar, unique, special	수
	歹	歼	殀	殊常	peculiar, odd, suspicious	수상
				特殊	special, unique	특수
歹 6 793	殊	殊	殊	殊勲	meritorious service	수훈

殉	⼐	⼎	⼎	죽을	be buried alive with a corpse; die for	순
	⼎	歼	列	殉教者 a martyr		순교자
				殉國	die for country	순국
歹 6 794	殉	殉	殉	殉職	die in the line of duty	순직

殺	⼂	⼂	⼿	죽일	kill; exceedingly	살
				감할	decrease; pare down	쇄
	杀	杀	杀	殺人	murder, kill	살인
				殺氣	violent temper	살기
殳 6 795	殺	殺	殺	相殺	offset, cancel each other out	상쇄

氣	一	仁	气	기운	steam, breath, gas	기
				空氣	air; the atmosphere	공기
	气	气	气	氣運	trend, tendency	기운
				氣象	weather,	기상
气 6 796	氣	氣	氣		weather conditions	

泰	二	三	丰	클	exalted; extreme; Thailand	태
				泰山	high mountain;	태산
	夫	夫	表		tremendous thing;	
					Mt. T'ai in Shantung	
				泰平	peace, tranquility	태평
水 5 797	泰	泰	泰	泰然自若	be perfectly calm, self-possessed	태연자약

流	丶	氵	氵	흐를	flow; current; descend,	류
					unstable; transport	
	氵	汰	法	流域	drainage basin	유역
				流行	popular, fashionable	유행
				上流	upper reaches of a	상류
水 7 798	流	流	流		stream; upper classes of society	

浦	丶	氵	氵	물가	riverbank; inlet, bay	포
				浦口	inlet; port, boat landing	포구
	氵	氵	洞	浦田	riverside field	포전
水 7 799	浦	浦	浦			

					바다	sea	해
海	冫	氵	汙		海岸	seashore, coast	해안
	沪	泛	泊		海外	overseas, abroad	해외
					海軍	navy, maritime forces	해군
水 7 800	泊	海	海				

					뜰	float; drift; light, volatile, insubstantial, frivolous	부
浮	冫	氵	氵		浮動	waft, float in the air; fluctuate	부동
	沪	氵	浮		浮遊	float, drift, waft	부유
水 7 801	浮	浮	浮		浮浪	wander about, float about, be a hobo	부랑

					넓을	vast; great, grand	호
浩	冫	氵	氵		浩然	vast; expansive, magnanimous	호연
	氵	浩	浩		浩浩白髮	old, hoary, "vast, vast white hairs"	호호백발
水 7 802	浩	浩	浩		浩蕩	vast, boundless, immense	호탕

					물결	wave; profligate, wasteful	랑
浪	冫	氵	氵		風浪	wind and waves, heavy seas	풍랑
	氵	沪	泪		浪漫	romance, romantic	낭만
水 7 803	浪	浪	浪		放浪	wander about, lead a Bohemian life	방랑

					목욕할	bathe, wash	욕
浴	冫	氵	氵		沐浴湯	public bath house	목욕탕
	氵	浴	浴		沐浴	bathe, take a bath	목욕
水 7 804	浴	浴	浴		浴室	bathing room	욕실

					젖을	soak, immerse; flood	침
浸	冫	氵	汀		浸入	penetrate, invade, raid	침입
	汀	浸	汗		浸水	be flooded, inundated	침수
水 7 805	浸	浸	浸		浸禮	baptism by immersion	침례

					끌	melt, thaw; disperse; cancel	소
消	氵	氵	氵				
	汀	沙	沙		消息	news, word, information	소식
					消化	digest, digestion	소화
水 7 806	消	消	消		消極的	negative, passive	소극적

					건널	wade, ford a stream; pass through, connected with; involve, concern, implicate; negotiate; interfere	섭
涉	氵	氵	氵				
	氵	沙	沙		干涉	meddle in, interfere with	간섭
					涉外	liaison; public relations	섭외
水 7 807	沙	洪	涉		交涉	negotiation	교섭

					까마귀	crow; black; "alas!"	오
烏	亻	户	白				
	鸟	鳥	鳥		烏鵲	crows and magpies	오작
					烏合之卒	hurriedly gathered crows, an unruly mob	오합지졸
火 6 808	烏	烏	烏		烏乎	Alas! Alack!	오호

					매울	burning, violent, impetuous; bright; meritorious, eminent; majestic, imposing	렬
烈	一	歹	歹				
	列	列	列		猛烈	violent; fierce; vehement	맹렬
					熾烈	intense, fierce	치열
火 6 809	烈	烈	烈		壯烈	heroic; glorious	장렬

					특별할	special	특
特	丿	牛	牛				
	牜	牜	牡		特別	special, extraordinary	특별
					特色	special feature, peculiarity	특색
牛 6 810	牪	特	特		特權	privilege, prerogative	특권

					이	this	자
玆	丶	丷	丷				
	六	玄	玄				
玄 6 811	玆	玆	玆		(Originally 玆.)		

163

班	二	于	王	나눌	class; squad; group; variegated	반
	班	班	班	班長	squad leader, class chief	반장
玉 6				班員	member of a neighborhood organization	반원
812	班	班	班	兩班	aristocrat, yangban	양반

畜	一	亠	玄	가축	cultivate, rear; domestic animals; store up	축
	玄	玄	斉	畜產	livestock; livestock breeding	축산
田 5				畜生	animals, beasts	축생
813	斉	畜	畜	畜類	domestic animals	축류

留	し	厶	幻	머무를	detain; entertain; keep; restrain; transmit	류
	纫	幻	留	留意	be attentive to; bear in mind	유의
田 5				留學	study abroad	유학
814	留	留	留	拘留	detention, custody	구류

疾	亠	广	广	병	disease, illness; urgency, haste	질
	疒	疒	疒	疾病	disease, sickness	질병
疒 5				疾走	run at full speed, speed	질주
815	疟	疾	疾	眼疾	eye disease, disorder of the eye	안질

疲	亠	广	广	피곤할	weary, tired	피
	疒	疒	疒	疲勞	fatigued, exhausted	피로
疒 5				疲困	fatigued, exhausted	피곤
816	疟	疲	疲	疲弊	be impoverished	피폐

病	亠	广	广	병들	disease; defect	병
	疒	疒	疒	病院	hospital; repair shop	병원
疒 5				病身	cripple; invalid	병신
817	病	病	病	傳染病	contagious disease, infectious disease	전염병

				증세	ailment, malady, disease	증
症	亠	广	疒	厭症	dislike, aversion	염증
	疒	疒	疒	症勢	symptoms of disease, the condition of the patient	증세
疒 5 818	疖	症	症	痛症	be severely ill, severe pain	통증
				더할	profit, advantage	익
益	ソ	丷	丷	無益	unprofitable, useless	무익
	兴	尖	谷	有益	profitable, beneficial	유익
皿 5 819	谷	益	益	公益	public good	공익
				참	true, real; likeness	진
眞	匕	匕	片	寫眞	photograph	사진
	片	盲	盲	眞正	genuineness	진정
目 5 820	眞	眞	眞	眞心	sincerity	진심
				잠잘	sleep; close the eyes	면
眠	刂	刂	月	睡眠	sleep, slumber	수면
	目	盯	盰	不眠不休	no sleep and no rest, work without surcease	불면불휴
目 5 821	眠	眠	眠	不眠症	insomnia, sleeplessness	불면증
				깰	break; destroy	파
破	厂	丆	石	破壞	destroy, demolish	파괴
	石	石	砂	破滅	ruin, destroy	파멸
石 5 822	砂	破	破	讀破	read all the way to the end	독파
				숨길	secret, mysterious, abstruse	비
祕	一	礻	礻	祕密	a secret	비밀
	禾	礼	礼	祕訣	secret; the key to, the secret of	비결
示 5 823	祕	祕	祕	祕方	secret process; secret formula	비방

165

祖	一 ラ テ	할아비 grandfather; ancestor; prototype; beginning	조
	ネ 乱 初	祖國 fatherland	조국
		祖父 grandfather	조부
示 5 824	袒 袒 祖	先祖 ancestor, forefather	선조

祝	一 ラ テ	빌 pray, invoke; bless	축
	ネ 利 初	祝賀 congratulate, felicitate	축하
		祝辭 congratulatory remarks	축사
示 5 825	初 祝 祝	祝願 supplicate, petition, pray for	축원

神	一 ラ テ	귀신 spirit, spirits, god; divine; supernatural; soul; mind; nerves; energy; genius	신
	ネ 利 初	神經 nerve, nerves	신경
		神父 Catholic priest/father	신부
示 5 826	袒 袒 神	神通 marvelous, extraordinary	신통

租	ニ 千 才	구실 tax; rent	조
	禾 利 利	租稅 taxes, taxation	조세
		租界 settlement, concession	조계
禾 5 827	利 租 租	租貢 pay taxes	조공

秩	ニ 千 手	차례 order, orderly; rank	질
	禾 秒 秒	秩序 order; system, method, regularity	질서
禾 5 828	秒 秩 秩		

並	丄 亠 立	아우를 together, side by side; and, also, at the same time	병
	立 並 並	並行 go abreast, run parallel with; perform two things at the same time	병행
立 5 829	並 並 並	並立 stand side by side; coexist (Also written 倂.)	병립

166

笑 竹 4 830	ノ	⺮	⺮	웃을	laugh, smile; ridicule	소
				微笑	smile	미소
	⺮	⺮	⺮	苦笑	forced smile, strained laugh	고소
	竺	竿	笑	談笑	visit, have a pleasant chat	담소

粉 米 4 831	⺊	⺌	半	가루	powder; meal; fragrance	분
				粉紅色	pink	분홍색
	米	米	米	粉炭	powdered coal	분탄
	粉	粉	粉	粉貼	powder puff; cardboard slate for writing practice	분첩

納 糸 4 832	幺	幺	幺	들일	receive	납
				納付	pay a fee, pay tax; deliver goods	납부
	糸	糸	糸	納品	deliver goods	납품
	糸	納	納	納入	pay tax; deliver goods	납입

純 糸 4 833	幺	幺	幺	순수할	pure, simple; unmixed	순
				純眞	pure, naive, genuine	순진
	糸	糸	糸	純全	pure, artless; wholly, completely	순전
	紅	紅	純	純情	a pure heart	순정

紙 糸 4 834	幺	幺	幺	종이	paper	지
				紙幣	paper money, bill	지폐
	糸	糸	糸	表紙	book cover	표지
	紅	紙	紙	白紙	paper, white paper, blank paper	백지

級 糸 4 835	幺	幺	幺	등급	degree, step, class	급
				級數	mathematical progression, a series	급수
	糸	糸	糸	等級	class, grade, rank	등급
	級	級	級	階級	rank, grade; social class	계급

索	十	亠	声	찾을	search into; think; demand; importune; inquire; index	색
糸 4 836	声	去	索	搜索 索引 索出	search for, go after an index seek out, ferret out, track down	수색 색인 색출
	索	索	索			

紛	幺	幺	幺	어지러울	confused; disorderly; mixed; numerous	분
糸 4 837	糸	糸	糸	紛爭 紛亂	dispute, quarrel disorderly, entangled, confused	분쟁 분란
	紛	紛	紛	紛雜	crowded, confused	분잡

素	二	圭	主	흴	white; plain, unadorned; commonly, usually	소
糸 4 838	丰	素	表	酸素 素質	oxygen temperament, character; constitution	산소 소질
	素	素	素	平素	ordinary times, peacetime	평소

缺	乞	二	午	이지러질	deficiency; defective; vacancy	결
缶 4 839	缶	缶	缶	缺點 缺乏	fault, defect be short, deficient; lack, want	결점 결핍
	缶	缺	缺	缺席	be absent, fail to attend	결석

翁	八	公	公	늙은이	old gentleman, old man, "sir"	옹
羽 4 840	今	翁	翁	翁主	princess (daughter of a king and a royal concubine)	옹주
	翁	翁	翁	翁壻	father-in-law and son-in-law	옹서

耕	二	三	丰	밭갈	a plow	경
耒 4 841	耒	耒	耒	耕作地 耕作 筆耕	land under cultivation cultivate, till, plow copy	경작지 경작 필경
	耒	耕	耕			

胸	丿	月	月	가슴	breast, chest	흉
	月	肑	肑	胸中	the breast, inmost heart	흉중
				胸部	chest, thorax	흉부
肉 6 842	胸	胸	胸	胸背	breast and back; embroidered rank insignia worn on breast and back	흉배

能	ㄥ	ㅿ	ㅿ	능할	able, may, can; ability, talent, power	능
	台	育	肖	能力	capability, ability	능력
				能率	efficiency, efficient	능률
肉 6 843	育	能	能	能熟	skillful, adept, expert	능숙

脅	力	刕	刕	위협할	rib, ribs; threat	협
	劦	劦	劦	威脅	threat, threaten	위협
				脅迫	intimidate, coerce	협박
肉 6 844	脅	脅	脅	脅迫狀	intimidating letter	협박장

脈	丿	月	月	맥	vein, artery; pulse; mountain range	맥
	肝	肝	肛	脈搏	pulse, pulsation	맥박
				山脈	mountain range	산맥
肉 6 845	脈	脈	脈	血脈	blood vessel	혈맥

臭	亻	竹	自	냄새	stink, smell	취
	自	自	自	惡臭	foul odor, stench	악취
				口臭	halitosis	구취
自 4 846	臭	臭	臭	乳臭	smell of milk	유취

致	工	云	云	이를	reach, extend to	치
	至	至	至	景致	scenic view, landscape	경치
				致命的	fatal	치명적
至 4 847	致	致	致	一致	agree, concur	일치

(9 strokes in original form, 致 .)

航	亻	方	方	쌍배	navigate	**항**
	月	舟	舟	航空	fly, navigate the air	항공
				航海	sail, navigate the sea	항해
舟 4 848	舟	舫	航	航母	aircraft carrier	항모

般	亻	方	月	일반	sort, manner, class; all kinds, all sorts	**반**
	月	舟	舟	一般	all, the whole; in general	일반
				諸般	all sorts	제반
舟 4 849	舩	般	般			

茫	十	扎	艹	아득할	vast, vague, boundless	**망**
	艹	芒	茫	茫茫	vast, boundless	망망
艸 6 850	茫	芒	茫			

草	十	刂	艹	풀	grass, weeds, herbs	**초**
	艹	艿	苎	草綠	grass-green, green	초록
				草家	straw-thatched house	초가
艸 6 851	苩	莗	草	蘭草	orchid; iris	난초

茶	十	刂	艹	차	tea plant, tea	**다(차)**
	少	火	太	茶房	tearoom, tea house	다방
				茶果	tea and cakes, light refreshment	다과
艸 6 852	茶	茶	茶	紅茶	tea, black tea	홍차

荒	十	刂	艹	거칠	wild, barren, deserted	**황**
	荒	荒	荒	荒廢	devastated, desolated	황폐
				荒野	wilderness, wilds; wasteland	황야
艸 6 853	荒	荒	荒	荒蕪地	barren tract, wasteland	황무지

衰 衣 4 854	亠	亠	序	쇠할	decrease, decline; deteriorate; small, decayed, weak		쇠
	亩	亩	户	衰弱	weakness		쇠약
	亨	亨	衰	衰亡 老衰	decline, decay, collapse grow old and infirm, be senile		쇠망 노쇠
被 衣 5 855	冫	礻	礻	입을	wear; bear, suffer; coverlet		피
	衤	衩	初	被害 被選	damage, loss be elected, be chosen		피해 피선
	神	被	被	被殺	be killed		피살
討 言 3 856	亠	亠	言	칠	beg, seek; punish		토
	言	言	言	討議 討論	discuss debate, discuss		토의 토론
	言	討	討	檢討	look into, examine		검토
訓 言 3 857	亠	亠	言	가르칠	instruct; admonish		훈
	言	言	言	訓練 訓戒	training teaching, instruction; precept, moral		훈련 훈계
	訓	訓	訓	訓示	instruct; direct		훈시
記 言 3 858	亠	亠	言	기록할	record, a record, a mark; remember		기
	言	言	言	記者	reporter, journalist; stenographer		기자
	訂	訂	記	記録 記事	a record, to record an article, an account		기록 기사
豈 豆 3 859	山	山	屮	어찌 승전악	how, how can it possibly be delighted; triumphant		기 개
	岂	岂	岂	豈歌	victory song; song of triumph; paean		개가
	岂	岂	豈				

171

10 strokes

貢 貝 3 860	一 吉 亩	工 吉 貢	干 青 貢	바칠 貢獻 貢米 朝貢	offer as tribute contribute to; render service to rice for government taxes pay tribute (to a larger state)	공 공헌 공미 조공
財 貝 3 861	刂 目 貝一	刀 貝 財	月 貝 財	재물 財政 財物 財産	property, wealth finance, fiscal matters property, goods an estate, property, possessions	재 재정 재물 재산
起 走 3 862	十 丰 起	土 走 起	丰 走 起	일어날 起原 起因 起訴	rise; start originate in, spring from cause indict, bring charges against	기 기원 기인 기소
軒 車 3 863	亠 亘 車	二 亘 軒	戸 車 軒	마루 烏竹軒	balcony; high *Ojukhŏn*, shrine of Yi Yul-gok in Kangnŭng	헌 오죽헌
辱 辰 3 864	厂 辰 辰	厂 辰 辱	戸 辰 辱	욕 辱說 屈辱 雪辱	disgrace, defile; abuse swear, curse humiliation, shame restore honor, clear oneself of shame	욕 욕설 굴욕 설욕
追 辶 6 865	亻 自 追	阝 自 追	自 自	따를 追加 追窮 追從	follow, pursue; seek out; look back on; press, dun add to, supplement; "moreover" press hard, probe to the heart of servilely obey, be a slave to	추 추가 추궁 추종

172

| 退 | ㅋ ㅋ 巳 / 巨 艮 艮 | 물러갈 withdraw; abate | 퇴 |
| 走 6 866 | 退 退 | 退職 retire (from employment)
退治 conquer; eliminate
退却 retreat, fall back | 퇴직
퇴치
퇴각 |

| 送 | ﾍ 二 ﾝ / 关 关 关 | 보낼 send; give to, hand over; send off, see off; accompany, escort | 송 |
| 走 6 867 | 送 送 | 送金 remit funds, send money
送還 repatriate, send back
送料 postage, shipping charge | 송금
송환
송료 |

| 逃 | ノ 刂 兆 / 兆 兆 兆 | 달아날 escape | 도 |
| 走 6 868 | 逃 逃 | 逃避 escape, flee; evade
逃走 escape
逃亡 escape, desert, decamp | 도피
도주
도망 |

| 逆 | ﾛ 二 丷 / 屰 屰 屰 | 거스를 oppose, disobey; contrary, refractory; anticipate | 역 |
| 走 6 869 | 逆 逆 | 逆情 anger
逆賊 rebels, traitors
逆境 adverse situation | 역정
역적
역경 |

| 迷 | 丷 二 半 / 半 米 米 | 수수께끼 bewildered; fascinated; deluded; lost | 미 |
| 走 6 870 | 迷 迷 | 迷信 superstition, superstitious belief
迷路 path of error; maze
迷惑 bewildered, confused; infatuated with | 미신
미로
미혹 |

| 郞 | ㄱ ㅋ ㅋ / 艮 良 良 | 사내 young man, young gentleman | 랑 |
| 邑 7 871 | 郞 郞 郞 | 新郞 bridegroom
花郞道 Way of the *Hwarang* (young knights of Silla)
婿郞 esteemed son-in-law (honorific) | 신랑
화랑도
서랑 |

173

郡	ㅋ	ㅋ	尹	고을	a county	군
	尹	君	君	郡守	county chief, magistrate	군수
				隣郡	neighboring county	인군
邑 7 872	君刁	君3	郡	郡民	citizens of a county	군민

配	一	一	丙	짝	match, mate, pair, fit; find a match; worthy, suitable; **suffer punishment**	배
	西	西	酉	配給	distribute supplies / rations	배급
酉 3 873	酉ᅵ	酉ᄀ	配	配當	apportion, allot	배당
				配定	allocate, assign	배정

酌	一	一	丙	잔질할	pour liquor; deliberate, consult	작
	丙	酉	酉	酌婦	barmaid	작부
酉 3 874	酉ᅳ	酉勺	酌	酌酒	fill a wine cup; serve wine	작주

酒	丶	氵	氵	술	liquor; wine	주
	沪	沪	沔	酒幕	tavern, inn	주막
				酒稅	tax on liquor	주세
酉 3 875	沔	酒	酒	麥酒	beer	맥주

針	人	今	今	바늘	a needle	침
	仐	余	余	針母	seamstress	침모
				短針	an hour hand, short hand of a clock	단침
金 2 876	金	金一	針	指針	pointer, indicator; guidance	지침

降	了	阝	阝	내릴	descend, send down	**강**
				항복할	surrender, fall	**항**
	阝	阬	阬	降服	surrender	항복
				降雨量	amount of rainfall	강우량
阜 6 877	隆	隆	降	降下	fall; drop; descend	강하

院	了 阝 阝' 阝' 阝'' 阝'' 阝'' 阝空 院	집	hall, public building; college; courtyard	원
阜 7 878		院内	within the building, within the institution	원내
		學院	academy, institute	학원
		退院	leave hospital	퇴원

陣	了 阝 阝一 阝一 阝豆 阝車 陣 陣 陳	진칠	file of soldiers; army; battle array; battle	진
阜 7 879		陣營	camp, military encampment	진영
		陣地	military position, fortification	진지

除	了 阝 阝' 阝人 阝人 阝人 阝个 除 除	덜	deduct; remove, do away with; subject	제
阜 7 880		除去	exclude, eliminate	제거
		解除	cancel, revoke	해제
		除名	expel, dismiss from membership	제명

馬	厂 F 厂 再 馬 馬 馬 馬 馬	말	horse	마
馬 0 881		馬力	horsepower	마력
		乘馬	ride a horse, riding	승마
		馬耳東風	east wind in a horse's ear, turn a deaf ear to	마이동풍

骨	冂 冂 冂 冎 冎 冎 骨 骨 骨	뼈	bone, bones	골
骨 0 882		眞骨	the "bone ranks" of Silla	진골
		白骨	a skeleton; whitened bones	백골
		氣骨	bones and spirit, body and soul; pluck, mettle, spirit	기골

高	亠 亠 亠 亠 亠 高 高 高 高	높을	high, tall; noble, proud	고
高 0 883		高等	high grade, high class	고등
		高級	high class; fancy	고급
		高尙	noble, elegant	고상

					귀신	spirit, spirits, ghost, disembodied spirits	귀
鬼					鬼神	spirit, spirits, demons; ghost	귀신
					鬼哭	the wailing of a ghost	귀곡
鬼 0 884					餓鬼	voracious demon; greedy person	아귀

11 Strokes

					하늘	heaven, one of the 8 trigrams	건
乾					마를	dry	간
					乾燥	dry; arid	건조
					乾魚	dried fish	건어
乙 10 885					乾物	dry foods	간물

					거짓	false, unreal; pretend	가
假					假裝	disguise oneself, wear a disguise	가장
					假令	if, supposing that; even if, granting that	가령
人 9 886					假拂	pay in advance, advance	가불

					머무를	delay, stop, desist	정
停					停戰	armistice, cease-fire	정전
					停止	stop, suspend; prohibit	정지
人 9 887					停留 場	a bus stop	정류장

					훌륭할	splendid, admirable	위
偉					偉人	great man; master thinker	위인
					偉大	grand, wonderful, great	위대
人 9 888					偉力	great power, mighty force	위력

健	亻	亻⺻	亻⺻	건강할 healthy, strong, vigorous; invigorate	건
	亻⺻	信	律	健康 health	건강
				健壯 robust, sturdy, healthy	건장
人 9 889	律	健	健	健在 be in good health	건재
側	亻	亻┐	佀	곁 side; askew; biased; perverted	측
	佀	佀	側	反側 betray; turn over in bed, toss and turn	반측
				側面 side, flank, lateral face	측면
人 9 890	側	側	側	兩側 both sides, the two sides, the two parties	양측
偶	亻	亻┐	佀	우연히 accidental, by chance; mate; even (numbers)	우
	佀	佀	偶	偶然히 accidentally, by chance	우연
				配偶者 mate, spouse; couple	배우자
人 9 891	偶	偶	偶	偶發 contingency; happen accidentally, come about by chance	우발
副	一	戸	戸	버금 the second; assistant, vice, subsidiary; aid	부
	呙	高	畐	副統領 vice-president	부통령
				副業 side job, side business	부업
刀 9 892	畐	副	副	副詞 adverb	부사
動	二	台	台	움직일 move; shake; excite	동
	台	重	重	動物 animal, living creature	동물
				動作 move members of the body, carriage, behavior	동작
力 9 893	重	動	動	不動産 real estate, fixed property	부동산
務	マ	予	矛	힘쓸 make efforts, devote attention to; duty, business, affairs	무
	矛	矜	矜	國務 affairs of state	국무
				任務 task, mission, duty; service	임무
力 9 894	矜	務	務	債務 indebtedness, liabilities, obligations	채무

區	一	戸	戸	구역	district, area; ward (of a city)	구
	吊	吊	品	區域	area, zone	구역
				區分	classify, divide up, section off	구분
匚 9 895	品	品	區	區廳	ward office	구청
參	厶	厽	厺	참여할	participate; consult; intervene; compare; blend; visit a superior	참
	厽	矣	矣	석	three (legal form)	삼
				參加	participate in, join	참가
				參席	attend; take part in	참석
厶 9 896	參	參	參	參拾	thirty (legal form)	삼십
唯	口	口'	听	오직	only; and, with; care for, consider	유
	听	听	听	唯一	be unique	유일
				唯物論	materialism	유물론
口 8 897	听	唯	唯	唯我獨尊	self-conceit	유아독존
唱	口	口	叩	노래부를	sing; call out	창
	叩	咀	唱	唱歌	a song; singing	창가
				齊唱	sing in unison	제창
				名唱	famous song; celebrated singer	명창
口 8 898	唱	唱	唱			
啓	丷	戸	戸	열	open, begin; explain	계
	所	所	改	啓蒙	enlighten, instruct, educate	계몽
				啓發	enlighten, edify	계발
口 8 899	啓	啓	啓	啓示	reveal, revelation	계시
商	亠	亠	亠	장사	trade, commerce; merchant; discuss, deliberate	상
	产	产	产	商業	commerce, business; engage in business	상업
				商人	merchant, shopkeeper	상인
口 8 900	商	商	商	商工業	commerce and industry	상공업

問 口 8 901	冂 門 門	日 門 問	月 門 問	물을 問題 質問 問招	ask, question problem; question question interrogate, question	문 문제 질문 문초
國 口 8 902	冂 冋 國	冋 回 國	同 國 國	나라 國民 國家 國會	nation, state, kingdom a people country, nation national assembly, congress	국 국민 국가 국회
域 土 8 903	十 圷 域	圹 圻 域	圹 垣 域	지경 地域 領域 聖域	frontier, boundary; region; country area, place, region territory, possession; sphere, jurisdiction sacred precincts	역 지역 영역 성역
執 土 8 904	十 查 幸)	圭 查 執	去 幸 執	잡을 執行 執權 執念	grasp, seize, hold; manage, direct execute, carry out hold political power concentrate the mind	집 집행 집권 집념
培 土 8 905	十 圹 培	圹 圹 培	圹 垃 培	북돋을 培養 栽培	bank up with earth; nourish, strengthen cultivate, nurture grow, raise	배 배양 재배
基 土 8 906	十 其 其	甘 其 基	甘 其 基	터 基礎 基本 基盤	foundation, base a foundation, a base basis, foundation; standard base, basis: foothold	기 기초 기본 기반

堂 土 8 907	⺌ ⺍ ⺌ ⺜ ⺜ ⺜ 堂 堂 堂	집 hall; temple; grave 食堂 restaurant; dining room 講堂 auditorium, hall 殿堂 palace, temple	당 식당 강당 전당
婚 女 8 908	女 女 妒 妒 婚 婚 婚 婚 婚	혼인할 marriage 結婚 marry, wed 約婚 engagement; become engaged 再婚 remarry	혼 결혼 약혼 재혼
婢 女 8 909	女 女 妒 妒 妒 妒 婶 婶 婢	계집종 female slave, maidservant 侍婢 lady-in-waiting, female attendant 奴婢 male and female slaves 官婢 female government slave	비 시비 노비 관비
婦 女 8 910	女 女 女 妇 妇 婦 婦 婦 婦	아내 wife, lady, woman; daughter-in-law 婦人 lady, married woman 婦女子 females; women; women and girls 婦德 womanly virtues	부 부인 부녀자 부덕
孰 子 8 911	亠 古 古 亨 亨 享 享 孰 孰	누구 who, which, what	숙
寂 宀 8 912	宀 宀 宀 宀 宀 宀 宗 宗 寂	고요할 silent, still 寂寞 lonely, solitary 閑寂 be retired, secluded 寂寂 lonely, deserted	적 적막 한적 적적

宿	宀 宀 宀 宀 疒 疒 宿 宿 宿	잘	lodge, stay for the night; halting place; old, in the past	숙
		宿命	fate; destiny	숙명
宀 8 913		宿題	homework assignment; pending question	숙제
		宿食	board and room, lodge, stay	숙식

寅	宀 宀 宀 宀 宀 宙 宙 寅 寅	범	3d of the 12 Earth's Branches; **tiger**	인
		甲寅	51st binary term of the sexagenary cycle	갑인
宀 8 914		寅年	Year of the Tiger	인년
		寅時	Watch of the Tiger, period between 3 and 5 A.M.	인시

寄	宀 宀 宀 宋 宋 宋 宧 宧 寄	붙을	send, mail; entrust; lodge at	기
		寄別	inform, report about, give information	기별
宀 8 915		寄宿舍	boardinghouse; dormitory	기숙사
		寄附	donate, contribute	기부

密	宀 宀 宓 宓 宓 窓 窓 密 密	빽빽할	secret; intimate, dense	밀
		密度	density (as of a population)	밀도
宀 8 916		密接	close to, intimate with	밀접
		密使	secret envoy, secret-service agent	밀사

將	丬 丬 丬 丬 丬 丬 丬 將 將	장수	a general; future; lead, escort	장
		將軍	a general, an admiral	장군
寸 8 917		將校	commissioned officer	장교
		將來	the future	장래

專	一 一 亘 車 車 車 重 專 專	오로지	alone, only, sole	전
		專門	a speciality; a major; a branch of learning	전문
寸 8 918		專務	senior managing director	전무
		專心	devote oneself to, put heart and soul into	전심

崩 山 8 919	山 山 屵 屵 肖 前 前 前 崩	무너질 collapse, fall; death of a monarch	붕
	崩壞 collapse, crumble; disintegrate	붕괴
	崩御 death of a king	붕어

崇 山 8 920	亠 山 屮 宀 峃 峃 峃 崇 崇	높일 venerate, honor; worship; reverence; lofty, noble	숭
	崇尚 revere, esteem	숭상
	崇高 sublime, noble	숭고
	崇仰 esteem	숭앙

帳 巾 8 921	冂 巾 巾 帄 帄 帳 帳 帳 帳	휘장 curtain, screen; scroll; tent	장
	帳簿 an account book	장부
	帳幕 tent; canopy; curtain hung from the ceiling	장막
	揮帳 a curtain, a curtain screen	휘장

常 巾 8 922	丷 小 当 尚 尚 尚 尚 常 常	항상 constantly, usually, frequently; regular; common; rule, principle	상
	恒常 always, constantly	항상
	常識 common sense, good sense	상식
	常用 commonly used, regularly used	상용

帶 巾 8 923	一 艹 卅 卅 卅 卅 帯 帯 帶	띠 belt, girdle; tape; bear, carry	대
	連帶 solidarity; joint liability	연대
	帶同 be accompanied by, take another with	대동
	帶劍 wear a sword; have a sword at one's side	대검

庸 广 8 924	广 庐 庐 庐 庐 庐 庐 庸	떳떳할 ordinary, commonplace, usual; simple; harmony	용
	庸劣 mediocrity; inferiority	용렬
	中庸 moderation, the golden mean, *The Doctrine of the Mean*	중용
	庸人 person of mediocrity	용인

庶	广 广 广 广 庐 庶 庶 庶 庶	무리 庶務 庶母 庶民	multitude, great number; whole; nearly, about; concubine general affairs concubine of one's father the common people, the masses	서 서무 서모 서민
广 8 925				

康	广 广 庐 庐 庚 庚 庚 康 康	평안할 康寧 健康 安康	peace, ease; health, vigor healthy and peaceful health well, healthy, safe	강 강녕 건강 안강
广 8 926				

張	ㄱ 引 弖 弔 弲 弲 張 張 張	베풀 張皇 張本人 誇張	stretch, extend out; display, publish; sheet long-winded, prolix ringleader, instigator exaggerate, overstate	장 장황 장본인 과장
弓 8 927				

彩	⼂ ⼂ 彐 爭 爭 采 采 彩 彩	채색 彩色 光彩 文彩	variegated colors; decorated, ornamented colored, in color; variegated colors luster, brilliance; splendor design, figure, pattern; beautiful coloring	채 채색 광채 문채
彡 8 928				

得	⼃ 彳 彳 彳 彳 彳 得 得 得	얻을 得點 得票 得失	obtain, gain, attain, acquire score, earn points; the score number of votes received gain and loss; advantages and disadvantages; merits and demerits	득 득점 득표 득실
彳 8 929				

御	⼃ 彳 彳 彳 彳 彳 徢 御 御	모실 御命 御前 御史	wait on, set before, offer to; drive a chariot; manage; attendant; imperial royal command in the royal presence royal emissary, secret royal inspector	어 어명 어전 어사
彳 8 930				

				字		音
從	⼻	⼻	⼻	좇을	follow, obey, comply; from; accessory; relatives	종
	⼻	從	從	從事	devote oneself to a task/profession	종사
				從來	up to now, before	종래
⼻ 8 931	從	從	從	從軍	follow the army, go to the front	종군
患	⼌	吕	吕	근심	anxiety; suffering; trouble	환
	吕	串	串	患者	a patient	환자
				憂患	anxiety; grief, sorrow	우환
心 7 932	患	患	患	患難	distress, misfortune	환난
悠	⼂	伜	伜	멀	distant; far-reaching; anxious thought	유
	似	悠	攸	悠悠	remote, distant; leisurely, deliberate	유유
				悠久	eternal, perpetual	유구
心 7 933	悠	悠	悠	悠然	calm, composed, self-possessed	유연
情	⼩	⼩	忄	뜻	feelings, emotions; circumstances, facts	정
	忄	忄	悻	感情	feeling, emotion, sentiment	감정
				情勢	situation, state of things	정세
心 8 934	情	情	情	情報	information; intelligence	정보
悽	⼩	忄	忄	슬플	grieved, suffering	처
	忄	悻	悻	悽然	sad, sorrowful; sadly, sorrowfully	처연
				悽慘	appalling, gruesome	처참
心 8 935	悽	悽	悽	悽絶	extremely sad, very sorrowful	처절
惜	忄	忄	⼩	아낄	be sparing of, begrudge; take care of; pity; love	석
	忄	忚	忄	哀惜	regret; regrettable	애석
				惜別	regret parting, part with regret	석별
心 8 936	惜	惜	惜	惜敗	regrettable defeat, lose by a narrow margin	석패

惟	忄 忄 忄 忄 忄 惟 惟 惟	생각할 think solemnly, care for, consider; only; and, with	유		
心 8 937		思惟 thought; thinking 惟獨 only, singly, uniquely	사유 유독		

戚 戈 7 938	厂 厂 厈 斤 厗 厗 厔 戚 戚	친척 relatives; mourning · 척 外戚 relatives on one's mother's side · 외척 姻戚 relatives by marriage; relatives on one's mother's side · 인척 親戚 relatives · 친척

掃 手 8 939	扌 扌 扫 扫 扫 扫 掃 掃 掃	쓸 sweep, clear away; exterminate · 소 掃除 clean up, sweep up · 소제 掃蕩 stamp out, get rid of, clean up · 소탕 掃萬 be rid of all hindrances · 소만

捨 手 8 940	扌 扌 扒 扲 拴 拴 捨 捨 捨	버릴 reject; forsake; spend; give alms; bestow · 사 取捨 take or leave; choose, select · 취사 喜捨 donate, give alms, give offerings · 희사 四捨五入 round off to the nearest whole number · 사사오입

授 手 8 941	扌 扌 扌 扴 抧 捋 授 授 授	줄 give to, confer; transmit · 수 授業 instruction, lessons · 수업 授受 give and receive; transfer, deliver · 수수 傳授 deliver, transmit; instruct, initiate · 전수

排 手 8 942	扌 扌 扌 扛 扞 排 排 排 排	물리칠 push, push out, clear out; open up; row, line; dispose; place in order · 배 排斥 reject, exclude; boycott · 배척 排除 remove, eliminate, oust · 배제 排擊 denounce, reject, strongly disapprove · 배격

185

				켈	pick, pluck, gather, choose	채
採	扌	扩	扩			
	扩	扩	扫	採用	adopt; employ	채용
				採集	gather, collect	채집
手 8 943	抖	採	採	採取	pick, harvest	채취

				찾을	inquire into, detect	탐
探	扌	扌	扩			
	扩	抔	抨	探險	exploration	탐험
				探偵	do detective work	탐정
手 8 944	探	探	探	探問	learn by inquiry; learn, hear, get wind of	탐문

				걸	hang, hang up	괘
掛	扌	扌	扩			
	扩	挂	拌	掛圖	wall map	괘도
				掛鐘	wall clock	괘종
手 8 945	挂	掛	掛	掛念	concerned, solicitous	괘념

				노략질할 rob, plunder		략
掠	扌	扌	扩			
	扩	抢	拍	擄掠	plunder	노략
				掠奪	plunder, pillage	약탈
手 8 946	掠	掠	掠			

				이을	meet, welcome; join, connect, contact; take, accept	접
接	扌	扌	扩			
	扩	拉	拉	接待	receive a guest, entertain	접대
				接受	receive (as visitors to a public place), accept applications	접수
手 8 947	挨	接	接	接觸	contact, keep in touch	접촉

				밀	push; expel; shirk; extend; deduce, promote; yield	추 (퇴)
推	扌	扌	扒			
	扒	抃	拃	推尋	take or receive what is one's own	추심
				推測	presume, conjecture	추측
手 8 948	推	推	推	推薦	recommend, sponsor	추천

11 strokes

敏 支 7 949	㇋	勹	勾	빠를	hasten, prompt, active; clever	민
	甸	每	每	敏捷	agile, nimble, sharp	민첩
	每	敏	敏	敏活	quick, agile, prompt	민활
				敏感	sensitive, susceptible	민감

敎 支 7 950	㇒	乂	耂	가르칠	teach, teaching; religion	교
	孝	孝	孝	敎育	education, instruction	교육
	孝	孝	孝	敎授	professor; teach, instruct	교수
				敎會	a church (the institution); a religious association	교회

敍 支 7 951	人	合	仐	펼	narrate; state; converse, chat; interview; meeting	서
	余	余	余	敍情	depict one's feelings	서정
	余	敍	敍	敍述	depict, narrate	서술
				敍事詩	descriptive poetry, epic poetry	서사시

救 支 7 952	寸	求	求	구원할	save, rescue, aid	구
	求	求	求	救濟	provide relief, help; save, deliver	구제
	救	救	救	救護	rescue, save	구호
				救出	aid, help, save	구출

敗 支 7 953	刂	目	目	패할	suffer defeat, lose; spoil	패
	貝	貝	貝	敗北	defeat; reversal	패배
	貝	敗	敗	敗戰	lose a battle, lose a war	패전
				敗亡	be defeated, annihilated	패망

斜 斗 7 954	人	合	仐	비낄	slanting, inclined, oblique; not upright, at an angle	사
	余	余	余	斜面	a slope, slanting surface, inclined plane	사면
	余	斜	斜	斜線	slanted line	사선
				斜陽	setting sun, evening light	사양

					돌	revolve, whirl; come back; forthwith; specially for that moment	선
旋	二	方	方				
	方	扩	扩		旋風	whirlwind; tornado; cyclone	선풍
方 7 955	扩	旋	旋		旋回	gyrate, turn, revolve	선회
					旋盤	a lathe	선반

					겨레	clan, tribe, family; class	족
族	亠	方	方		民族	race, ethnic group, a people	민족
	方	扩	扩		族譜	genealogy; genealogical table, clan register	족보
方 7 956	扩	族	族		同族	of the same race, from the same country	동족

					이미	since, already	기
旣	亻	白	白				
	白	白	白		旣往	the past, bygone days	기왕
					旣成服	ready-made clothing	기성복
无 7 957	旣	旣	旣		旣婚	already married	기혼

					낮	daytime	주
晝	㓷	聿	聿				
	書	書	書		晝夜	day and night	주야
					晝食	a midday meal, lunch	주식
日 7 958	書	書	晝		白晝	broad daylight	백주

					새벽	daybreak, dawn	신
晨	冂	曰	旦				
	戸	戸	戸		晨星	morning star	신성
日 7 959	晨	晨	晨				

					늦을	late; evening	만
晚	刂	日	旷				
	旷	昀	昀		晚學	a late education	만학
					晚秋	late autumn	만추
日 7 960	昭	晔	晚		晚餐	dinner, the evening meal	만찬

朗	㇇	㇕	良	밝을	bright, clear		랑
	艮	良	朗	朗讀	read aloud, recite	낭독
				明朗	bright, clear, cheerful	명랑
月 7 961	朗	朗	朗	朗報	good news	낭보

望	亠	亡	亾	바랄	hope, expect, look towards; full moon	망
	込	动	动	失望	disappointment; despair, lose hope	실망
				可望	hopes, prospects, likelihood	가망
月 7 962	望	望	望	希望	hope, desire; expectation; aspiration	희망

梁	氵	汀	㲀	다리	bridge; beam; ridge	량
	沏	沏	㳀	橋梁	a bridge	교량
				棟梁	small and great beams; pillars of the state, great ability	동량
木 7 963	梁	梁	梁	跳梁	rampant, dominant; prevailing	도량

梧	才	木	杧	오동나무	paulownia tree	오
	杧	杯	梧	梧桐	paulownia tree	오동
				碧梧桐	sultan's parasol (*firmiana platanifolia*)	벽오동
木 7 964	梧	梧	梧			

梨	二	禾	禾	배	pear	리
	利	利	利	梨花	pear blossom	이화
				梨園	the theatrical world; institute of court music in former days	이원
木 7 965	梨	梨	梨			

梅	才	木	杧	매화	plum, prune	매
	杧	柸	栂	梅花	plum tree; plum blossom	매화
				梅實	a plum	매실
木 7 966	梅	梅	梅	白梅	white plum blossoms; salted plums	백매

條	仁 亻 亻 亻 伀 佟 修 木 7 967 俢 俢 條	가지	branch, twig; section, clause, item; orderly, regular; a long thing	조
		條件	stipulation, term	조건
		條目	articles, items, clauses	조목
		條約	treaty, agreement	조약

| 械 | 扌 木 杧 杧 杧 枅 木 7 968 栻 械 械 | 기계 | machine, implement | 계 |
| | | 機械 | machine, machinery | 기계 |

欲	八 父 父 谷 谷 谷 欠 7 969 谷 欲 欲	하고자할	desire, wish	욕
		欲望	ambition, desire	욕망
		情欲	lust, desire	정욕
		欲求	craving, want, desire	욕구

毫	亠 亠 亠 亠 宣 宣 毛 7 970 毫 毫 毫	터럭	the finest hair, the smallest bit	호
		秋毫	autumn down (the lightest down); a bit, a whit, a hair, an atom	추호
		揮毫	"wield a brush"; write, paint	휘호

涙	氵 氵 氵 氵 沪 沪 水 8 971 泹 涙 涙	눈물	tears; weep, cry	루
		落涙	shed tears, weep	낙루
		感涙	tears of gratitude, tears of emotion	감루

涯	氵 氵 氵 沪 沪 涯 水 8 972 涯 涯 涯	물가	shore, bank; border, edge, limit	애
		生涯	a life, a lifetime; living	생애
		天涯	the horizon; a distant land	천애

淨				깨끗할	clean, pure	정
				淨化	purify	정화
				淨潔	cleanliness	정결
水 8 973				淨書	make a clean copy, write out neatly	정서

淡				맑을	clear, light in color; tasteless	담
				淡淡	clear (water); bright (moon); flat (taste); unconcerned	담담
				淡泊	candid, ingenuous	담박
水 8 974				淡水	fresh water	담수

淑				맑을	clear, pure; virtuous	숙
				淑女	a lady	숙녀
				貞淑	chaste, virtuous	정숙
水 8 975						

混				섞일	confused; turbid	혼
				混亂	confusion, chaos	혼란
				混沌	confused, mixed up	혼돈
水 8 976				混線	crossed lines, entangled wires	혼선

深				깊을	deep; profound, abstruse; intimate; long; extreme	심
				深刻	serious, acute, grave	심각
				深甚	deep, profound	심심
水 8 977				深呼吸	breathe deeply, take deep breaths	심호흡

淺				얕을	shallow; light	천
				深淺	deep and/or shallow; relative depth	심천
				淺薄	shallow, superficial	천박
水 8 978				淺見	shallow view, superficial idea	천견

淫	シ	ジ	ジ	음란할	lewd, lascivious, immoral, obscene; sex; dissolute; debauch	음
	ジ	涇	涇	淫亂	lewd, lascivious, lecherous	음란
水 8 979	淫	浮	淫	賣淫 姦淫	prostitution adultery, illicit intercourse	매음 간음

添	シ	ジ	ジ	더할	add, increase	첨
	汙	沃	添	添付 添加	add, append, annex affix, add	첨부 첨가
水 8 980	添	添	添	添削	correct, revise	첨삭

淸	シ	ジ	ジ	맑을	clear, pure	청
	洼	洼	洼	淸掃 淸新	clean, sweep new and fresh	청소 청신
水 8 981	淸	淸	淸	淸雅	elegant, refined; mellifluous	청아

焉	丁	正	正	어찌	how; why; where; in it, at it; in that situation	언
	또	焉	焉	於焉	quickly, in no time at all, before one is aware	어언
火 7 982	焉	焉	焉			

猛	犭	犭	犭	사나울	fierce, cruel, savage, violent; courageous	맹
	猂	猂	猛	猛獸 猛爆	beast of prey, fierce animal fierce bombardment, heavy bombing	맹수 맹폭
犬 8 983	猛	猛	猛	猛擊	violent attack; a savage blow	맹격

率	亠	玄	玄	거느릴	lead; follow and obey; universally, all, generally	솔
	玄	宏	宏	등분	rate, ratio (as suffix)	률
				比率	ratio, percentage	비율
				率直	candid, frank	솔직
玄 6 984	宏	率	率	率先	take the initiative, be first to	솔선

球	二	王	玒	구슬	ball, sphere, globe	구
	玎	玎	球	地球	the earth, the globe	지구
玉 7	球	球	球	電球	light bulb, electric lamp	전구
985				排球	volleyball	배구

現	二	王	玑	나타날	appear; now	현
	珇	珇	玥	現象	a phenomenon; a happening	현상
玉 7	珇	現	現	現金	cash, ready funds	현금
986				現實	actuality; reality	현실

理	二	王	玉	다스릴	manage, regulate; reason, principle; right (as an abstract principle)	리
	玎	珇	珇			
玉 7	玾	理	理	理由	reason, cause, grounds	이유
987				理致	principle, reason	이치
				理論	theory	이론

產	亠	文	立	낳을	give birth, bear offspring; produce; native; estate, possessions; livelihood	산
	产	产	产	產業	industry	산업
生 6	产	産	產	產出	produce, turn out	산출
988				產物	product; manufactured item	산물

畢	丷	田	田	다할	complete, finish, exhaust; all, together	필
	甲	毕	畀	畢生	lifelong	필생
田 6	畢	畢	畢	未畢	unfinished; unfulfilled	미필
989						

略	丨丨	田	田	간략할	abbreviated; summary; outline, sketch; plan; slightly, little	략
	畊	畋	畋	略圖	map, diagram	약도
田 6	畋	略	略	略字	an abbreviation; a simplified character	약자
990				概略	summary, gist	개략

193

異	冂	甲	田	다를	different; extraordinary; foreign; heterodox	이
	田	畀	畀	異狀	abnormal, extraordinary	이상
				異性	the opposite sex	이성
田 6	畧	異	異	異國	strange country, alien land	이국
991				(13 strokes in original form, 異 .)		

眼	冂	目	目	눈	eye; hole; eyelet; space	안
	目	目	目	眼鏡	glasses, spectacles	안경
				眼目	sense of discrimination, an appreciative eye	안목
目 6	眼	眼	眼	眼前	before one's eyes	안전
992						

票	一	一	西	표	ticket; slip of paper; banknote	표
	两	西	酉	投票	vote, cast a ballot	투표
				開票	count votes	개표
示 6	覀	票	票	票決	put to a vote, take a vote on	표결
993						

祥	礻	礻	礻	상서로울	happiness, good luck, good omen; sacrificial service for deceased parents	상
	礻	衫	衫	祥瑞롭다	auspicious, lucky	상서
				發祥地	cradle, birthplace; birthplace of a king	발상지
示 6	裇	裇	祥	吉祥	auspicious sign, lucky omen	길상
994						

祭	夕	夕	夕	제사	sacrifice	제
	夕	叕	癶	祭祀	sacrificial rite; ancestor veneration ceremony	제사
				祭主	director of an ancestor veneration ceremony	제주
示 6	癶	祭	祭	祭文	funeral oration, funeral ode	제문
995						

移	一	禾	禾	옮길	move; shift; transmit; influence, change	이
	利	秒	移	移動	move; remove; transfer	이동
				移民	emigrate; shift people about	이민
禾 6	移	移	移	移徙	move, move one's domicile	이사
996						

窓 穴 6 997	宀 宏 窓	宀 宏 窓	穴 宏 窓	창 窓門 窓戸紙 窓口	window; door a window window paper wicket, window at a box office	**창** 창문 창호지 창구
章 立 6 998	亠 音 音	立 音 音	立 音 章	글 文章 勳章 樂章	document; chapter; badge; medal sentence; composition, article medal, award **a movement** (in music)	**장** 문장 훈장 악장
竟 立 6 999	亠 音 音	立 音 章	立 音 竟	마침내 畢竟 究竟	at last, finally after all, in the final analysis the ultimate fundamental (Buddhism); ultimately, in the end	**경** 필경 구경
第 竹 5 1000	ノ 竹 笻	竹 竺 第	竹 笂 第	차례 第一 第三者 落第	order, series, grade, degree, …th; a house; an examination degree first, number one; primary third person, disinterested party fail an examination	**제** 제일 제삼자 낙제
笛 竹 5 1001	ノ 竹 笘	竹 竹 笛	竹 竹 笛	피리 汽笛 胡笛 號笛	flute, whistle siren; steam whistle a kind of clarinet siren, horn; whistle	**적** 기적 호적 호적
符 竹 5 1002	𠂉 竹 竹	竹 笀 符	竹 竹 符	붙을 符號 符籍 符合	agree with; tally; a written charm mark, sign, symbol Buddhist or Taoist amulet on paper with designs in red ink correspond to, agree with	**부** 부호 부적 부합

				가늘	thin, slender; small, fine, minute; careful	세
細	幺	幺	幺			
	糸	紀	紀	仔細	in detail, minutely	자세
				細菌	germ, bacterium	세균
糸 5 1003	絅	細	細	細密	detailed, minute, elaborate	세밀
				포갤	tie, bind; accumulate; implicate, involve; trouble; tired, weary	루
累	冂	用	田			
	뽀	里	畧	累進	steady progress, gradual advance	누진
糸 5 1004	畧	界	累	累積	accumulate, accumulation	누적
				連累	be involved in crime	연루
	幺	幺	糸	마칠	conclude, end; the end; finally, at last	종
終	糸	紀	紹	終日	all day, through the whole day	종일
				終點	terminal point, terminus	종점
糸 5 1005	終	終	終	最終	last, final	최종
	幺	糸	糸	줄	musical string	현
絃	糸	紀	紹	絃樂器	stringed instruments	현악기
				絃樂	string music	현악
糸 5 1006	紝	絃	絃	絃琴	six-stringed Korean harp	현금
	幺	幺	糸	짤	silk cord; tissue; group, section, department	조
組	糸	紹	細	組織	structure, organization	조직
				組合	union, guild	조합
糸 5 1007	組	絹	組	組長	foreman	조장
	丁	켜	케	익힐	practice, study; customs, practices	습
習	켜커	켜커	켜커	習慣	customs, practices	습관
				練習	practice, drill	연습
羽 5 1008	習	習	習	學習	study, drill	학습

11 strokes

脚	刀 月 刖 刖 肚 胼 胠 脚 脚	다리	base, leg, foot	각
		立脚	be based on, rest on the basis of	입각
肉 7 1009		脚本	play, drama	각본
		脚色	plot of play; dramatization	각색

脣	厂 戸 辰 辰 辰 辰 脣 脣 脣	입술	lips	순
		口脣	mouth and lips; lips	구순
肉 7 1010		脣音	a labial sound	순음

脫	刀 月 月 月' 肝 肝 肸 胖 脫	벗을	undress, strip; remove; cast off	탈
		脫出	escape; extricate oneself from; parachute from	탈출
肉 7 1011		脫線	derail, run off the line; deviate	탈선
		脫衣	disrobe, undress	탈의

船	亻 冎 角 舟 舟 舡 舡 船 船	배	boat, ship	선
		船舶	boat, vessel, ship	선박
舟 5 1012		船員	ship's crew; crewman	선원
		船長	ship's captain	선장

莊	屮 艹 艹 艹 艹 艹 莊 莊 莊	집	brave; serious; farm, place	장
		莊嚴	majestic; solemn	장엄
艸 7 1013		山莊	mountain village	산장
		別莊	cottage, villa, country house	별장

荷	一 艹 艹 艹 荷 荷 荷 荷 荷	멜	load; lotus	하
		荷主	baggage owner; shipper	하주
艸 7 1014		荷物	cargo, freight, baggage	하물
		荷役	stevedoring, loading and unloading	하역

197

莫	十	艹	艹	말	don't; not; large, huge	막
	艻	苩	甘	莫大	enormous, immense	막대
				莫重	extremely important	막중
				莫逆	intimate, familiar	막역
艸 7 1015	莒	莫	莫			

處	上	卢	卢	곳	a place; stay; decide; punish; manage, attend to	처
	卢	虍	虏	處女	virgin, maiden	처녀
				處所	place; residence, living place	처소
虍 5 1016	處	處	處	處分	deal with, handle, dispose of	처분

蛇	口	中	虫	뱀	snake	사
	虫	虫	虫	毒蛇	poisonous snake, viper	독사
				龍頭蛇尾	"dragon head snake tail", start with a flourish end with a whimper	용두사미
虫 5 1017	虫	蚧	蛇	長蛇陣	"long snake formation"; a long line, a queue	장사진

術	彳	行	什	재주	device, artifice; trick; mystery; art, method; profession, occupation	술
	衍	術	術	術策	artifice, stratagem	술책
				術語	terms; specialized terminology	술어
行 5 1018	術	術	術	術法	magic, magical tricks	술법

規	二	夫	扫	법	regulations; scale	규
	却	却	却	規定	regulation, rule	규정
				規模	scale, size; rule, pattern	규모
				規格	standard, norm, criterion	규격
見 4 1019	규	規	規			

訟	亠	言	言	소송할	litigation; dispute; demand justice	송
	言	言	言	訴訟	litigate, go to the law; file suit	소송
				訟事	sue, file suit	송사
言 4 1020	訟	訟	訟	爭訟	dispute	쟁송

設	亠	言	言	베풀	establish, found; supposing, what if	설
	言	言	言	設置	establish, found, create	설치
				設計	design, plan, blueprint	설계
言 4 1021	訊	訍	設	設立	establish, set up	설립

訪	亠	言	言	찾을	search out, visit; inquire about, ask after	방
	言	言	言	訪問	call on, visit	방문
				來訪	a visit, a call	내방
言 4 1022	訪	訪	訪	探訪	a visit; interview, inquiry	탐방

許	亠	言	言	허락할	permit; place	허
	言	言	言	許諾	permit, approve; consent	허락
				許多	many, vast numbers	허다
言 4 1023	許	許	許	特許	license, permit, charter	특허

豚	丿	月	月	돼지	pig	돈
	月	肵	脉	豚肉	pork	돈육
				養豚	hog breeding, hog farming	양돈
豕 4 1024	脉	豚	豚	豚兒	my son (humble form)	돈아

貧	八	分	今	가난할	impoverished, poor	빈
	貧	貧	貧	貧弱	poor, limited, meagre	빈약
				貧困	indigent, destitute	빈곤
貝 4 1025	貧	貧	貧	貧富	poverty and wealth, the haves and the have-nots	빈부

貪	八	今	今	탐낼	covet, show greed	탐
	貪	貪	貪	貪吏	greedy official, grasping official	탐리
				貪心	avarice, greed, cupidity	탐심
貝 4 1026	貪	貪	貪	貪慾	avarice, rapacity	탐욕

貨	イ	化	化	재물	goods; cargo, freight	화
	佧	貨	貨	貨幣	money, currency	화폐
				外貨	foreign goods; foreign currency	외화
貝 4 1027	貨	貨	貨	財貨	goods, commodities; property, wealth	재화

貫	口	毌	毌	꿸	penetrate, go through, thorough; Korean unit of weight: 8.27 pounds	관
	貫	貫	貫	貫徹	penetrate, pierce; accomplish, achieve	관철
貝 4 1028	貫	貫	貫	貫通	pass through, penetrate	관통
				一貫	consistent, unswerving	일관

販	刂	月	目	판매할	sell, deal in	판
	貝	貝	貝	販賣	sell merchandise, deal in	판매
				販路	market for goods, outlet	판로
				販賣人	seller, agent	판매인
貝 4 1029	財	販	販			

責	二	圭	丰	꾸짖을	responsibility; punish, rebuke	책
	青	青	青	責任	responsibility	책임
				職責	official duties, position	직책
貝 4 1030	責	責	責	重責	heavy responsibility	중책

軟	一	百	百	부드러울	soft, yielding, pliable; weak	연
	亘	車	車	軟弱	gentle, tender; weak	연약
				軟粉紅	soft pink	연분홍
車 4 1031	軟	軟	軟	軟膏	ointment, salve	연고

途	人	今	今	길	road	도
	余	余	余	途中	on the way, in progress	도중
				壯途	ambitious undertaking; important mission	장도
辵 7 1032	途	途		前途	road before one, prospects, outlook	전도

透	二	禾	禾	투철할 penetrate; transparent; understand; thoroughly	투
	禾	秀	透	透視 see through; see, divine, sense	투시
辶 7 1033	透	透		透徹 penetrating, lucid, limpid; thorough, thoroughgoing	투철
				透明 transparent, diaphanous	투명

通	マ	孑	甬	통할 go through; communicate; intercourse; all, whole	통
	甬	甬	涌	通信 communications; news	통신
				通過 pass, carry, be approved	통과
辶 7 1034	涌	通		通商 commerce, commercial intercourse	통상

速	一	曰	束	빠를 fast, quick	속
	束	束	束	速度 speed, velocity	속도
				速力 speed, velocity, rate	속력
辶 7 1035	涑	速		速成 a quick course; rapid completion	속성

逐	一	歹	豕	쫓을 expel; pursue; in order, in succession, one by one	축
	豕	豕	豕		
				逐出 drive out, oust, evict	축출
辶 7 1036	逐	逐		角逐 compete, vie, contend	각축
				驅逐 expel, drive away, oust	구축

連	一	曰	百	이을 connect, join	련
	亘	車	車	連絡 keep contact with, keep in touch	연락
				連結 join, link, connect	연결
辶 7 1037	渾	連		連載 publish serially	연재

造	㇉	生	牛	지을 build, make, create	조
				構造 build, construct; structure, framework	구조
	告	告	造	造成 make, manufacture	조성
辶 7 1038	浩	造		造化 creative energy of the universe, creation, nature; the mysterious	조화

				만날	meet with; happen	봉
逢	夂	冬	夆	逢着	meet; encounter, be confronted with	봉착
	冬	夆	逢	逢變	meet with mishap; be insulted, humiliated	봉변
辵 7 1039	逢	逢		相逢	meet each other, meet with	상봉
	一	스	亠	우편	posthouse; post office; postal, mail	우
郵	亠	垂	垂	郵便	postal service, mail	우편
				郵票	postage stamp	우표
邑 8 1040	垂	郵	郵	郵送	mail, post, send by mail	우송
	亠	古	台	성곽	citadel; the surname: Kwak	곽
郭	亨	亨	享	外郭	outer defended wall; outer defenses	외곽
				輪郭	contours of the human body; an outline	윤곽
邑 8 1041	享	郭	郭			
	亠	立	立	나눌	division, section, class, kind, sort, genus; part, portion; government department; public court	부
部	立	音	音			
				部分	part, portion	부분
邑 8 1042	音	部	部	部隊	military unit	부대
				部長	department director	부장
	口	日	旦	들	field, wilderness; rustic, savage; wild, undomesticated	야
野	甲	里	野			
				野心	ambition; mad ambition	야심
里 4 1043	野	野	野	野菜	vegetables, greens	야채
				野球	baseball	야구
	冂	月	門	닫을	close, shut, obstruct	폐
閉	門	門	門	閉幕	bring down the curtain, bring to an end	폐막
				閉會	close a meeting	폐회
門 3 1044	閉	閉	閉	閉鎖	lock out; close, shut	폐쇄

陸	阝	阝	阝	뭍	continent; dry land; continuous	륙
	阝土	陆	阮	陸地	land	육지
阜 8 1045	陸	陸	陸	陸軍 上陸	army, ground forces land, disembark; amphibious landings	육군 상륙

陷	阝	阝	阝	빠질	sink; fall	함
	阝勹	阝	陷	陷落	sink in, fall in, collapse	함락
阜 8 1046	陷	陷	陷	陷穽 謀陷	pit, trap, pitfall plot to injure	함정 모함

陰	阝	阝	阝	그늘	the female or negative principle, Yin	음
	阝人	阝今	陰	陰陽	Yin and Yang, the positive/ negative principle of Chinese philosophy	음양
阜 8 1047	陰	陰	陰	陰數 陰散	negative number dreary, dismal, gloomy	음수 음산

陶	阝	阝	阝	질그릇	kiln; pottery	도
	阝勹	阝	陶	陶磁器	ceramic ware, pottery	도자기
				陶醉	drunkenness, inebriation; fascinated, enraptured	도취
阜 8 1048	陶	陶	陶	陶工	potter, maker of ceramics	도공

陵	阝	阝	阝	언덕	mound; tumulus; tomb	릉
	阝土	陵	陵	王陵	royal tomb	왕릉
				陵線	ridge	능선
阜 8 1049	陵	陵	陵	陵所	royal mausoleum, place of royal tombs	능소

陳	阝	阝	阝	베풀	spread out, arrange; old, seasoned; make a statement or plea	진
	阝	阝	阝	陳列	display, put on show	진열
				陳情書	a petition	진정서
阜 8 1050	陳	陳	陳	陳述	make a statement; state, explain	진술

雪 雨 3 1051	一	示	雪	눈	snow; whiten; wipe out 　　a grievance	설
	雨	雨	雪	雪糖 雪害 雪辱	sugar snow damage vindicate oneself	설탕 설해 설욕
	雪	雪	雪			
頂 頁 2 1052	丁	丁	圢	정수리	top, head; extreme	정
	顶	顶	頂	頂點 頂上 頂禮	zenith, apex peak, summit a deep bow	정점 정상 정례
	頂	頂	頂			
頃 頁 2 1053	匕	圠	圻	이랑	a short time; 　　approximate time	경
	圻	頃	頃	頃刻 萬頃 頃步	an instant, a moment immensity, boundlessness half-step	경각 만경 경보
	頃	頃	頃			
飢 食 2 1054	人	今	今	주릴	hunger, famine; dearth	기
	今	食	食	飢饉 飢餓 飢渴	famine; scarcity, dearth starvation, hunger hunger and thirst, starvation	기근 기아 기갈
	食	飢	飢			
魚 魚 0 1055	⺈	乌	刍	고기	fish	어
	角	魚	魚	魚族 魚物 魚肉	fish, fishes dried fish, stockfish fish and meat	어족 어물 어육
	魚	魚	魚			
鳥 鳥 0 1056	亻	白	白	새	bird	조
	自	鳥	鳥	鳥銃 鳥類 白鳥	fowling piece, bird gun birds, fowl swan	조총 조류 백조
	鳥	鳥	鳥			

鹿

鹿 0
1057

사슴	deer, stag	록
馴鹿	reindeer	순록
鹿茸	deer antlers in velvet	녹용
鹿角	deer horn, antlers	녹각

麥

麥 0
1058

보리	barley, wheat	맥
麥酒	beer	맥주
小麥	wheat	소맥
麥粉	wheat flour	맥분

麻

麻 0
1059

삼	hemp	마
麻藥	narcotic; anesthetic	마약
麻織物	hemp cloth	마직물
麻衣	hemp clothes	마의

12 Strokes

傍

人 10
1060

곁	the side; nearby; depend on	방
傍觀	look on, remain indifferent	방관
傍聽	listen to, sit in on, audit	방청
傍證	circumstantial evidence	방증

備

人 10
1061

갖출	prepare; complete; perfection	비
準備	prepare	준비
備考	a note, remarks (for reference)	비고
備品	furnishings, fixtures	비품

傑	亻 仃 伄	뛰어날	superior; hero, heroic			걸
	仁 休 俳	傑作	a masterpiece; buffoonery			걸작
	俳 傑 傑	女傑	heroine, brave woman			여걸
人 10 1062		豪傑	hero, gallant man, extraordinary man			호걸

割	宀 宁 审	벨	cut up; divide			할
	宔 宭 害	割引	discount, price-reduction			할인
	害 害 割	割當	allocate, apportion, assign			할당
刀 10 1063		割愛	share generously			할애

創	人 今 仝	비롯할	begin, create, make; wound, stab			창
	仑 仓 倉	創造	create, call into being			창조
	倉 創 創	創作	create; creative writing, composition			창작
刀 10 1064		創立	found, establish			창립

勝	刀 月 朤	이길	be victorious, overcome; superior to; scenic beauty			승
	朕 朕 朕	勝利	win, be victorious			승리
	朕 勝 勝	勝敗	victory and/or defeat			승패
力 10 1065		勝戰	win a war, a successful war			승전

勞	丶丶 火 火丶	수고로울	toil; weary; cause trouble; give trouble to; console			로
	火丷 炒 炒	勞力	strive, work hard			노력
	燃 塋 勞	勞動	labor, work			노동
力 10 1066		慰勞	console, comfort; recognize the services of another			위로

博	十 扣 㧖	넓을	wide, extensive, ample; wide learning, erudition; museum; gamble			박
	㩦 博 博					
		博士	a doctor, Ph.D.			박사
十 10 1067	博 博 博	博物館	museum			박물관
		博識	erudite, learned			박식

卿				벼슬	noble, high officer: term of respect	경
卩 10 1068				公卿	court noble	공경

厥				그	it, its; his	궐
厂 10 1069						

善				착할	good, virtuous; expert; whole; perfect	선
口 9 1070				善良	good, virtuous, right	선량
				善心	generous; good-hearted	선심
				善惡	good and evil	선악

喜				기쁠	happiness, joy	희
口 9 1071				喜劇	a comedy, a farce	희극
				喜悲	joy and/or sorrow	희비
				喜悦	joy, delight	희열

喉				목구멍	the throat	후
口 9 1072				喉頭	the larynx	후두
				咽喉	the throat	인후

喪				잃을	lose by death; mourning	상
口 9 1073				喪服	mourning attire	상복
				喪主	chief mourner	상주
				喪家	house in mourning, bereaved family	상가

				홀	single; simple	단
單	口	吅	吅	單純	simple, simpleminded	단순
	吅	吅	閏	單獨으로	singly, unilaterally	단독
口 9 1074	習	閏	單	單一	sole, unilateral	단일

				에울	surround, besiege, invest; circumference; span	위
圍	冂	囝	周			
	周	周	圉	範圍	scope, extent	범위
口 9 1075	圍	圍	圍	包圍	surround, encircle	포위

				언덕	dike, embankment	제
堤	土	圵	坦	堤防	dike, bank, dam	제방
	坦	坦	埠	防波堤	a breakwater	방파제
土 9 1076	埠	堤	堤			

				알릴	inform, report, declare, announce; reward; retribution; recompense	보
報	土	查	查			
	幸	幸	報	報道	news report; report, inform	보도
土 9 1077	報	報	報	報告	a report; submit a report	보고
				報酬	remuneration, compensation	보수

				굳을	firm, hard, strong	견
堅	厂	臣	臣	堅固	firm, solid, strong	견고
	臣	堅	堅	堅實	steady, sound, reliable	견실
土 8 1078	堅	堅	堅	堅持	firmly maintain; adhere to, stick to	견지

				마당	open space; place; threshing floor	장
場	土	圵	坦	場面	place, setting; a scene	장면
	坦	坦	場	場所	place, spot; location, site	장소
土 9 1079	場	場	場	場內	inside the hall, on the premises	장내

壹	士	志	吉	전일할 one (legal form); unity; unify; the same	일
	吉	壱	吉	壹千 one thousand 壹萬 ten thousand	일천 일만
士 9 1080	壹	壹	壹		

媒	女	女+	女世	중매할 match-maker, go-between; decoy	매
	女世	妒	姓	仲媒 match-maker; arrange a marriage	중매
女 9 1081	媒	媒	媒	媒介物 medium, agency, vehicle	매개물

富	宀	宀	宁	부자 wealth; enrich	부
	宁	宫	宫	富者 a rich man 富貴 wealth and position 富强 rich and powerful	부자 부귀 부강
宀 9 1082	富	富	富		

寒	宀	宀	宀	찰 cold	한
	宋	空	実	寒帶 arctic regions, frigid zone 寒流 a cold current 寒氣 cold weather; chill, chilliness	한대 한류 한기
宀 9 1083	寒	寒	寒		

尋	⼅	⼅	글	찾을 seek, search for, investigate; a fathom	심
	灵	寻	寻	尋常 ordinary, commonplace, mediocre	심상
寸 9 1084	盂	尋	尋	尋訪 visit, pay a call	심방

尊	⼂	亠	前	높을 honor, exalt, venerate	존
	芮	酋	酋	尊敬 respect, esteem 尊待 treat with respect 尊嚴 majesty, dignity	존경 존대 존엄
寸 9 1085	尊	尊	尊		

就	亠	吉	亨	나아갈	go for a purpose, come for a purpose	취
	亨	京	京	就職	gain employment	취직
				就任	assume a post, assume an office	취임
尤 9 1086	尌	就	就	就業	enter an occupation; go to work	취업

幅	冂	巾	帄	넓이	width; strip of cloth	폭
	帄	帄	帄	大幅	in one big jump, sharply, steeply; full width	대폭
				全幅	full width of cloth; full, fully	전폭
巾 9 1087	帄	幅	幅			

幾	幺	幺	絲	몇	some, few; almost, about; how much, how many	기
	絲	丝	丝			
				幾何學	geometry	기하학
幺 9 1088	幾	幾	幾	幾百	hundreds	기백

強	口	弓	弘	굳셀	strong; violent	강
	弘	弘	弘	強力	powerful, strong	강력
				強調	emphasize, stress	강조
				強國	a great power, a strong nation	강국
弓 8 1089	強	強	強			

復	彳	彳	彳	회복할	restore; return; reply; repeat; make good	복
	彳	彳	彳	다시	again, repeatedly	부
				回復	recover, get well; regain	회복
				復興	be revived, restored	부흥
彳 9 1090	復	復	復	復活	resurrect, return to life; revive	부활

循	彳	彳	彳	좋을	comply with, follow; in order	순
	彳	彳	循	循環	rotate, revolve	순환
				惡循環	a vicious circle	악순환
彳 9 1091	循	循	循	循環期	a cycle	순환기

悲 心 8 1092	亅 非 非	非 非 非	非 非 悲	슬플 悲劇 悲哀 悲壯	sad, sorry, grieved; lament tragedy sorrow, grief pathetic, tragic	비 비극 비애 비장
惑 心 8 1093	一 或 惑	一 或 惑	豆 或 惑	미혹할 迷惑 疑惑 惑星	delude, bewitch; doubt doubtful, confused; infatuated, captivated mistrust, doubt a planet	혹 미혹 의혹 혹성
惡 心 8 1094	一 亞 惡	亞 亞 惡	亞 亞 惡	악할 미워할 惡魔 惡質 憎惡	evil, wicked hate, dislike Satan; evil spirit, devil wickedness, evil nature hate, abhor	악 오 악마 악질 증오

惠 心 8 1095	一 重 惠	日 重 惠	申 重 惠	은혜
				
				恩惠
				
				惠澤
				惠存
					favor, grace, kindness;
					  graciousness
					grace, favor; obligation,
					  moral indebtedness
					favor, benevolence
					"with the compliments
					  of the author"
						혜
						
						은혜
						
						혜택
						혜존

惱 心 9 1096	忄 忄 惱	忄 忄 惱	忄 忄 惱	번뇌할
				
				煩惱
				
				苦惱
				惱殺
					vexed, grieved, irritated;
					  anger
					agony; harassed by evil
					  passions
					anguish, affliction
					fascinate, bewitch, enchant
						뇌
						
						번뇌
						
						고뇌
						뇌쇄

掌 手 8 1097	𝅭 尚 堂	𝅭 尚 堂	𝅭 尚 掌	손바닥 掌握 車掌 管掌	palm of the hand; manage, control seize; grasp, hold conductor, conductress manage, take charge of	장 장악 차장 관장

提	才	扣	担	들	pick up, lift up, pull up; mention; suggest; propose	제
	担	担	捍	提供	provide, furnish	제공
手 9 1098	捍	捍	提	提案	propose, suggest	제안
				提出	submit, turn in, present	제출

揚	才	扣	担	날릴	let fly, scatter; raise, display; brandish, flourish; winnow; publish aboad; praise	양
	担	担	捍	揚揚	exultant, triumphant	양양
手 9 1099	揚	揚	揚	宣揚	proclaim; enhance, heighten	선양
				揭揚	hoist, raise; fly, display	게양

揮	才	扌	扣	휘두를	shake; wield; sprinkle; wipe away	휘
	扝	捐	捐	揮發	volatile, volatility	휘발
				揮毫	wield a brush, write	휘호
手 9 1100	捐	揎	揮	發揮	display; demonstrate, make manifest	발휘

換	才	扚	扚	바꿀	exchange	환
	挌	扚	换	轉換	convert, switch over; switch	전환
				換氣	ventilation, changing air	환기
手 9 1101	换	换	換	換算	convert, change, exchange	환산

援	才	扚	扚	구원할	rescue, pull up, assist; lead	원
	扚	捗	捗	救援	rescue, deliver, relieve	구원
				援護	relief; protection; support, backing	원호
手 9 1102	捗	揖	援	援助	aid, assist; support	원조

敢	ʼ	ʼ	斉	감히	dare, presume, venture	감
	盲	育	育	敢히	daringly, boldly, without hesitation	감
				果敢	bold, daring	과감
支 8 1103	斉	敢	敢	敢行	take decisive action	감행

敦 支 8 1104	亠	亠口	亨	두터울 thick, growing thickly; generous; honest, sincere; to esteem	돈
	亨	享	享		
	享	敦	敦	敦篤 sincere, simple and honest	돈독
				敦厚 straightforward, sincere	돈후

散 支 8 1105	艹	艹	芇	흩어질 scatter, disperse; wander; dismiss; miscellaneous; fall to pieces; break up an association	산
	芇	芇	肯		
	肯	散	散	分散 break up; decentralize	분산
				散步 a walk, a stroll	산보
				散散이 break to pieces	산산

斯 斤 8 1106	一	甘	甘	이것 this, these; thus; such	사
	其	其	其	斯界 this world; this field	사계
				斯道 Confucian morality; this subject, this art, this profession	사도
	斯	斯	斯	瓦斯 gas	와사

普 日 8 1107	丷	꾸	並	넓을 universal, general; all; everywhere	보
	꾜	並	並	普通 common, ordinary; normal, usual	보통
				普及 propagate, popularize, spread	보급
	普	普	普	普遍 universal; ubiquitous	보편

智 日 8 1108	亻	二	矢	슬기 wisdom, knowledge	지
	矢	知	知	智能 intelligence, intellect	지능
				智慧 wisdom, sagacity	지혜
	智	智	智	智勇 wisdom and courage	지용

晴 日 8 1109	刂	日	日	갤 clear sky, fair weather	청
	日	晴	晴	晴天 cloudless sky, fair weather	청천
				晴曇 clear or cloudy, relative cloudiness	청담
	晴	晴	晴		

景	冂	日	旦	볕	bright, luminous	**경**
	昂	景	景	景氣	business conditions; prosperity	경기
日 8 1110	景	景	景	景致	scenery, landscape	경치
				景品券	a gift certificate	경품권

曾	丷	宀	丙	일찍	already; duplicate; add to, additional	**증**
	两	兩	逆	曾祖父	paternal great-grandfather	증조부
				曾孫	great-grandson	증손
日 8 1111	兩	曾	曾	曾孫女	great-granddaughter	증손녀

最	冂	曰	旦	가장	most; extremely; collect, assemble	**최**
	旱	昌	昌	最近	latest, most recent; nearest	최근
				最高	highest; best; most expensive	최고
日 8 1112	晷	最	最	最初	first, initial	최초

替	夫	夫	尗二	대신할	substitute	**체**
	扻	奜	扻	代替	alternate; substitute	대체
				交替	replace; shift (as personnel)	교체
日 8 1113	梺	替	替			

期	十	甘	甘	기약할	pledge; term, period; date, time; limit	**기**
	其	其	其	期約	pledge, promise; engagement	기약
				期日	fixed time, appointed day	기일
月 8 1114	期	期	期	期待	expectation; anticipation	기대

朝	宀	古	古	아침	morning; the court; visit a superior; a dynasty	**조**
	直	卓	軺	朝鮮	Korea, title of the Yi Dynasty	조선
				王朝	dynasty; king's direct rule	왕조
月 8 1115	朝	朝	朝	朝夕	morning and evening; breakfast and supper	조석

棄	一 云 卒 夲 查 査 室 章 章 棄	버릴	abandon; reject	기
		抛棄	forsake, abandon, give up; relinquish, forfeit	포기
木 8 1116		棄權	waive rights; abstain from voting	기권
		棄兒	abandon a child	기아
森	十 才 木 木 森 森 森 森 森 森	수풀	forest; overgrown	삼
		森林	forest, a wood	삼림
木 8 1117		森羅萬象	the universe, all creation, everything in nature	삼라만상
		森嚴	solemn, awe-inspiring	삼엄
植	才 木 朴 朽 柿 植 植 植 植	심을	to plant; implant, set up; trees, plants	식
		植物	plants, vegetation	식물
木 8 1118		植木	planting trees, forestation	식목
		植字	compose, write	식자
欺	十 甘 其 其 其 其 欺 欺 欺	속일	deceive, cheat	기
		欺瞞	deceive, hoodwink	기만
欠 8 1119		詐欺	defraud, swindle	사기
殘	一 歹 歹 殘 殘 殘 殘 殘 殘	남을	remnant, residue; injure, destroy	잔
		殘額	remaining balance, remainder	잔액
歹 8 1120		殘滓	remnants; leftovers; dregs	잔재
		殘惡	cruel, inhumane	잔악
渴	氵 氵 氵 氵 渴 渴 渴 渴 渴	목마를	thirsty, thirst	갈
		渴望	thirst after, crave	갈망
水 9 1121		解渴	slake one's thirst	해갈
		渴症	thirst	갈증

215

港 水 9 1122	항구 港口 港灣 港都	bay port, harbor harbor a port city	항 항구 항만 항도
渡 水 9 1123	건널 渡河 讓渡 賣渡	cross over; ferry; hand over, transmit cross a river transfer, convey, cede sale and delivery	도 도하 양도 매도
減 水 9 1124	덜 減少 減速 減免	decrease, subtract, lessen reduce, decrease; drop, go down reduce speed exempt; remit	감 감소 감속 감면
湖 水 9 1125	호수 湖水 江湖 湖畔	a lake a lake rivers and lakes lakeside, lakeshore	호 호수 강호 호반
湯 水 9 1126	끓일 熱湯 雜湯 湯器	boil, scald; hot water; soup boiling water, boiling broth a mixed soup; pot-au-feu; jumble, potpourri a soup bowl	탕 열탕 잡탕 탕기
測 水 9 1127	헤아릴 測定 測量 測地	measure; fathom; estimate measure, calibrate, plumb survey, measure; estimate, guess survey land	측 측정 측량 측지

然

火 8
1128

그럴	so, that way;...like,...ly; yes, certainly; still, nevertheless, although	연
然後	after that, afterwards	연후
必然的	surely, definitely, certainly	필연적
泰然	calm, composed	태연

無

火 8
1129

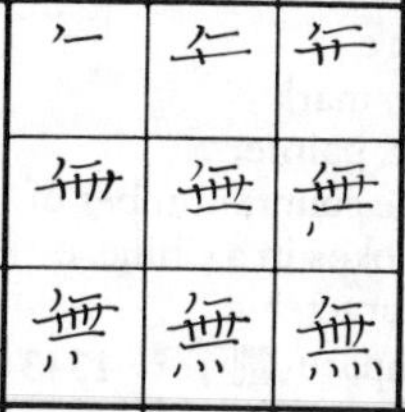

없을	nothing, nil; not having	무
無視	ignore, disregard	무시
無線	radio, wireless	무선
無事	safely, without incident	무사

爲

瓜 8
1130

하	do; make; cause; be; by; to	위
行爲	conduct, behavior	행위
人爲的	artificial, man-made	인위적
爲主	stress, give prime importance to	위주

猶

犬 9
1131

오히려	yet; even; like, as	유
猶豫	a reprieve; extension, postponement	유예
猶太教	Judaism	유태교

琢

玉 8
1132

쪼을	polish, cut (as gems)	탁
琢磨	polish; cultivate virtue, improve one's mind	탁마
琢木鳥	woodpecker	탁목조

琴

玉 8
1133

거문고	lute, guitar, harp	금
弦琴	a type of harp	현금
琴瑟	harp and lute	금슬
彈琴	play the harp	탄금

番	⺌	⺜	釆	차례	turn (as in "my turn"), duty, shift; change; repeat	번
	釆	釆	番	番地	number assigned to an area, address	번지
田 7 1134	番	番	番	番號	a number	번호
				番番히	habitually; all the time	번번

畫	⺹	⺕	聿	그림	picture	화
	書	書	書	그할 피할	draw, mark	획
				畫家	artist, painter	화가
田 7 1135	書	畫	畫	畫數	stroke count, number of strokes in a Chinese character	획수
				(Compare 劃, 획 1343.)		

疏	了	了	正	소홀할	negligent, careless; state to a superior; statement; distant, separate; sparse; distribute, spread out; dredge	소
	正	距	距	疏忽	negligent, careless	소홀
疋 7 1136	踈	踈	疏	疏開	disperse; remove, evacuate	소개
				(Also written 疎.)		

痛	⺊	疒	疒	아플	painful, sore	통
	疒	疒	病	痛歎	bitterly lament, deeply regret	통탄
				痛快	be most pleasant, extremely delightful	통쾌
广 7 1137	痛	痛	痛	痛感	feel keenly, realize acutely	통감

登	彐	癶	癶	오를	rise; mount; advance	등
	癶	啓	啓	登錄	register, enroll	등록
				登記	register (as a title)	등기
癶 7 1138	啓	登	登	登山	mountain-climbing	등산

發	彐	癶	癶	필	become; put forth, send forth, issue; arise, develop; depart; manifest	발
	癶	登	癹	發展	develop; prosper	발전
				發行	publish, circulate	발행
癶 7 1139	發	發	發	發見	discover; detect, spot, chance upon	발견

					도둑	rob, steal; robber, pirate	도
盗	シ	汐	汐		盜難	theft, robbery	도난
	次	次	盗		盜賊	thief, robber; stealing	도적
皿 7 1140	盗	盗	盗		强盜	robber, burglar	강도

					창성할	abundant, flourishing, plenteous	성
盛	厂	厉	成		繁盛	prosper, thrive, flourish	번성
	成	成	盛		盛大	grand, magnificent	성대
皿 7 1141	盛	盛	盛		盛衰	prosperity and decline, vicissitudes	성쇠

					붙을	contact; arrive; detach; put on, wear; put, place	착
着	⺷	兰	羊		着手	begin, commence, put one's hand to	착수
	羊	羊	养		着陸	land (by aircraft)	착륙
目 7 1142	着	着	着		着實	stable, steady, honest	착실

					짧을	short	단
短	ノ	二	矢		短期	short time, short period	단기
	矢	矢	矢		短刀	dagger, short sword	단도
矢 7 1143	短	短	短		短命	short-lived	단명

					굳을	solid, hard; obstinate	경
硬	厂	石	石		硬度	degree of hardness, solidity	경도
	石	硞	硁		硬化	harden, stiffen	경화
石 7 1144	硒	硬	硬		硬質	strong, tough, hard	경질

					벼루	ink stone	연
硯	厂	石	石		硯滴	water receptacle for use with an ink stone	연적
	矵	硏	硯		硯石	a Chinese ink stone	연석
石 7 1145	硯	硯	硯		硯池	the well of an ink stone	연지

稀	禾 禾 禾 禾 秆 秆 禾 7 1146 秆 稀 稀	드물	sparse, rare; thin	희
		稀微	indistinct, dim, faint	희미
		稀薄	weak, thin	희박
		稀貴	rare	희귀

稅	禾 禾 禾 禾 秆 秖 禾 7 1147 秘 秘 稅	세금	taxes, revenue; duty on goods	세
		稅金	tax; duty	세금
		稅務	tax affairs	세무
		國稅	national tax	국세

程	禾 禾 禾 和 和 和 禾 7 1148 秤 秤 程	길	road; journey; career; grade; standard, pattern; amount	정
		程度	extent, degree, amount; level, grade; limit	정도
		過程	task; course of study; course	과정
		日程	daily activities; day's schedule	일정

童	亠 亠 立 音 音 音 立 7 1149 音 童 童	아이	child; virgin, pure	동
		童謠	children's songs	동요
		童詩	poems for children, nursery rhymes	동시
		童心	mind of a child; childish-minded	동심

筆	丶 𥫗 𥫗 笁 笁 筌 竹 6 1150 筌 筌 筆	붓	writing brush; pen; pencil	필
		筆者	writer, author	필자
		筆頭	tip of a writing brush; the top name on a list or roster	필두
		筆記	jot down, take notes	필기

等	丶 𥫗 𥫗 竺 竺 竺 竹 6 1151 筜 等 等	무리	group; class; wait; " etc."	등
		同等	equality; of the same rank	동등
		等分	classify; divide equally, share evenly	등분
		等差	difference in rank	등차

策				피	plan, scheme	책
				策動	scheme, maneuver	책동
				策略	strategy, maneuver, scheme	책략
竹 6 1152				上策	best policy, wisest plan	상책

答				대답	answer, reply; recompense	답
				對答	answer, reply	대답
				答辯	reply; defend and explain oneself	답변
竹 6 1153				答案	written examination answers	답안

粟				조	millet	속
				粟米	millet	속미
米 6 1154						

粧				단장할	adorn; use cosmetics	장
				丹粧	dress up, perform one's toilette	단장
				化粧	apply make-up	화장
米 6 1155				粧飾	adorn, ornament	장식

紫				보랏빛	purple	자
				紫朱	maroon; purple, violet	자주
				紫桃	plum tree, plum	자도
糸 6 1156				紫外線	ultraviolet rays	자외선

統				거느릴	govern, rule; unite; all; clue, end of the thread; start	통
				統一	unification	통일
				統計	statistics, numerical data	통계
糸 6 1157				統治	administer, govern, rule	통치

結	糹	糸	幺	맺을	tie up, a knot; bear fruit, result	결
	紅	糹	糸一	結果	results, outcome	결과
				結局	finally, ultimately; end	결국
糸 6 1158	結	結	結	結婚	marriage	결혼

絶	糹	糸	幺	끊을	cut off, end; absolutely; the top, the best	절
	糹	糸	糸	絶對	absolute	절대
				絶望	despair, hopelessness	절망
糸 6 1159	絶	絡	絡	絶命	pass away, die	절명

給	糹	糸	幺	줄	give, provide, grant	급
	給	糸	糸	給水	supply water; piped water	급수
				給食	provide meals	급식
糸 6 1160	給	給	給	給與	grant, allowance; pay; supply	급여

絡	糹	糸	幺	이을	connect; continuous; cotton fiber; unreeled silk cord; spin silk	락
	絡	糸	糸			
				籠絡	toy with, victimize, make a person one's puppet	농락
糸 6 1161	絡	絡	絡	連絡	contact, liaison, connections	연락

絲	糹	糸	糸	실	thread, fiber, wire; silk	사
				絹絲	silk thread	견사
	糸	絲	絲	鐵絲	wire	철사
				毛絲	wool yarn	모사
糸 6 1162	絲	絲	絲			

菊	艹	艹	艹	국화	chrysanthemum	국
				菊花	a chrysanthemum, a mum	국화
	菊	菊	菊	菊版	small octavo book format (21 by 15 cm)	국판
艸 8 1163	菊	菊	菊	黃菊	winter chrysanthemum	황국

菌	ナ	サ	芍	세균	germ, bacterium; mushroom, fungus, mildew	균
	芍	芮	菡	細菌	bacterium, germ	세균
				保菌	infected, germ-carrying	보균
艸 8 1164	茵	菌	菌	菌類	fungus, fungi	균류

菜	ナ	サ	サ	나물	vegetables	채
	サ	芯	芯	菜蔬	vegetables, garden products	채소
				菜毒	vegetable poisoning	채독
艸 8 1165	芊	莩	菜	菜食	vegetable diet; vegetarianism	채식

華	ユ	サ	世	빛날	splendid; flowery; China	화
	芋	芏	荜	華麗	magnificent, splendid	화려
				華僑	overseas Chinese	화교
艸 8 1166	荜	菙	華	華燭	painted candles; wedding ceremony	화촉

虛	ト	广	卢	빌	empty; vain	허
	虍	虎	虗	虛空	empty sky, air	허공
				虛無	futile, vain; nil, nonexistent	허무
虍 6 1167	虗	虗	虛	虛榮	vanity, vainglory	허영

衆	宀	血	血	무리	crowd, multitude; all, the whole of	중
	罒	衆	衆	大衆	the general public, the masses	대중
				衆生	all living things	중생
血 6 1168	衆	衆	衆	公衆	the public, public	공중

街	彳	彳	往	거리	street	가
	往	往	徍	街路樹	trees along a street	가로수
				街頭	a street	가두
行 6 1169	徍	徍	街	街路燈	street lights	가로등

裁	十	土	圭	마를	cut out clothes; diminish, reduce, moderate; regulate; decide, settle, judge	재
	圭	圭	表	裁判	trial, judgment; administer justice	재판
衣 6 1170	裁	裁	裁	裁決	ruling, judgment	재결
				裁斷	cut out a garment; judge	재단

裂	一	歹	歹	찢을	split, crack; rip open, tear, rend	렬
	列	列	裂	破裂	burst, rupture	파열
				裂傷	laceration, cut	열상
衣 6 1171	裂	裂	裂	分裂	break up, divide, disunite	분열

裕	ﾎ	ﾎ	ﾈ	넉넉할	abundant; wealthy; generous; in good circumstances	유
	衤	衤	衿	餘裕	extra time, extra money, leeway, margin	여유
衣 7 1172	裕	裕	裕	富裕	be wealthy, enjoy plenty	부유
				裕福	affluent, well-to-do	유복

補	ﾎ	ﾎ	ﾈ	기울	fill, fill in, fill a vacancy; repair, patch; add to, supplement; help	보
	衤	衦	袻	補給	supply, furnish	보급
				補缺	supplement, fill a vacancy; make up a deficiency	보결
衣 7 1173	補	補	補	補助	assist, aid, subsidize	보조

視	ﾎ	ﾎ	ﾈ	볼	look at, inspect	시
	初	神	神	視線	line of sight; gaze	시선
				視力	strength of vision, eyesight	시력
				視覺	vision, sense of sight	시각
見 5 1174	視	視	視			

訴	亠	言	言	소송할	accuse; complain; tell, inform, state	소
	言	訁	訁	訴訟	sue, take legal proceedings	소송
				訴請	petition	소청
				訴追	file charges	소추
言 5 1175	訴	訴	訴			

詐	言	言	言	속일	deceive; false, artful	사
	言	言	言	詐欺罪	fraud	사기죄
				詐取	obtain by fraud, defraud	사취
言 5 1176	訐	詐	詐	詐稱	misrepresent oneself, falsely assume another's name	사칭

評	言	言	言	평할	criticize, comment	평
	言	言	言	評論	criticism, review and comment on	평론
				評價	appraise, rate, assess	평가
言 5 1177	訂	証	評	評判	reputation, repute	평판

詞	言	言	言	말씀	word, phrase, idiom; part of speech; expression; tales, stories; kind of poem	사
	言	訂	詞	歌詞	lyric poetry, poetry intended to be sung; poetry; lyrics	가사
				弔詞	words of condolence	조사
言 5 1178	訂	詞	詞	品詞	part of speech, word class	품사

詠	言	言	言	읊을	chant, recite; sing, hum	영
	言	言	訂	詠誦	recitation	영송
				詠歎	exclaim; admire	영탄
言 5 1179	詞	詠	詠	詠唱	an aria	영창

象	⺈	⺈	禸	형상	appearance; phenomenon; image, representation; omens; elephant; ivory	상
	免	免	象	象徵	symbol; symbolize	상징
				象牙	ivory	상아
豕 5 1180	象	象	象	象形	image; simple pictographs	상형

貯	刀	月	貝	쌓을	store up; hoard	저
	貝	貝	貝	貯藏	store, stock	저장
				貯蓄	save money	저축
貝 5 1181	貯	貯	貯	貯水	store water; reservoir water	저수

貳	一	二	三	버금	two (legal form)	이
	亖	弎	貳	貳拾	twenty	이십
貝 5 1182	貳	貳	貳	貳萬	twenty thousand	이만

貴	口	虫	串	귀할	valued, esteemed, honorable, "your"; costly, high-class	귀
	貴	貴	貴	貴重	precious, valuable	귀중
				貴族	aristocracy, nobility; your esteemed family lineage (honorific)	귀족
貝 5 1183	貴	貴	貴	貴賤	noble and mean, high and low	귀천

買	冖	罒	四	살	buy, purchase; suborn	매
	罗	胃	胃	買入	purchase, buy	매입
				買受	bribe, buy someone	매수
				買氣	inclination to buy	매기
貝 5 1184	買	買	買			

貸	亻	代	代	빌릴	lend; borrow	대
	代	佟	貸	貸借	debt and credit; let and hire	대차
				貸與	loan, lend	대여
				貸付	lend, loan	대부
貝 5 1185	貸	貸	貸			

費	一	弓	弗	소비할	expenditure; expend; waste; extensive	비
	弗	費	費	消費	consume; expend	소비
				費用	cost, expense	비용
貝 5 1186	費	費	費	會費	dues, membership fee	회비

貿	乚	𠄔	卯	무역할	trade, barter	무
	貿	貿	貿	貿易	trade, international commerce	무역
				貿易港	trade port	무역항
貝 5 1187	貿	貿	貿	貿易會社	trading company	무역회사

賀	力	加	賀	하례할 congratulate		**하**
	智	智	智	賀禮	congratulate, hold a ceremony of congratulation	하례
				祝賀	congratulate, felicitate, "congratulations"	축하
貝 5 1188	智	賀	賀	賀客	well-wisher	하객

超	十	土	丰	넘을 jump over; stride; excel		**초**
	走	起	起	超過	exceed; excessive	초과
				超越	transcend, go beyond; excel, surpass	초월
走 5 1189	起	超	超	超然	aloofness, stand-offish	초연

越	十	土	丰	넘을 pass over, cross, exceed; transgress, encroach; Vietnam		**월**
	走	赴	起	越冬	pass the winter	월동
				越境	cross the border, violate the border	월경
走 5 1190	越	越	越	越權	exceed one's authority	월권

距	口	尸	足	떨어질 distance between; go to, reach		**거**
	昆	足	距	距離	distance, range; gap, interval	거리
足 5 1191	距	距	距			

逸	ク	鸟	色	편안할 leisure, leisurely; ease, idleness; let go, lose, loose; retire, withdraw		**일**
	兔	兔	兔	逸品	outstanding item, excellent piece	일품
				逸話	anecdote	일화
辶 8 1192	兔	逸	逸	安逸	life of ease; life of idleness	안일

進	亻	仁	仁	나아갈 go forward, advance		**진**
	住	住	佳	進出	advance into, launch into	진출
				進行	progress; advance	진행
				進步	progress, improve	진보
辶 8 1193	住	進	進			

都 邑 9 1194	十	土	耂	도읍 metropolis; all; main 都邑 capital city 都市 city; towns and cities 都心地 heart of the city, 　　　downtown area	도 도읍 도시 도심지
	耂	者	者		
	者	都	都		

量 里 5 1195	冂	曰	旦	헤아릴 measure; limit; amount 計量器 meter, gauge 大量 large quantity; 　　　magnanimity 測量 measure; estimate	량 계량기 대량 측량
	昌	昌	量		
	量	量	量		

鈍 金 4 1196	人	仝	全	둔할 dull-witted; obtuse; blunt 鈍角 obtuse angle 鈍感 dull, thick-skinned 鈍濁 dull-witted, stupid	둔 둔각 둔감 둔탁
	金	金	釒		
	釼	釼	鈍		

間 門 4 1197	冂	卩	門	사이 interval, space, between 間接 indirect, indirectly 間隔 interval, gap, space 間諜 espionage agent	간 간접 간격 간첩
	門	門	門		
	間	間	間		

閏 門 4 1198	冂	卩	門	윤달 extra month inserted to 　　　rationalize calendar; 　　　intercalary, extra, 　　　inserted; "leap year" 閏年 leap year, intercalary year 閏月 leap month, intercalary month 閏日 leap day, intercalary day	윤 윤년 윤월 윤일
	門	門	門		
	閏	閏	閏		

閑 門 4 1199	冂	卩	門	한가로울 leisure 閑暇 have spare time, 　　　have leisure 閑寂 be retired, sequestered 閑散 inactive; leisurely, quiet	한 한가 한적 한산
	門	門	門		
	閑	閑	閑		

				열	open; explain; begin	개
開	門 門 門 門 閂 閂 閂 門 4 1200			開拓 開催 開始	bring under cultivation; develop, colonize, pioneer open a meeting start, inaugurate, begin	개척 개최 개시
隆	阜 9 1201			높을 隆盛 隆起 隆崇	eminent, surpassing; prosperous; exalt prosperous, thriving bulge, rise up highly esteem, deeply respect	륭 융성 융기 융숭
陽	阜 9 1202			볕 太陽 陽地 夕陽	Yang (of Yin and Yang), the male principle, the sun the sun a sunny place the setting sun	양 태양 양지 석양
隊	阜 9 1203			떼 軍隊 隊長 隊伍	file of soldiers, company of soldiers; army the military, the army, the armed services leader, section commander file, rank	대 군대 대장 대오
階	阜 9 1204			섬돌 階級 階段 階層	stairs, steps; rank, grade rank; class stairs, steps; stage, phase stairs; class; rank	계 계급 계단 계층
雄	隹 4 1205			수컷 雄壯 雄大 雄辯	male (of birds, etc.); virile, strong; brave; martial magnificent, grand majestic, magnificent oratory; eloquence	웅 웅장 웅대 웅변

229

雅
 	
隹 4
1206
	于	矛	矛	닭을	fine, elegant, polished,
					  refined, polite; constantly;
					  your esteemed
						아

	矛	邪	邪	雅樂	classical court music	아악
	邪	雅	雅	雅淡	elegant, graceful	아담
				雅量	magnanimity, broad-mindedness	아량

集 隹 4 1207	亻	仁	信	모을	assemble, gather; compile, edit	집
	佳	佳	隹	集團	bloc, group, collective body	집단
	隼	隼	集	蒐集	compile, collect	수집
				集中	concentrate, mass; focus, converge	집중

雁 隹 4 1208	厂	厂	厃	기러기	wild goose	안
	厃	雁	雁	雁行	esteemed brothers(honorific)	안항
	雁	雁	雁	鴻雁	wild geese	홍안

				奠雁	presentation by the
					  groom of a goose to
					  the bride as part of
					  the wedding rite
						전안

雲 雨 4 1209	一	雨	雨	구름	clouds; numerous; gather	운
	雨	雲	雲	雲集	throng, gather in swarms	운집
				風雲兒	adventurer, soldier of fortune	풍운아
	雲	雲	雲	雲母	mica	운모

須
 	
頁 3
1210
	彡	汀	奷	모름지기	necessary; necessarily,
					  by all means; must;
					  moment; wait, expect
						수

	須	須	須			
	須	須	須	必須	required, compulsory	필수

項 頁 3 1211	工	工	功	목	back of the neck; item	항
	項	項	項	事項	items, details, matters	사항
				項目	an item; a heading	항목
	項	項	項	條項	article, clause	조항

順	川	川	川	순할	smooth, gentle; favorable; fluent; obey; accord with	순
	川	川	順	順應	accommodate to, adapt to	순응
				順調롭다	smoothly, without friction	순조
頁 3 1212	順	順	順	順從	obey, comply with	순종

黃	十	廿	世	누를	yellow	황
	苗	苗	苗	黃金	gold	황금
				黃昏	dusk, twilight	황혼
				黃泉	death, the ''yellow spring'' of Hades	황천
黃 0 1213	苗	黃	黃			

黑	冂	四	四	검을	black; evil	흑
	四	里	黑	黑字	black letters; boldface; in the black (not in the red)	흑자
黑 0 1214	黑	黑	黑	黑人	a black, a Negro	흑인
				黑板	blackboard	흑판

13 Strokes

亂	⺈	⺈	台	어지러울	disorderly; reckless; rebellion; confusion	란
	舌	爲	爲	反亂	rebellion, revolt	반란
				亂暴	violent; reckless	난폭
				亂舞	wild dancing; run wild; rampage	난무
乙 12 1215	爲	爲	亂			

催	亻	仙	仙	재촉할	pressure, urge	최
	件	件	件	催促	importune, press, urge	최촉
				催眠術	hypnotism	최면술
				催告	demand, press for	최고
人 11 1216	催	催	催			

231

傲	亻	亻ʼ	仹	업신여길 haughty, proud		오
	傲	傲	傲	傲慢 arrogant, haughty 傲氣 proud; cocky; obstinate		오만 오기
人 11 1217	傲	傲	傲			

傳	亻	仁	俥	전할 transmit, hand down; preach, propagate		전
	俥	俥	傳	宣傳 publicity; advertising; propaganda		선전
人 11 1218	傳	傳	傳	傳統 tradition, convention 傳說 legend, myth		전통 전설

債	亻	仁	佳	빚 debt		채
	倩	倩	倩	公債 public loan; government bond		공채
				債券 bond, debenture		채권
人 11 1219	債	債	債	債務 debt, indebtedness, liabilities		채무

僅	亻	亻ʼ	亻世	겨우 barely, hardly enough		근
	借	借	借	僅少 small, few, scanty 僅僅 only, merely, no more than; barely		근소 근근
人 11 1220	僅	僅	僅			

傷	亻	亻ʼ	佰	슬플 grieve, distress; injure, wound		상
	伯	恒	傅	傷處 wound, cut, bruise 負傷 be injured, be wounded		상처 부상
人 11 1221	傷	傷	傷	重傷 serious injury		중상

傾	亻	化	化	기울 incline, lean; tip over, collapse		경
	伺	傾	傾	傾向 tendency; inclination 傾斜 slope, slant		경향 경사
人 11 1222	傾	傾	傾	傾聽 give ear to, pay attention		경청

募	十	艹	芹	모을	summon, round up, raise, solicit	모
	节	营	草	募集	recruit, hire, enlist	모집
力 11	莫	募	募	募金	money-raising	모금
1223				募兵	conscript, draft	모병

勢	十	圥	去	기세	power, influence, authority, strength; circumstances; aspect	세
	去	剚	執	氣勢	spirit, vigor	기세
力 11	執	勢	勢	勢力	strength, power; force, energy	세력
1224				權勢	power, influence, authority	권세

勤	廿	芐	苫	부지런할	diligence; duty	근
	革	堇	革	勤勞者	laborer	근로자
力 11	菫	勤	勤	勤務	serve, be on duty, be at work	근무
1225				勤勉	diligence	근면

嗚	口	口'	听	탄식할	sobbing; "alas!"	오
	咋	嗚	嗚	嗚呼	Alas! Alack!	오호
口 10	嗚	嗚	嗚	嗚咽	sobbing, choking	오열
1226						

園	门	冂	周	동산	garden, orchard; park	원
	周	園	園	園藝	gardening; horticulture	원예
口 10	園	園	園	公園	public park, public gardens	공원
1227				植物園	botanical garden	식물원

圓	门	冂	同	둥글	round, circular; basic unit of Korean money	원
	同	同	員	圓滿	satisfaction, contentment; perfection; harmony	원만
口 10	圓	圓	圓	圓形	a circle, round shape	원형
1228				圓筒	cylinder, cylindrical	원통

塔 土 10 1229	土 圵 圤 圢 坎 坎 塔 塔 塔	탑 塔載 塔乘 石塔	pagoda, tower load; embark, entrain embark, board, ride stone pagoda, stupa, tower	탑 탑재 탑승 석탑
塊 土 10 1230	土 圤 坥 坥 坥 坥 塊 塊 塊	덩어리 金塊 塊石 塊炭	lump, piece, clod nugget; ingot of gold a rock, stone lump coal	괴 금괴 괴석 괴탄
塞 土 10 1231	宀 宀 宇 窜 宲 寒 寒 寒 塞	변방 要塞 閉塞 窘塞	block; stop up, clog; cork; stopper, plug fortress, stronghold block a harbor, blockade indigent, poor	새 (색) 요새 폐색 군색

幹 干 10 1232	宀 方 百 草 軺 軺 軺 軺 幹	줄기 幹部 幹線 幹事	tree trunk; trunk of a body
			managing staff,
			  executive management
			trunk line, main line
			administrative affairs;
			  administrator,
			  executive secretary
				간
				간부
				간선
				간사

廊 广 10 1233	广 庁 庌 庌 庌 庌 庌 庌 廊	행랑 行廊 廊下 畫廊	verandah, porch; corridor
			servants' quarters, esp.
			  on both sides of an
			  entry gate; lines of
			  shops along a street
			corridor, hallway
			art gallery
				랑
				행랑
				낭하
				화랑

廉 广 10 1234	广 庁 庄 庌 庌 庌 庿 廉	청렴할 低廉 廉恥 廉探	pure, uncorrupted;
			  modest; investigate;
			  reasonable in price
			inexpensive, cheap
			sense of shame;
			  sense of honor
			secretly observe, spy on
				렴
				저렴
				염치
				염탐

微	彳	彳	彳	작을	small, fine; microscopic; subtle; lowly, humble	미
	彳	彳	彳	微笑 smile, a smile		미소
				微妙 subtle, delicate		미묘
彳 10 1235	微	微	微	微賤 lowly, humble		미천

慈	丶	丷	䒑	사랑	compassion; love	자
	兹	兹	兹	慈悲心 benevolence; mercy		자비심
				慈善 charity, benevolence		자선
				慈愛 affection, kindness, love		자애
心 9 1236	慈	慈	慈	(14 strokes in original form, 慈 .)		

想	十	才	机	생각	think; expect	상
	相	相	相	想像 imagine; suppose		상상
				感想 impressions, feelings, thoughts		감상
心 9 1237	想	想	想	想起 recall, remember		상기

愁	千	禾	利	근심	concern, anxiety; melancholy; grieving, sad; depressing, gloomy	수
	利	秋	秋	愁心 grief, sadness; melancholy		수심
				愁色 melancholy air, worried look		수색
心 9 1238	愁	愁	愁	憂愁 sorrow		우수

愈	人	今	會	어질	surpass, excel, more; heal	유
	俞	俞	俞			
心 9 1239	愈	愈	愈			

意	亠	立	立	뜻	purpose, will; meaning; idea	의
	音	音	音	意味 meaning, significance		의미
				意見 opinion, view		의견
心 9 1240	意	意	意	意思 intention; idea		의사

235

				사랑	love; be fond of, like; affection; desire, covet; grudge; beloved daughter	애
愛				愛情	affection, love; devotion	애정
				愛國	patriotism, love of country	애국
心 9 1241				愛慾	love and lust, passion	애욕

				어리석을	stupid, foolish; simple, rude	우
愚				愚昧	stupid and ignorant	우매
				愚劣	stupidity	우열
心 9 1242				愚鈍	stupid, dull	우둔

				느낄	feel; feeling, emotion	감
感				感謝	"thank you", be grateful	감사
				感覺	sense, perception; sensibility	감각
心 9 1243				感激	be deeply moved; deeply grateful	감격

				부끄러울	bashful; ashamed	괴
愧				愧赧	be ashamed, blush with shame	괴란
心 10 1244						

				삼갈	cautious, act with care	신
愼				愼重	cautious, prudent	신중
				謹愼	prudent, discreet; behave properly	근신
心 10 1245						

				흔들	shake, agitate, toss; wave, sway; scull, row	요
搖				動搖	shake, quake; be perturbed, restless	동요
				搖籃	cradle; birthplace	요람
手 10 1246				搖動	roll and pitch, rock; shake, quake	요동

損	扌	扩	护	덜	loss; disadvantage, drawback; injure, destroy, spoil; injury, disability, impairment	손
	扪	捐	捐			
手 10 1247	捐	損	損	損害 損失 損傷	damage, loss loss, suffer loss suffer damage, incur injury	손해 손실 손상

携	扌	扑	护	이끌	lead; carry; take along	휴
	扩	挫	拃	携帯 提携	carry along, take along act in harmony, move in concert	휴대 제휴
手 10 1248	推	携	携			

敬	亠	艹	芍	공경	respect, reverence	경
	苟	苟	苟	恭敬 敬意 敬語	respect, revere, venerate respect, regard highly honorific expressions, terms of respect	공경 경의 경어
攴 9 1249	敬	敬	敬			

新	亠	六	立	새	new; fresh; recent	신
	亲	亲	亲	新聞	newspaper; news in the papers	신문
斤 9 1250	亲	新	新	新鮮 新綠	fresh fresh green, tender green	신선 신록

暇	丨	日	日	겨를	leisure, relaxation	가
	旷	昖	昖	閑暇 餘暇 休暇	leisure, spare time spare time vacation, leave, holiday, furlough	한가 여가 휴가
日 9 1251	昖	暇	暇			

暑	冂	曰	早	더울	hot	서
	昇	昇	昇	酷暑 避暑	wilting heat avoiding summer heat, summering	혹서 피서
日 9 1252	暑	暑	暑	大暑	intense heat, 12th of the 24 seasonal divisions, midsummer	대서

| 暖 日 9 1253 | 丨丨 日 日丶 日丶 日丶 日丶 日丶 日丶 日丶 日丶 日丶 日丶 日丶 暖 | 따뜻할 warm; genial

暖流 a warm current
暖房 room heating | 난
난류
난방 |

| 暗 日 9 1254 | 丨丨 日 日丶 日丶 日立 日音 暗 暗 暗 | 어두울 dark; obscure; hidden; secret

暗黑 darkness, blackness
暗示 hint, suggestion; intimation
暗室 darkroom; a dark room | 암
암흑
암시
암실 |

| 會 日 9 1255 | 人 今 命 命 金 金 會 會 會 | 모을 assemble, meet; society

會社 corporation, company
會議 conference, meeting
會談 talks, conference | 회
회사
회의
회담 |

| 楊 木 9 1256 | 十 木 村 相 担 棋 楊 楊 楊 | 버들 willow; poplar; aspen

垂楊 weeping willow
白楊 white poplar
楊貴妃 poppy, opium poppy | 양
수양
백양
양귀비 |

| 楓 木 9 1257 | 十 木 机 枫 枫 枫 楓 楓 楓 | 단풍나무 maple tree

楓嶽 Diamond Mountains in autumn
丹楓 maple tree; autumnal tints | 풍
풍악
단풍 |

| 業 木 9 1258 | 丨丨 业 业 业 业 业 業 業 業 | 업 trade, line of business, profession, occupation

職業 occupation, job
業者 businessman
業務 business operations, business matters | 업
직업
업자
업무 |

Character	Stroke order	Word	Meaning	Reading
極 木 9 1259		지극할	utmost; extremely; pole, utmost point, end	극
		極度	highest degree, zenith	극도
		極盡히	cordially, kindly	극진
		極致	acme, zenith; ideal perfection	극치
歲 止 9 1260		해	year; harvest; age	세
		歲月	time, time and tide	세월
		歲拜	formal bow on New Year's Day	세배
		年歲	age (honorific)	연세
毁 殳 9 1261		헐	ruin; slander	훼
		毁謗	slander, villify	훼방
		毁損	damage, injure; defame	훼손
源 水 10 1262		근원	source; spring	원
		財源	funds, source of revenue; economic resources	재원
		源泉	source, fountainhead	원천
		根源	source, origin	근원
溪 水 10 1263		시내	stream	계
		溪谷	valley, ravine	계곡
		溪流	mountain stream	계류
		淸溪路	major east-west road in Seoul	청계로
準 水 10 1264		법	rule; regularize, adjust; exact, true; weigh, measure; grant, allow; quasi…, semi…	준
		準備	prepare, arrange	준비
		水準	level, standard; water level	수준

13 strokes

滄 水 10 1265	⟨strokes⟩	바다	ocean; vast; cold	창
		滄波	ocean waves, billows	창파
		滄海	the vast blue sea	창해
		滄浪	blue waves	창랑

溫 水 10 1266	⟨strokes⟩	따뜻할	warm; warm up; gentle; revive	온
		溫度	temperature	온도
		溫順	be genial	온순
		溫度計	thermometer	온도계

滅 水 10 1267	⟨strokes⟩	멸망할	destroy; exterminate	멸
		滅亡	be destroyed, cease to exist	멸망
		消滅	become extinct, disappear, cease to exist	소멸
		滅種	exterminate a race of people, genocide	멸종

煙 火 9 1268	⟨strokes⟩	연기	smoke; mist, vapor; tobacco	연
		煙氣	smoke	연기
		煙草	tobacco	연초
		吸煙	smoke tobacco	흡연

熙 火 9 1269	⟨strokes⟩	밝을	bright, splendid	희
		熙宗	21st king of Koryŏ (1181-1237)	희종
		光熙門	name of Little South Gate in Seoul	광희문

照 火 9 1270	⟨strokes⟩	비칠	reflect; look after; a permit; according to, referring to	조
		照明	illuminate, light up	조명
		照會	make inquiries about	조회
		照準	to aim, to sight	조준

煩 火 9 1271	번거로울 troublesome, vexing; vexed	번
	煩惱 suffer agony, agonize; be harassed by evil passions	번뇌
	煩悶 suffer, agonize, worry	번민
	煩雜 vexatious, annoying; confused, crowded	번잡

當 田 8 1272	마땅할 suitable; correct; ought	당
	當身 you (to equal or inferior); thou, thee	당신
	當座 the assembled, the seated; the place, the spot	당좌
	當局 authorities concerned, responsible officials	당국

盟 皿 8 1273	맹세할 swear, covenant, contract; oath; league	맹
	盟誓 vow, pledge; give one's word of honor	맹서
	盟約 pact, covenant; alliance, league	맹약
	盟友 ally, sworn friend	맹우

睡 目 8 1274	잠잘 sleep	수
	睡眠 sleep, slumber	수면
	睡魔 drowsiness, sleepiness	수마
	昏睡 become comatose, lapse into coma	혼수

睦 目 8 1275	화목할 harmony, peace, concord, friendship	목
	親睦 friendly association; foster friendship	친목
	和睦 be in harmony, be at peace with each other	화목

督 目 8 1276	감독할 oversee; enforce	독
	督促 urge, press; dun	독촉
	督勵 stimulate, encourage	독려
	提督 admiral	제독

241

碑 石 8 1277	厂 石 石ノ 矿 碑 碑 硬 碑	비석 stone tablet; gravestone 碑石 large stone tablet, stone monument 碑文 inscription on a stone tablet; epigraph 碑閣 tablet house, structure protecting a stone tablet	비 비석 비문 비각
祿 示 8 1278	二 ネ ネ' ネ ネ' 禄 禄 禄 禄	녹 official stipend, salary; happiness, prosperity 祿俸 stipend, salary 國祿 government salary 貫祿 commanding appearance; dignity; weight of character	록 녹봉 국록 관록
禁 示 8 1279	十 木 村 林 楚 楚 禁 禁 禁	금할 prohibit, forbid 禁止 prohibit, forbid 禁物 contraband 禁錮 imprisonment, confinement	금 금지 금물 금고
禽 內 8 1280	入 仝 今 含 禽 禽 禽 禽 禽	날짐승 winged animals, birds 禽獸 birds and beasts; beast, brute	금 금수
稚 禾 8 1281	千 禾 利 利 秆 秤 稚 稚 稚	어릴 young, tender 幼稚 infantile, childish 幼稚園 kindergarten	치 유치 유치원
經 糸 7 1282	幺 糸 糸一 紅 經 經 經 經 經	경서 classic books; Buddhist sutras; pass through; manage 經濟 economy, economics 經費 expenses; expenditures 經驗 experience	경 경제 경비 경험

絹 糸 7 1283	幺 幺 幺 糹 糹 糹 絹 絹 絹	비단 絹織物 人絹 絹絲	thin silk silk fabrics, silk goods rayon, synthetic silk silk thread	견 견직물 인견 견사
置 网 8 1284	一 罒 罒 罕 罕 罙 胃 置 置	둘 置重 置簿 放置	put aside, put away; place, establish; dismiss, disregard stress, attach importance to keep books, keep accounts; enter, write down let alone, leave to chance	치 치중 치부 방치
罪 网 8 1285	一 罒 罒 罪 罪 罪 罪 罪 罪	허물 犯罪 罪惡 罪人	sin; crime; transgression; misdeed, offense commit crime, violate law crime; sin; vice criminal, convict; sinner; I, me (as used by son mourning his father)	죄 범죄 죄악 죄인
群 羊 7 1286	⺻ 尹 君 君 君ˇ 君ˇ 君ˇ 君兰 群	무리 群衆 群島	flock, herd; multitude crowd; masses, the public archipelago	군 군중 군도
義 羊 7 1287	﹀ ⺍ 半 差 羊 莑 義 義 義	옳을 義務 義理 義兵	right conduct; justice; morality, righteousness; duty to one's neighbor obligation; duty justice; sense of duty; loyalty; integrity righteous army; loyal troops	의 의무 의리 의병
聖 耳 7 1288	厂 巨 巨 耴 耴 耴 聖 聖 聖	성인 聖經 聖地 聖賢	saint, sage; holy, sacred; divine the Bible; a holy book sacred ground; the Holy Land sages; saints	성 성경 성지 성현

				부를	invite with presents, invite with rewards; engage someone	빙
聘				招聘	engage, employ, invite with due rewards	초빙
耳 7 1289				聘母	wife's mother	빙모
				聘丈	wife's father	빙장

				엄숙할	solemn; reverential; respectful; majestic; awesome	숙
肅				嚴肅	solemn, grave, serious	엄숙
聿 8 1290				肅清	purge; liquidate	숙청
				肅正	enforce, regulate	숙정

				뇌	brain	뇌
腦				腦溢血	stroke, cerebral hemorrhage	뇌일혈
肉 9 1291				腦炎	encephalitis, brain inflammation	뇌염
				腦膜炎	meningitis, brain fever	뇌막염

				허리	waist; lower back; middle; loins	요
腰				腰痛	backache	요통
				腰帶	sash; belt, waistband	요대
肉 9 1292				腰絶	be spoiled, go to ruin	요절

				배	abdomen, stomach	복
腹				腹膜	the peritoneum	복막
				腹痛	stomachache	복통
肉 9 1293				腹部	abdomen, abdominal region	복부

				창자	intestines	장
腸				腸器	viscera, internal organs; the bowel	장기
				盲腸	appendix	맹장
肉 9 1294				腸炎	enteritis	장염

| 與 臼 7 1295 | 줄 | give, grant; with, by, to; wait for | 여 |
| | 與否 參與 附與 | whether or not; yes or no participate, take part in confer, grant | 여부 참여 부여 |

| 萬 艸 9 1296 | 일만 | ten thousand | 만 |
| | 萬一 萬歲 萬物 | if; unexpected 10,000 years, "long live…" everything, all things | 만일 만세 만물 |

| 落 艸 9 1297 | 떨어질 | fall, drop; lose; scatter; die; village | 락 |
| | 部落 落心 落成 | village, community discouraged, downhearted completion of a building | 부락 낙심 낙성 |

| 葬 艸 9 1298 | 장례 | funeral service; bury | 장 |
| | 葬禮 葬事 葬地 | funeral service, funeral ceremony bury burial ground | 장례 장사 장지 |

| 葉 艸 9 1299 | 잎사귀 | leaf; petal; slip, card; page; hinge; generation, period | 엽 |
| | 葉書 葉錢 落葉 | a postcard brass coin formerly used in Korea fallen leaves, dead leaves | 엽서 엽전 낙엽 |

| 著 艸 9 1300 | 나타날 붙을 | to manifest; write put on, wear | 저 착 |
| | 著者 著述 | author, writer compose, write | 저자 저술 |

號	口	号	号	이름	name, designation, mark	호
	号	号	號	號令	command, order; yell, shout	호령
				記號	mark, sign, symbol	기호
虍 7 1301	號	號	號	口號	slogan; password; extemporaneously compose poetry	구호
蜂	口	中	虫	벌	bee, hornet, wasp	봉
	虫ク	蚁	蚁	蜂起	revolt, insurrection, uprising	봉기
				蜂蜜	honey	봉밀
虫 7 1302	蜂	蜂	蜂	蜂巢	a beehive	봉소
裏	亠	亠	盲	속	within, inside; lining	리
	言	車	車	裏面	background, inside story; the inside; the back, the reverse side	이면
				表裏	inside and outside, front and back; duplicity	표리
衣 7 1303	裏	裏	裏	裏書	endorsement	이서
裝	ㅓ	ㅓ	壯	꾸밀	pretend, dress as; costume; load, pack	장
	壯	壯	壯	裝置	equip, fit, install; fixtures, fittings	장치
				裝備	equipment; furnishings; fittings	장비
衣 7 1304	裝	裝	裝	裝飾品	ornaments, decorations	장식품
解	ク	角	角	풀	explain; deliver; loosen, release	해
	角	解	解	解放	liberate	해방
				解決	solve, settle	해결
角 6 1305	解	解	解	解釋	interpret, explicate	해석
試	言	言	言	시험할	examination, test; examine; try, experiment; use; trained, disciplined	시
	言	訂	訂	試驗	examination, test; try out	시험
				試練	trial, test, ordeal	시련
言 6 1306	訂	試	試	試圖	attempt, try	시도

246

詩 言 6 1307	二 言 訁 言 訁 詩 詩	글 詩人 詩集 詩想	poetry, poem, ode poet anthology poetic sentiment; the idea of a poem	시 시인 시집 시상
該 言 6 1308	二 言 言 訁 訁 該 該	그 該當 該博 當該	that, the said applicable, pertinent erudite, learned the concerned, the interested	해 해당 해박 당해

詳 言 6 1309	二 言 言 訁 訁 詳 詳	자세할
		
		詳細
		詳察
		
		詳報
			particulars, detail;
			    examine with care,
			    judge; carefully
			minute, detailed
			fully consider; carefully
			    observe
			detailed report
				상
				
				상세
				상찰
				
				상보

話 言 6 1310	二 言 言 訁 訁 話 話	말씀
		話題
		
		對話
		會話
			words, talk
			topic of conversation,
			    a subject raised or
			    discussed
			converse with, talk to
			conversation
				화
				화제
				
				대화
				회화

誇 言 6 1311	二 言 言 訂 訮 詝 誇	자랑할 誇大 誇張 誇示	boast, brag; praise exaggerate, overstate stretch the truth, exaggerate display; show off	과 과대 과장 과시
賊 貝 6 1312	刂 月 貝 貝一 貯 財 賊 賊	도둑 盜賊 海賊 山賊	thief; to plunder thief, robber; theft pirate brigand, bandit	적 도적 해적 산적

賃 貝 6 1313	亻 亻 任 任 倩 倩 倩 債 賃	삵	rent, lease	임
		賃金	salary, wage; rent	임금
		勞賃	wages	노임
		賃貸	hire out; lease, charter	임대
資 貝 6 1314	冫 次 冷 泞 浒 资 资 資 資	재물	property, wealth; assistance; disposition; qualifications	자
		資金	capital, funds	자금
		資格	competence, capability; qualifications	자격
		資産	assets, property	자산
跡 足 6 1315	口 무 足 足 趵 趵 跡 跡 跡	자취	traces, footsteps; follow up	적
		痕跡	traces, indications, evidence	흔적
		行跡	achievements of a lifetime, one's contributions	행적
		人跡	human traces (tracks, footprints)	인적
跳 足 6 1316	口 무 足 趴 趴 趴 趴 跳 跳	뛸	jump	조
		건널	cross	도
		跳躍	jump, leap	도약
		跳梁	rampant, dominant; prevail	도량
		捧高跳	the pole vault	봉고도
路 足 6 1317	口 무 足 足 趵 趵 趵 路 路	길	road, path	로
		路資	road money, traveling expenses	노자
		路上	on the road, on the way	노상
		路線	route, course, line	노선
較 車 6 1318	一 曰 車 車 軒 軒 車 軒 較	비교할	compare; test; check	교
		比較	compare	비교

248

載	十	土	吉	실을	load, to load; contain; to record	재
	吉	亘	車	記載	record, note down	기재
				滿載	fully loaded, full to capacity	만재
車 6 1319	軒	載	載	轉載	reproduce, reprint	전재

農	冖	曲	曲	농사	agriculture; farm; farmer	농
	严	严	農	農作物	crops, agricultural products	농작물
				農業	agriculture, farming	농업
				農民	farmer, peasant	농민
辰 6 1320	農	農	農			

遇	冂	日	咼	만날	meet; happen, occur; entertain, receive	우
	禺	禺	禺	待遇	reception, treatment; pay, remuneration	대우
				不遇	unfortunate, ill-fated	불우
辶 9 1321	遇	遇	遇	千載一遇	rare opportunity	천재일우

遂	丷	丷	艼	다할	complete, reach; proceed to; end up at; forthwith	수
	芗	豕	豙	遂行	execute, perform	수행
				完遂	complete, accomplish	완수
辶 9 1322	㒸	遂	遂	未遂	attempted; unconsummated	미수

遊	亠	方	方	놀	play, amuse oneself; roam, travel, saunter	유
	扩	斿	斿	遊戲	play, play at a game	유희
				遊覽	sightsee, tour	유람
辶 9 1323	斿	遊	遊	遊興	amuse oneself, make merry	유흥

運	冖	尸	冒	운전할	transport, convey; luck; revolve, turn around; period of time	운
	昌	宣	軍	運轉	drive; operate	운전
				運命	destiny, fate, fortune	운명
辶 9 1324	軍	渾	運	運動	physical exercise, athletic sports	운동

13 strokes

過	⼔	⽇	咼	지날	pass, cross over	과
	咼	咼	咼	過去	the past	과거
				過誤	mistake, error	과오
⾡ 9 1325	渦	過	過	過半	majority, greater part	과반

達	十	土	击	통달할	penetrate, apprehend; intelligent; thorough	달
	查	查	幸	達成	achieve, accomplish	달성
				傳達	convey, forward, deliver	전달
⾡ 9 1326	幸	達	達	配達	deliver, distribute	배달

遍	⼾	戶	启	두루	everywhere; whole; time, occasion	변(편)
	启	扁	扁	普遍	universal; ubiquitous	보편
				遍歷	roam, travel about	편력
⾡ 9 1327	扁	徧	遍			

違	⼑	卉	吾	어길	disobey; disregard; oppose; avoid; abandon a purpose; offend against	위
	音	宣	韋	違反	violate, break	위반
				違法	break the law	위법
⾡ 9 1328	韋	違	違	非違	violation	비위

道	⼉	⾋	芮	길	road, way, path; truth, principle; province	도
	芮	首	首	道理	reason; duty; way, means	도리
				道路	road, street	도로
⾡ 9 1329	首	道	道	道義	morality, moral justice, moral principles	도의

鄉	⼷	⼺	幺り	고을	village; country	향
	幼	绉	绉	鄉愁	homesickness, nostalgia	향수
				鄉土	native country; birthplace	향토
				鄉歌	"native songs", 25 extant Korean folk songs dating from before the 12th century	향가
邑 10 1330	绑	鄉	鄉			

Korean word spacing

鉛 金 5 1331	人 金 釦	亼 釦 鉛	余 釦 鉛	납 鉛筆 黑鉛	lead (the metal) pencil graphite	연 연필 흑연
雌 隹 5 1332	止 屮 雌	屮 屮 雌	此 雌 雌	암컷 雌雄	female male and female; victory or defeat	자 자웅
零 雨 5 1333	雨 雨 雨	雨 雰 零	雨 雰 零	영 零落 零細 零點	zero; fragments; fractional; rainfall, dewfall go to ruin, lose one's fortune paltry, petty zero; nothing; freezing point	령 영락 영세 영점
電 雨 5 1334	雨 雨 霄	雨 雨 霄	雨 雨 電	번개 電氣 電流 電燈	lightning; electricity electricity electric current electric light	전 전기 전류 전등
雷 雨 5 1335	雨 雨 雷	雨 雷 雷	雨 雷 雷	우뢰 雷同 雷雨 雷聲	thunder chime in with, blindly echo another rain and thunder, a thunderstorm the crack of thunder	뢰 뇌동 뇌우 뇌성
頌 頁 4 1336	八 頌 頌	公 頌 頌	公 頌 頌	욀 頌歌 讚頌歌 頌德	praise, commend; hymn, ode hymn hymn eulogize, praise for virtue	송 송가 찬송가 송덕

飲 食 4 1337	人 今 今 食 食 食' 飲' 飲 飲	마실 drink, swallow 飲食物 food and drink, foodstuff 飲料水 soft drinks; drinking water 飲酒 drink liquor	음 음식물 음료수 음주
飯 食 4 1338	人 今 今 食 食 食' 飯 飯 飯	밥 cooked rice; food; provisions 飯饌 side dishes, dishes served with rice 飯床 dining table 朝飯 breakfast	반 반찬 반상 조반
鼓 鼓 0 1339	十 吉 吉 吉 壴 壴 壴十 鼓 鼓	북 drum 鼓膜 eardrum 鼓笛 drum and flute 鼓手 drummer	고 고막 고적 고수

14 Strokes

| 像 人 12 1340 | 亻 伫 倅 俊 伄 像 像 像 像 | 형상 appearance, resemblance, similar; likeness, portrait, statue
肖像 portrait, likeness
銅像 bronze statue
現像 develop film | 상
초상
동상
현상 |
| 僧 人 12 1341 | 亻 伫 伵 伵 伵 僧 僧 僧 僧 | 승려 Buddhist priest
僧侶 Buddhist monk, Buddhist priest
僧舞 monk dance, a dance in Buddhist attire | 승
승려
승무 |

				거짓	false, simulated	위
僞				僞造	forged, counterfeit; falsify	위조
人 12 1342				僞善	hypocrisy	위선
				僞證	perjury, false testimony	위증

				그을	draw, mark	획
劃				劃期的	epochal, epoch-making	획기적
				劃策	scheme, plan, stratagem	획책
刀 12 1343				劃一	uniform, standard	획일

(Also written 畫, 화, 1135.)

				맛볼	taste; try; already	상
嘗				未嘗不	truly, indeed, certainly	미상불
口 11 1344						

				그림	map, picture, diagram	도
圖				圖謀	plan; seek to, strive for	도모
				圖表	chart, graph, diagram	도표
口 11 1345				圖案	a design, a sketch	도안

				둥글	sphere; mass; surround; party	단
團				團體	organization, association	단체
				團束	control, supervise	단속
口 11 1346				團合	unite, stand together	단합

				무덤	grave, tomb	묘
墓				墓地	burial ground, graveyard	묘지
				墓碑	gravestone, tombstone	묘비
土 11 1347				墓祭	memorial service held at a grave	묘제

境	土	扩	圹	지 경	boundary; region; circumstances	경
	圹	培	培	境遇	circumstances, situation; in the event of	경우
				境界	boundary, border	경계
土 11 1348	培	境	境	境地	condition, state; territory, sphere	경지

壽	士	吉	壹	목 숨	longevity, long life, old age	수
	壽	壽	壽	壽福	long life and happiness	수복
				壽命	life, the span of life	수명
士 11 1349	壽	壽	壽	長壽	live a long time	장수

夢	⺈	꾸	芅	꿈	dream	몽
	芇	莔	蓝	夢想	reverie, day dream	몽상
				夢遊病	somnambulism, sleepwalking	몽유병
夕 11 1350	萝	夢	夢	吉夢	lucky dream, auspicious dream	길몽

獎	丬	爿	爿夕	권 할	encourage, exhort	장
	肞	將	將	獎勵	encourage, stimulate	장려
				獎學	encourage learning	장학
大 11 1351	獎	獎	獎	獎學金	scholarship	장학금

奪	大	衣	本	빼앗을	take away, snatch, wrest away	탈
	奓	奮	奞	强奪	plunder, loot, rob	강탈
				奪取	seize, capture	탈취
大 11 1352	奞	奪	奪	奪還	recapture, recover	탈환

寢	宀	宀	宎	잠잘	sleep, rest; bedchamber	침
	寍	㝷	寍	寢室	bedroom, bedchamber	침실
				寢臺	bed; couch	침대
宀 11 1353	寍	寢	寢	寢食	sleep and food, bodily comfort	침식

察 宀 11 1354	宀 ⼾ 宀 宓 宓 寃 寮 寮 察	살필	investigate	찰
		警察	the police	경찰
		視察	inspection, inspect	시찰
		檢察	prosecute; public prosecutor	검찰

寡 宀 11 1355	宀 宀 宀 宦 宣 寅 寅 寡 寡	적을	few, little; lessen; alone	과
		寡婦	a widow	과부
		寡人	term used by a monarch when speaking of himself, "We"	과인
		寡默	taciturn, reticent	과묵

寧 宀 11 1356	宀 宀 忄 忘 窈 窞 窞 窞 寧	편안할	peace, peaceful; repose; better, rather	녕
		安寧	an initial address: peaceful, well, in good health	안녕
		康寧	healthy and peaceful	강녕

實 宀 11 1357	宀 宀 宔 宭 宭 實 曾 實 實	열매	fruit, nut; solid, substantial, hard; real, true, sincere	실
		實習	actual practice; internship, apprenticeship	실습
		實施	execute, put into effect	실시
		實際	actual condition of things; actuality; truth	실제

對 寸 11 1358	⺌ 业 ㄓ 业 业 业 业 對 對	대할	face, oppose; opposite	대
		對立	be facing; antagonistic	대립
		對策	means or measure to counter a recognized problem	대책
		對象者	object (as of a policy), subject (as of an investigation)	대상자

屢 尸 11 1359	尸 尺 屄 屚 屚 屚 屢 屢 屢	여러	frequently, repeatedly, constantly	루
		屢屢이	frequently, often	누누
		屢次	repeatedly, time after time	누차

幕 巾 11 1360			장막	screen, curtain; private secretary	막
			天幕	tent	천막
			幕間	interval between acts or scenes	막간
態 心 10 1361			태도	attitude; behavior	태
			態度	attitude; mien, behavior	태도
			態勢	situation, state of affairs	태세
			狀態	condition, situation	상태
慚 心 11 1362			부끄러울 shame		참
			無慚	ashamed, mortified	무참
			(Also written 慙 .)		
慢 心 11 1363			거만할 rude, arrogant, haughty; slow, gradually		만
			倨慢	haughty, arrogant, proud	거만
			慢性	long lasting, chronic	만성
			怠慢	careless, negligent, inattentive	태만
慘 心 11 1364			슬플 sorrowful, pitiful		참
			慘事	tragedy, disaster	참사
			慘敗	suffer defeat, be miserably beaten	참패
			慘憺	miserable, wretched, piteous	참담
慨 心 11 1365			슬퍼할 saddened, regretful; public-spirited; noble-minded, generous		개
			感慨	deep emotion	감개
			慨嘆	lament, regret	개탄
			憤慨	indignation, resentment	분개

慣	忄	忄口	忄毌	익숙할 accustomed, experienced		관
	忄毌	忄貫	忄毌	慣習	usual practice, custom	관습
				慣例	convention, usage	관례
				習慣	habit	습관
心 11 1366	忄貫	忄貫	慣			

摘	扌	扩	护	딸	pick, pluck; extract; deprive of	적
	抏	摘	摘	指摘	point out, indicate	지적
				摘要	sum up, summarize	적요
手 11 1367	摘	摘	摘	摘發	expose, unmask, lay bare	적발

旗	亠	方	扩	기	flag, banner	기
	旆	旆	旃	國旗	national flag	국기
				旗幟	flag, banner; view, position, stand	기치
方 10 1368	旌	旗	旗	旗艦	flagship	기함

暢	日	申	申	화창할 pleasant; joyful; luxuriant, flourishing		창
	申旦	申旦	申旦	和暢	balmy, sunny; contented and happy	화창
				暢達	rapid growth; activity	창달
日 10 1369	暢	暢	暢	流暢	fluent	유창

榮	火	炏	炏	영화 glory, honor; flourishing; beautiful		영
	炏	熒	熒	榮華	glory, splendor	영화
				榮譽	honor; distinction	영예
木 10 1370	榮	榮	榮	榮光	honor, glory	영광

構	扌	木	栱	얽을 construct, compose; structure		구
	栱	栱	構	構想	envision, visualize	구상
				構成	constitute, organize, compose	구성
木 10 1371	構	構	構	構造	construct, build	구조

歌	哥	可	哥	노래	song; sing	가
	哥	哥	哥	歌謠	song, ballad	가요
				歌曲	tune, melody; song, aria	가곡
欠 10 1372	哥'	歌	歌	歌劇	opera; lyric drama	가극

滿	氵	氵	滿	찰	full; complete; satisfied	만
	滿	滿	滿	滿點	perfection; best mark, highest grade	만점
				滿員	capacity crowd	만원
水 11 1373	滿	滿	滿	滿足	satisfaction, contentment	만족

滴	氵	氵	滴	물방울	to drip; a drop	적
	滴	滴	滴	硯滴	water receptacle for use with an ink stone	연적
				餘滴	drippings	여적
水 11 1374	滴	滴	滴	滴水	drops of water	적수

漂	氵	氵	漂	뜰	float, drift	표
	漂	漂	漂	漂流	drift along, drift about	표류
				漂白	bleach	표백
水 11 1375	漂	漂	漂	浮漂	float	부표

漆	氵	十	木	옻	lacquer	칠
	柒	漆	漆	漆器	lacquerware	칠기
				漆工	painter, lacquerer	칠공
水 11 1376	漆	漆	漆	漆板	blackboard	칠판

漢	氵	艹	艹	한나라	Han Dynasty of China	한
	漢	漢	漢	漢文	classical Chinese, classical Korean	한문
				漢藥	Chinese medicine, herb medicine	한약
水 11 1377	漢	漢	漢	漢詩	Chinese poetry	한시

258

漏				샐	leak; drip; disclose; smuggle; funnel	루
水 11 1378				漏落 漏泄 漏電	omit, leave out disclose, leak, divulge short circuit (electricity leak)	누락 누설 누전

漁				고기잡을	catch fish; fish	어
水 11 1379				漁場 漁業 漁夫	fishing grounds fishing, the fishing industry fisherman	어장 어업 어부

漫				어수선할	overflow, spread, be diffused; far and wide	만
水 11 1380				漫談 漫畫 散漫	comedy routine; chitchat comic book, comic strip discursive, wandering, vague	만담 만화 산만

演				익힐	drill, exercise, practice; wide, widen, extend; perform	연
水 11 1381				演說 演劇 演士	deliver a speech, speak publicly drama; a play lecturer, public speaker	연설 연극 연사

漸				점점	gradually; flow; soak	점
水 11 1382				漸漸 漸次 漸進	gradually, by degrees gradually gradual progress	점점 점차 점진

漠				아득할	vast, boundless; sandy desert; indifferent	막
水 11 1383				沙漠 漠然 漠漠	a desert ambiguous, vague vast, boundless	사막 막연 막막

疑 疋 9 1384	ヒ ヒマ 矣	ヒヒ 矣コ 疑	矣 矣ヌ 疑	의심할 doubt, distrust, suspect 疑心 doubt; suspicion 疑訝다 mistrust, doubt 疑問 a question; interrogation; doubt		의 의심 의아 의문
獄 犬 10 1385	犭 猏 獄	犷 猏 獄	狢 狢 獄	감옥 prison; trial at law 監獄 prison, jail 地獄 Hades, hell 獄死 die in prison		옥 감옥 지옥 옥사
盡 皿 9 1386	ヨ 聿 盡	聿 肃 盡	肃 盡 盡	다할 all, entirely; exhaust; utmost 盡力 endeavor, render services 賣盡 sell out of 盡終日 all day long		진 진력 매진 진종일
監 皿 9 1387	⌐ 臣 監	戸 臣 監	臣 臣 監	감독할 oversee，manage; inspect 監督 director, superintendent; manage 監視 surveil; watch, inspect 監査 inspect; superintend		감 감독 감시 감사
碧 石 9 1388	王 珀 碧	王' 珀 碧	玏 珀 碧	푸를 green, blue; jade 碧梧桐 sultan's parasol (*firmiana platanifolia*) 碧溪 a blue stream 碧海 the blue sea, azure ocean		벽 벽오동 벽계 벽해
禍 示 9 1389	ネ ネ 禍	ネ 祸 禍	初 禍 禍	재앙 calamity 禍福 vicissitudes, fortune and misfortune 災禍 calamity, disaster 禍根 source of evil, root of misfortune		화 화복 재화 화근

| 福 示 9 1390 | 礻 礻 祠 福 禍 | 衤 衤 福 福 福 | 祚 祸 福 福 福 | 복
福利
祝福
福音 | happiness, prosperity, good luck; blessed
public welfare
blessing, bless
glad tidings; the Christian Gospel | 복
복리
축복
복음 |

| 種 禾 9 1391 | 千 秆 稆 種 | 禾 秆 稆 種 | 和 秆 稆 種 | 씨
種類
人種
種子 | seed, sow, plant; kind, sort
kind, variety
a human race; the human species
a seed; strain, breed | 종
종류
인종
종자 |

| 稱 禾 9 1392 | 千 秤 稱 | 禾 秤 稱 | 和 秤 稱 | 일컬을
稱讚
稱呼
稱頌 | declare, designate, call; price; weigh, estimate; suitable; raise
praise, speak highly of
title, name, designation
praise, compliment | 칭
칭찬
칭호
칭송 |

| 端 立 9 1393 | 亠 端 端 | 立 端 端 | 立 端 端 | 끝
極端
端正히
發端 | extreme, end; extremely; beginning; upright, correct
the farthest limit, the extremity, the extreme
correctly; neatly
start, begin | 단
극단
단정
발단 |

| 算 竹 8 1394 | 𥫗 筧 筧 | 𥫗 筧 算 | 竹 筧 算 | 수놓을
算出
計算
算術 | calculate, reckon; consider as; plan, scheme
calculate, compute
calculate; calculation for services (as in a restaurant)
arithmetic | 산
산출
계산
산술 |

| 管 竹 8 1395 | 𥫗 筦 管 | 𥫗 管 管 | 竹 管 管 | 대롱
管下
管理
主管 | tube, flute; govern
under the jurisdiction of, under the control of
administer, manage, supervise
superintend, manage | 관
관하
관리
주관 |

精	丷	半	米	정할	spirit; fine, delicate; essence, essential, unadulterated, refined; skill; extreme, extremely; secretions	정
	粗	粘	精	精神	mind, spirit, soul	정신
米 8 1396	精	精	精	精誠 精力	sincerity, a true heart vigor, energy, vitality	정성 정력

綠	幺	幺	糹	푸를	green	록
	綵	綷	綠	綠色 綠陰	green green of trees in early summer	녹색 녹음
糸 8 1397	綠	綠	綠	綠化	afforestation, planting trees and shrubs, beautification	녹화

綱	幺	幺	糹	벼리	large rope of a fishing net; tie; laws, principles	강
	納	納	網	大綱	in general, generally	대강
				綱領 三綱	general principle the 3 basic human relationships in Confucianism	강령 삼강
糸 8 1398	網	綱	綱			

維	幺	幺	糹	얽을	tie, hold fast; only, but	유
	紓	綷	緋	維持 維新	maintain reinvigorate, revitalize	유지 유신
糸 8 1399	維	維	維	纖維	textiles; fiber, strands	섬유

綿	幺	幺	糹	솜	cotton, the cotton plant	면
	絇	絇	絈	綿花 綿絲	cotton cotton thread	면화 면사
糸 8 1400	絹	綿	綿	綿密	detailed, minute; meticulous, careful	면밀

緊	臣	臤	臤	요긴할	important; urgent; prompt; tight, taught, strained	긴
	堅	堅	堅	緊急	urgent, pressing; an emergency	긴급
				緊張	tension, tenseness	긴장
糸 8 1401	緊	緊	緊	緊密	close (as a relationship); strict, stringent	긴밀

罰	四	四	罒	벌	punish, punishment, fine	벌
	罰	罰	罰	刑罰 punishment by law, penalty 罰金 a fine; a penalty 處罰 punish, impose penalty	형벌 벌금 처벌
网 9 1402	罰	罰	罰			

署	四	四	罒	관청서 public office, bureau; write, sign; acting, temporary appointment	서
	罝	署	署	署長 police chief; director of a government office	서장
网 9 1403	署	署	署	署名 signature 部署 place of duty, post	서명 부서

聞	門	門	門	들을 hear	문
	門	門	聞	醜聞 scandal 見聞 information, experiences, that seen and heard	추문 견문
耳 8 1404	聞	聞	聞	所聞 rumor, gossip, hearsay	소문

腐	广	庁	府	썩을 rotten; corrupt; worthless	부
	府	腐	腐	腐敗 rot, putrefication; corruption (as political)	부패
肉 8 1405	腐	腐	腐	腐蝕 rust, corrode; erode 腐心 vexed, worried; take pains, rack the brain	부식 부심

臺	士	吉	吉	집 tower, terrace, stage, platform, elevation	대
	臺	臺	臺	臺帳 ledger, register 臺詞 words spoken from the stage	대장 대사
至 8 1406	臺	臺	臺	土臺 foundation, basis, cornerstone	토대

舞	仁	午	無	춤출 dance; posture; brandish; fence	무
	無	舞	舞	舞臺 stage, arena 舞踊 dance, dancing	무대 무용
舛 8 1407	舞	舞	舞	舞蹈 dance, dancing	무도

263

蒙	亠	艹	艹	입을	cover, conceal; stupid; receive from a superior; meet with; Mongolia	몽
	芧	荸	荸	啓蒙	enlighten, educate	계몽
				蒙昧	unenlightened, uncivilized	몽매
艸 10 1408	蒙	蒙	蒙	蒙古	Mongolia	몽고

蒸	亠	艹	艹	찔	steam	증
	蒸	蒸	蒸	蒸氣	steam; vapor	증기
				蒸發	evaporate	증발
艸 10 1409	蒸	蒸	蒸	蒸溜水	distilled water	증류수

蒼	亠	艹	艹	푸를	green, blue	창
	苍	蒼	蒼	蒼白	pale, pallid	창백
				蒼空	blue heaven, blue sky	창공
艸 10 1410	蒼	蒼	蒼			

蓄	亠	艹	艹	쌓을	store up	축
	蓄	蓄	蓄	蓄電池	electric storage battery	축전지
				蓄積	stockpile, store up	축적
艸 10 1411	蓄	蓄	蓄	貯蓄	save (money)	저축

蓋	亠	艹	艹	덮을	to cover; cover, lid; hide	개
	蓋	蓋	蓋	覆蓋	a cover	복개
				蓋然性	probability	개연성
艸 10 1412	蓋	蓋	蓋			

蜜	宀	宓	宓	꿀	honey; sweet	밀
	蜜	蜜	蜜	蜜月	a honeymoon	밀월
				蜜酒	drink made from honey and buckwheat flour	밀주
虫 8 1413	蜜	蜜	蜜	蜜柑	tangerine, mandarin orange	밀감

裳 衣 8 1414			치마	skirt		상
			衣裳	clothes, clothing		의상
			紅裳	red-colored skirt		홍상

製 衣 8 1415			지을	make, construct		제
			製造	manufacture, make		제조
			製品	products, manufactured goods		제품
			製粉	mill, grind		제분

複 衣 9 1416			겹칠	double; repeat, reiterate		복
			複雜	complicated, tangled, knotty		복잡
			複寫	duplicate, reproduce, photocopy		복사
			複線	double line; double tracks		복선

認 言 7 1417			인정할	recognize; endure, bear; repress, hold back		인
			認定	recognize; acknowledge		인정
			認識	realize, recognize; perceive		인식
			是認	approve, endorse		시인

誌 言 7 1418			기록	to record; annals, official gazette		지
			誌面	page of a magazine, pages in a periodical		지면
			月刊誌	monthly magazine, a monthly		월간지
			日誌	diary, journal		일지

誘 言 7 1419			꾈	entice, induce, mislead		유
			誘惑	temptation, allurement		유혹
			誘引	induce, entice; allure, seduce		유인
			誘拐	abduct, kidnap		유괴

誠 言 7 1420	二 言 言 訁 訐 訮 訫 誠 誠	정성	sincere; true, honest; certainly	성
		精誠	earnest, sincere	정성
		忠誠	loyalty	충성
		誠意	good faith, honesty	성의

語 言 7 1421	二 言 言 訁 訝 語 誤 語 語	말씀	language; talk, words, phrases	어
		國語	national language; Korean	국어
		語調	tone ; accent	어조
		語感	feel for words, sensitivity for language	어감

誦 言 7 1422	二 言 言 訁 訝 訽 詢 誦 誦	외울	recite; intone; hum over; refrain, song	송
		暗誦	recite from memory	암송
		詠誦	recitation	영송
		朗誦	sonorous recitation	낭송

誤 言 7 1423	二 言 言 訂 誯 誯 誤 誤 誤	그릇	mistake, error; erroneous; bungle; miss	오
		誤解	misinterpret, misunderstand	오해
		錯誤	error, mistake	착오
		誤謬	mistake, error; fallacy	오류

說 言 7 1424	二 言 言 訁 訝 訝 詋 誯 說	말씀	say, speak	설
		달랠	persuade	세
		기쁠	happy	열
		說明	explain, elucidate	설명
		說教	preach	설교
		遊說	canvass, campaign	유세

豪 豕 7 1425	亠 亠 亩 亭 亭 豸 豪 豪 豪	호걸	brave, chivalrous	호
		豪傑	hero, gallant man, extraordinary man	호걸
		豪華	splendid, elegant	호화
		豪奢	enjoy the good life, luxuriate in	호사

貌	모양	form; face; manner, appearance	모
	貌襲	features, looks; shape, appearance	모습
豸 7	外貌	outward appearance; exterior aspects	외모
1426	容貌	facial features, looks	용모

賓	손님	visitor, guest	빈
	貴賓	honored guest, important visitor	귀빈
貝 7	來賓	guest, visitor	내빈
1427	賓客	honored guest	빈객

輕	가벼울	light in weight; frivolous, disrespectful	경
	輕率	frivolous, flippant	경솔
	輕視	slight, ignore	경시
車 7	輕音樂	light music	경음악
1428			

遙	멀	distant, remote; long	요
	逍遙	stroll, walk leisurely	소요
辵 10	遙遠	far, distant, remote	요원
1429			

遣	보낼	send; chase away	견
	派遣	dispatch, send	파견
辵 10	分遣隊	detachment, contingent	분견대
1430			

遠	멀	far, distant, remote; far-reaching; keep away from	원
	遠距離	long distance, long range	원거리
辵 10	遠大	far-reaching	원대
1431	遠洋	deep sea, ocean	원양

酸	厂	西	酉	실	sour; acid; distressed, grieved	산
	酚	酚	酚	酸素	oxygen	산소
				酸性	acidity	산성
酉 7 1432	酸	酸	酸	酸化	oxidize, oxygenate	산화

銃	𠆢	全	金	총	gun	총
	釒	釒	釷	銃殺	shoot to death; execute by shooting	총살
				拳銃	pistol	권총
金 6 1433	銃	銃	銃	銃傷	bullet wound	총상

銀	𠆢	全	金	은	silver; money; riches, treasure	은
	釒	釘	釘	銀行	a bank	은행
				銀色	silver color	은색
金 6 1434	銀	銀	銀	銀幕	silver screen; moviedom	은막

銘	𠆢	全	金	새길	engrave, carve	명
	釒	釣	釞	銘心	bear in mind, inscribe on the heart	명심
				銘記	bear in mind	명기
金 6 1435	銘	銘	銘	感銘	moved, deeply impressed, engraved on the feelings	감명

銅	𠆢	全	金	구리	copper; brass; bronze	동
	釗	釦	銅	銅錢	a copper coin	동전
				銅像	bronze statue	동상
金 6 1436	銅	銅	銅	銅鑛	copper mine	동광

閨	門	門	門	안방	women's quarters	규
	門	閨	閨	閨秀	unmarried young woman	규수
				閨房	boudoir; woman's living room	규방
門 6 1437	閨	閨	閨			

閣 門 6 1438	尸 門 閃 閣	月 閃 閣 閣	門 閂 閣 閣	누각 內閣 閣下 閣僚	pavilion; council chamber; vestibule; studio the cabinet; the government Your Excellency, His Excellency cabinet ministers	각 내각 각하 각료
際 阜 11 1439	阝 陘 際	阝 陘 際	阦 降 際	사귈 國際 交際	associate; time; occasion; border, limit international, international relationship associate with	제 국제 교제
障 阜 11 1440	阝 陪 隌	阝 陪 隌	阝 陪 障	막힐 障碍物 障害 支障	obstruct, screen; barricade obstacle, barrier obstruct, hinder impediment, hindrance, trouble	장 장애물 장해 지장
需 雨 6 1441	一 雫 霅	雨 雫 需	雫 雫 需	쓸 需要 需給 婚需	need, require; essential demand (as in supply and demand) supply and demand expenses essential to a marriage	수 수요 수급 혼수
頗 頁 5 1442	屮 皮 頗	皮 頗 頗	皮 頗 頗	자못 頗多 偏頗的	partial; rather abundant; a good many; quite frequently partiality, favoritism	파 파다 편파적
領 頁 5 1443	亼 領 領	今 領 領	令 領 領	거느릴 大統領 領土 領收證	lead, guide; receive chief executive, president (of a nation) territory (of a nation) receipt, voucher	령 대통령 영토 영수증

飽 食 5 1444	亽 今 食 食 食 飲 飽 飽 飽	배부를 be full from eating 飽和 be saturated 飽滿 satiated, full 飽食 sate the appetite; gorge, overeat	포 포화 포만 포식
飾 食 5 1445	亽 今 食 食 食 食 飲 飾 飾	꾸밀 adorn, adornment; ornament 裝飾 decorate, ornament, adorn 假飾 two-faced, hypocritical; pretend; dissimulate 修飾 decorate, ornament; embellish	식 장식 가식 수식
魂 鬼 10 1446	云 云 动 云勿 云由 云鬼 云鬼 魂 魂	혼 soul, spirit; wits 魂靈 the spirit, the soul 招魂 invoke the spirit of the deceased 鎭魂 repose of souls	혼 혼령 초혼 진혼
鳳 鳥 3 1447	几 凡 凡 凡 鳳 鳳 鳳 鳳 鳳	새 phoenix 鳳仙花 touch-me-not, a balsam 鳳凰 phoenix (mythical bird)	봉 봉선화 봉황
鳴 鳥 3 1448	口 叫 叱 呼 鳴 鳴 鳴 鳴 鳴	울 cry of a bird or animal 悲鳴 shriek; scream; cry in distress 共鳴 resonant, resonates; echo, chime in with 自鳴鐘 an alarm clock	명 비명 공명 자명종
鼻 鼻 0 1449	门 自 自 鳥 鼻 鼻 鼻 鼻 鼻	코 nose 鼻笑 sneeze 鼻孔 the nostrils	비 비소 비공

齊	亠 亠 亣 亦 瓶 瓶	나라	name of ancient Chinese state; even, regular, uniform	제
齊 0 1450	瓶 齊 齊	一齊	uniformly, equally; wholly; all at one time	일제
		齊唱	sing in unison	제창

15 Strokes

價	亻 亻 価 價 價 價	값	price; trade; merchant	가
		價格	price; cost	가격
人 13 1451	價 價 價	物價	prices, cost of goods	물가
		原價	original price; cost price	원가

儀	亻 亻 伴 佯 佯 佯	거동	deportment, manners; ceremony; usage; rule	의
		儀式	ceremony, ritual, rite	의식
		禮儀	courtesy, etiquette; propriety; formality	예의
人 13 1452	儀 儀 儀	儀仗隊	honor guards, guards of honor	의장대

儉	亻 亻 佥 僉 僉 儉	검소할	frugal; economical; temperate	검
		儉素	thrift, frugality	검소
		勤儉	diligence and frugality, thrift and industry	근검
人 13 1453	儉 儉 儉	儉約	frugality, economy	검약

億	亻 亻 位 倍 億 億	억	a hundred million	억
		億兆蒼生	the teeming millions, the masses, the people	억조창생
人 13 1454	億 億 億	億萬長者	a very rich man, a hundred-millionaire	억만장자

271

劇	上	庐	虍	심할	severe, intense; drama	극
	虐	虘	豦	劇場	a theater; a movie theater	극장
刀 13 1455	豦	豦刂	劇	喜劇	farce, comedy	희극
				劇的	theatrical, dramatic	극적

劍	스	合	合	칼	double-edged sword	검
	命	僉	僉	劍術	the art of swordsmanship	검술
刀 13 1456	僉	劍	劍	劍道	fencing, swordsmanship	검도
				寶劍	a valuable sword; formal dress sword	보검

墨	口	四	里	먹	ink; black, dark	묵
	里	黑	黑	白墨	chalk	백묵
土 12 1457	黑	墨	墨	墨畫	paintings done in Chinese ink	묵화
				墨紙	carbon paper; copying paper	묵지

增	土	圹	圹	더할	add to, increase, augment	증
	圹	塇	増	增加	increase, augment	증가
土 12 1458	增	增	增	增大	enlarge, increase	증대
				增産	increase production	증산

墮	阝	阝十	阼	떨어질 fall, sink		타
	阼	隋	隋	墮落	become degraded, become corrupted	타락
土 12 1459	隋	隋	墮			

墳	土	圵	坆	무덤	grave, mound; heap up; soil	분
	垆	墳	墳	墳墓	grave, tomb	분묘
土 12 1460	墳	墳	墳	墳土	earth over a tomb	분토
				古墳	old tomb, ancient mound	고분

寬	宀	宀	宵	너그러울 broad, spacious; generous; magnanimous		관
	宵	宵	寬	寬大 magnanimous, broad-minded		관대
宀 12 1461	寬	寬	寬	寬容 generously pardon, show leniency		관용
審	宀	宀	空	살필 investigate, examine; inquiry; judge		심
	宋	宋	宋	審査 judge, screen 審判 judge; referee		심사 심판
宀 12 1462	審	審	審	審問 interrogate, question		심문
寫	宀	宀	宫	베낄 trace, write, sketch; dispel, drain		사
	宮	寫	寫	寫眞 photograph 寫本 manuscript, handwritten work		사진 사본
宀 12 1463	寫	寫	寫	描寫 portray, describe, depict		묘사
層	尸	尸	屄	층 level, story, layer; degree; item, clause		층
	屄	屆	屚	層階 stairs, steps 高層 upper floors		층계 고층
尸 12 1464	層	層	層	層層 all layers, all stories		층층
履	尸	尺	屄	밟을 walk, walk on; shoe; actions; conduct		리
	屝	屝	屝	履行 execute, put into practice 履歷 personal history, curriculum vitae		이행 이력
尸 12 1465	履	履	履			
幣	小	沿	尙	돈 money; silk; gifts; wealth		폐
	尙'	敝	敝	紙幣 paper money; a bank note		지폐
				造幣 coinage, coin		조폐
巾 12 1466	敝	幣	幣	貨幣 money, currency		화폐

					넓을	broad, wide, extensive	광
廣	广	庁	庐		廣告	announce, advertise, publicize	광고
	庶	廗	庸		廣大	vast, immense	광대
广 12 1467	庸	廣	廣		廣範	extensive, far-reaching, broad	광범

					사당	shrine, temple	묘
廟	广	广	庐		廟堂	the government, the court (prior to 1910)	묘당
	盾	庫	廂		宗廟	ancestral shrine of the royal family of the Yi Dynasty	종묘
广 12 1468	廟	廟	廟				

					폐할	dispose of, dispense with; destroy; abrogate; waste	폐
廢	广	庐	庐				
	庶	廃	廃		廢止	abolish, repeal	폐지
					廢墟	a ruin	폐허
广 12 1469	廢	廢	廢		廢物	waste, refuse	폐물

					폐단	corruption, abuse; worn out; distressed	폐
弊	小	尚	尚		弊端	corrupt practices, abuses	폐단
	尚	敝	敝		弊習	bad habit; corrupt customs; evils	폐습
廾 12 1470	敝	弊	弊		語弊	faulty expression, misuse of words	어폐

					탄약	bullet; bounce, spring; pluck a stringed instrument	탄
彈	弓	引	弹				
	彈	彈	彈		彈藥	ammunition	탄약
					彈丸	bullet; shell; projectile	탄환
弓 12 1471	彈	彈	彈		彈壓	suppress, coerce	탄압

					그림자	shadow; image; reflection	영
影	日	日	昙				
	昌	景	景		影響	influence, effect	영향
					撮影	to photograph	촬영
彡 12 1472	景	影	影		幻影	a vision; a phantom	환영

德	彳	彳	彳	큰	virtue, goodness; power	덕
	徫	徫	德	德澤	kind concern; help, aid	덕택
				美德	grace of character, noble virtue	미덕
彳 12 1473	德	德	德	德望	reputation for virtue, high moral repute	덕망

徹	彳	彳	彳	통할	penetrate; intelligible; remove; recall; degrade	철
	徫	徫	徫	徹底	thorough, thoroughly	철저
				徹夜	stay up all night, keep vigil through the night	철야
彳 12 1474	徫	徫	徹	貫徹	penetrate, pierce; attain, accomplish	관철

徵	彳	彳	彳	부를	summon; conscript; levy, collect; seek, solicit; prove, verify	징
	徫	徫	徫	徵收	levy, collect	징수
				徵兵	conscript, draft	징병
彳 12 1475	徫	徫	徵	徵稅	collect taxes	징세

慕	艹	艹	芐	사모할	yearn, long for, desire; love, affection	모
	苩	莫	莫	思慕	long for, yearn for	사모
				追慕	cherish the memory of one who is deceased	추모
心 11 1476	慕	慕	慕	戀慕	love and yearn for, become attached to	연모

慶	广	庐	庐	경사	happiness, luck, good fortune; congratulate	경
	庐	庱	慶	慶事	a happy event, an event of happy fortune	경사
				慶祝	congratulation, felicitation	경축
心 11 1477	庼	慶	慶	國慶日	national holiday	국경일

慧	彐	彗	彗	지혜	wisdom; cleverness; wit	혜
	彗	彗	彗	智慧	wisdom, sagacity	지혜
				慧星	a comet	혜성
心 11 1478	慧	慧	慧	慧智	wisdom	혜지

慮 心 11 1479	卢 慮 慮	庐 虍 慮	虍 虙 慮	생각 考慮 憂慮 思慮	think; plan; anxiety; anxious consider, mull over concern, apprehension think, consider	려 고려 우려 사려
慾 心 11 1480	夕 谷 慾	父 欲 慾	谷 欲 慾	욕심 慾心 慾望 慾情	greedy, covetous; desire, lust, passion greed, covetousness desire; craving; ambition sexual desire, passion	욕 욕심 욕망 욕정
憂 心 11 1481	丆 頁 憂	百 憂 憂	百 憂 憂	근심할 憂鬱 憂患 憂慮	worry; grief; sad; melancholy depressed, gloomy anxiety; distress anxiety, concern	우 우울 우환 우려
慰 心 11 1482	尸 屌 慰	尼 尉 慰	尿 尉 慰	위로할 慰勞 慰安 慰問	console, comfort, soothe, pacify console, comfort console, comfort; amuse inquire after another's health, visit and show solicitude	위 위로 위안 위문
憎 心 12 1483	忄 忄 忄	忄 忄 憎	忄 憎 憎	미워할 憎惡 可憎	hate, detest detest, abhor contemptible, despicable	증 증오 가증
憐 心 12 1484	忄 忄 憐	忄 憐 憐	忄 憐 憐	불쌍히여길 可憐 哀憐	have compassion for, pity; sympathize pathetic, pitiful piteous, touching	련 가련 애련

憫	忄	忙	忙	딱할	pity, sympathize; grieve	민
	憫	憫	憫	憫惘	embarrassed, sorry, sad	민망
心 12 1485	憫	憫	憫	憐憫	compassion, mercy	연민

憤	忄	忭	忙	분할	very angry; exasperated; zeal	분
	憤	憤	憤	憤怒	wrath, fury	분노
				憤慨	rage; indignation	분개
心 12 1486	憤	憤	憤	憤激	exasperated; enraged	분격

播	扌	扩	拉	뿌릴	sow; disseminate	파
	抵	採	搓	傳播	propagate	전파
				播遷	royal refuge	파천
手 12 1487	播	播	播	播種	sow, plant seeds	파종

敵	亠	亠	商	원수	enemy; to oppose	적
	商	商	商	敵軍	enemy forces	적군
				敵陣	enemy positions	적진
攴 11 1488	敵	敵	敵	敵兵	enemy soldiers	적병

數	口	吕	昌	수	a number; count; frequently; some; fate, destiny	수
	婁	婁	婁	數量	quantity, volume	수량
				數學	mathematics	수학
攴 11 1489	數	數	數	運數	fortune, luck	운수

暴	口	旦	昇	사나울	cruel, violent	포(폭)
	昇	暴	暴	드러낼	expose, be exposed; dry in the sun	폭
				暴擊	bombing attack, to bomb	폭격
				暴風	gale, violent wind	폭풍
日 11 1490	暴	暴	暴	暴惡	barbarous, ruthless	포악

暮	一 艹 苩 苩 莫 莫 莫 莫 莫 莫	저물	evening, sunset; end of a period of time	모
日 11 1491		歲暮 朝令暮改	end of the year unpredictable, issue an order in the morning and change it that night	세모 조령모개
暫	一 亘 車 車 斬 斬 斬 暫 暫 暫	잠시	a short time, a short while	잠
日 11 1492		暫時 暫間 暫定	short time, short while, temporarily a little while, a moment, a minute tentative, provisional	잠시 잠간 잠정
樣	才 木' 栏 样 样 样 栐 様 様 様	모양	kind, manner, style; pattern, sample, example	양
木 11 1493		模樣 樣式 各樣	shape, pattern; design form, style variety, a variety of	모양 양식 각양
概	才 术 栶 栶 栶 栶 椴 椴 概	대개	generally, all in all, for the most part	개
木 11 1494		大概 概要	generally, in general outline, summary	대개 개요
標	才 本 栖 栖 栖 標 標 標 標	표	mark; signal; notice, sign, signboard	표
木 11 1495		標準 標本 標語	standard, norm a specimen (as in natural sciences) slogan, motto	표준 표본 표어
樓	才 朾 栖 栖 栖 椚 樓 樓 樓	다락	tower; upper story; pavilion	루
木 11 1496		樓閣 望樓 樓上	tall building, many-storied building watchtower upstairs; balcony	누각 망루 누상

樂	𠂊	白	𢇍
	𢆉	𢆫	樂
木 11 1497	樂	樂	樂

즐길 pleasure, pleased, enjoy 락
풍류 music 악
좋아할 delight in, like 요

樂器 musical instrument 악기
樂山 enjoy mountaineering 요산
快樂 pleasure, delight 쾌락

模	扌	村	柑
	栉	栉	槽
木 11 1498	槽	模	模

본뜰 pattern, mould; style; example 모

模樣 shape, form; pattern, design 모양
模範 model, pattern; paragon 모범
模型 model, pattern 모형

歎	艹	芐	苦
	莒	菓	菓
欠 11 1499	歎	歎	歎

탄식할 sigh 탄

歎息 sigh; lament, deplore 탄식
歎服 admiration 탄복
歎聲 sigh, sigh of admiration; groan 탄성

潛	氵	氵	氵
	氵	潜	潜
水 12 1500	潜	潜	潛

잠길 hide; submerge 잠

潛水 dive; submerge 잠수
潛在 potential; latent 잠재
潛伏 conceal oneself; dormant, latent 잠복

潤	氵	氵	氵
	潤	潤	潤
水 12 1501	潤	潤	潤

불을 shining, sleek, glossy; moisten; enrich 윤

潤澤 lustrous; abundant 윤택
潤氣 luster, gloss 윤기
潤滑 smooth, lubricious 윤활

潭	氵	氵	氵
	氵	潭	潭
水 12 1502	潭	潭	潭

못 pool, lake; deep 담

潭陽 county in South Chŏlla Province 담양

潔				깨끗할 clean, pure		**결**
				純潔	purity; innocence	순결
				淸潔	clean; a cleanup, a purge	청결
				潔白	pure, innocent	결백
水 12 1503						

潮				밀물	the tide	조
				潮水	the tides, tide water	조수
				潮流	tidal current; current	조류
				思潮	drift of public opinion; trend of thinking	사조
水 12 1504						

熟				익을	ripe; cooked; prepared, manufactured; experienced, accustomed to; intimate	숙
				熟練	skillful, dexterous	숙련
				熟考	consider, deliberate	숙고
火 11 1505				熟達	proficient, skillful	숙달

熱				더울	hot; heat; fever	**열**
				熱烈	fervent, fiery	열렬
				熱心	enthusiasm, earnestness	열심
				熱意	enthusiasm, zeal	열의
火 11 1506						

畿				왕터	royal domain; capital area	기
				京畿道 Kyŏnggi Province		경기도
田 10 1507						

盤				쟁반	tray, plate, dish	**반**
				小盤	small dining table; tray	소반
				盤石	rock, crag	반석
				音盤	phonograph record	음반
皿 10 1508						

確				확실할 definite, sure	확
				確實 certain, sure; trustworthy	확실
				確信 believe firmly, be convinced of	확신
石 10 1509				確認 confirm; affirm	확인

穀				곡식 grain, corn	곡
				穀食 grain, cereals	곡식
				穀物 cereals, grains	곡물
禾 10 1510				穀倉 granary; district rich in grain	곡창

稿				원고 manuscript; grain stalks; straw	고
				原稿 manuscript; a draft	원고
				寄稿 contribute, submit (a manuscript)	기고
禾 10 1511				稿料 payment for a manuscript	고료

稻				벼 paddy, rice growing in the field	도
				稻熱病 riceplant fever	도열병
禾 10 1512				稻作 rice culture, farming rice	도작

窮				궁할 poor; exhausted	궁
				窮理 study the laws of nature; ponder	궁리
				窮極 final, ultimate	궁극
穴 10 1513				窮乏 poor, destitute	궁핍

節				마디 bamboo joint; section, chapter, verse; token; time, season; festival; moderation, restraint	절
				節次 procedure	절차
				節約 conserve, cut down on	절약
竹 9 1514				節制 moderation, restraint	절제

範	⺮	⺮	竺	법	law, rule; custom; pattern, model	범
	笁	笁	笪	範圍	scope, extent	범위
				示範	model, sample	시범
竹 9	軍	範	範	規範	rule; standard, norm	규범
1515						

篇	⺮	⺮	竺	책	book	편
	竺	笢	笢	長篇	long work, lengthy book	장편
				玉篇	character dictionary	옥편
竹 9	篤	篇	篇	篇首	the first page of a book	편수
1516						

練	幺	幺	糸一	익힐	practice, drill; select	련
	糸ヲ	綿	綿	訓練	train, drill; practice	훈련
				洗練	polishe, refine	세련
糸 9	綷	練	練	練習	practice, drill	연습
1517						

緒	幺	幺	糸十	실마리	the end of a ball of thread; clue; connect	서
	糸十	緂	緂	情緒	emotion, sentiment	정서
				端緒	commencement, beginning; a clue	단서
糸 9	緒	緒	緒	緒論	introduction, prefatory remarks	서론
1518						

緣	幺	幺	糸ㄅ	인연	affinity, connection; destiny; cause, reason; hem, border	연
	緣	綠	緣	因緣	affinity; origin; karma, fate	인연
				緣分	predestined tie; relationship; marriage	연분
糸 9	緣	緣	緣	緣故	reason, cause; relationship, tie-in	연고
1519						

線	幺	幺	糸'	줄	thread, line, wire, ribbon; clue; fuse; length	선
	糸力	綿	綿	直線	straight line	직선
				曲線	curved line	곡선
糸 9	綿	線	線	電線	electric wire, telephone cord	전선
1520						

緩 糸 9 1521	幺 糸 綏	糸 絆 緩	糸 絲 緩	늘어질 slow, tardy, leisurely, easily, gradually; delay; neglect; retard	완
				緩和 mitigate, ease	완화
				緩急 slow and fast; tempo	완급
				緩慢 dull, listless	완만

緯 糸 9 1522	幺 結 繪	幺 絡 緯	幼 結 緯	씨줄 parallels of latitude; transverse lines; woof of a web; fringe, tassels	위
				緯度 latitude	위도
				經緯 longitude and latitude; warp and woof; details	경위
				緯線 a parallel of latitude	위선

編 糸 9 1523	幺 糸 絹	幺 糸 編	糸 糸 編	얽을 weave; arrange; compile	편
				編輯 edit; compile	편집
				編成 organize, form	편성
				編曲 arrange music	편곡

罷 网 10 1524	罒 罪 罷	四 罪 罷	罒 罪 罷	파할 stop, finish	파
				罷業 go out of business; go on strike	파업
				罷免 dismiss, discharge, fire	파면
				罷場 conclude; close (as a market, examination)	파장

膚 肉 11 1525	上 虍 膚	卢 虘 膚	虎 膚 膚	살갗 skin; flesh	부
				皮膚 the skin	피부
				皮膚科 dermatology	피부과

蓮 艸 11 1526	屮 昔 革	屮 萱 蓮	芒 革 蓮	연꽃 lotus; waterlily	연
				蓮根 lotus root	연근
				蓮花 lotus blossom	연화
				蓮池 lotus pond	연지

蝶 虫 9 1527	中 虫卄 蝴	虫 虫也 蝶	虫一 虫也 蝶	나비 蜂蝶 胡蝶 黃蝶	butterfly bees and butterflies a butterfly a yellow butterfly	접 봉접 호접 황접
衝 行 9 1528	彳 徍 徍	彳 徆 徍	行 徆 衝	찌를 衝突 衝動 衝擊	collide, rush against; insult; thoroughfare collision; quarreling incite, stir up shock, trauma; strike against	충 충돌 충동 충격
誰 言 8 1529	亠 訁 訨	言 訏 誰	言 誰 誰	누구 誰謀 誰何	who; anyone so and so, certain persons who; what person; a challenge (who is there?)	수 수모 수하
課 言 8 1530	亠 言 譚	言 訌 課	言 記 課	공부 課稅 課題 課長	a lesson; a section, a department, an office taxes, duties subject, theme; a problem, a question section chief	과 과세 과제 과장
談 言 8 1531	亠 言 談	言 診 談	言 談 談	말씀 面談 談話 談判	chat, converse have an interview with converse with, talk to negotiate, bargain	담 면담 담화 담판
調 言 8 1532	亠 訓 調	言 訂 調	言 調 調	고를 調査 調節 調和	harmonize; investigate investigate adjust, regulate harmony, accord	조 조사 조절 조화

| 諒 言 8 1533 | 言 言 言 諒 諒 諒 諒 諒 諒 | 살필 | consider; excuse; faithful; believe | 량 |
| | | 諒解 諒察 諒知 | understanding
sympathetic understanding, consideration
understanding, appreciation | 양해
양찰
양지 |

| 請 言 8 1534 | 言 言 言 請 請 請 請 請 請 | 청할 | request; invite | 청 |
| | | 要請 請求 請婚 | request, demand
claim, request
propose marriage | 요청
청구
청혼 |

| 論 言 8 1535 | 言 言 言 訟 訟 論 論 論 論 | 논의할 | discuss; argue; speak of; arrange; reason; essay, article | 론 |
| | | 論議 討論 論文 | discuss; debate
debate, discuss
thesis; dissertation | 논의
토론
논문 |

| 賦 貝 8 1536 | 貝 貝 貝 貯 斯 賦 賦 賦 賦 | 지을 | levy; taxes; diffuse; give, bestow | 부 |
| | | 賦課 賦與 天賦 | levy, impose
contribution, contribute
natural endowment, native ability | 부과
부여
천부 |

| 賞 貝 8 1537 | 小 尚 尚 尚 尚 尚 賞 賞 賞 | 상줄 | reward, prize, award; enjoy, appreciate; praise | 상 |
| | | 賞狀 鑑賞 賞金 | certificate of merit
enjoy, appreciate
award, prize | 상장
감상
상금 |

| 賢 貝 8 1538 | 臣 臣 臣又 賢 賢 賢 賢 賢 賢 | 어질 | worthy; wise | 현 |
| | | 賢明 賢母 賢淑 | wise, sagacious
wise mother
have wisdom and virtue (of women) | 현명
현모
현숙 |

285

賜 貝 8 1539	刖 貝刂 賜	月 貝刂 賜	貝 貝旦 賜	줄
				下賜
				賜死
				
				賜藥
					bestow, confer upon an inferior
					grant, bestow (by the king)
					present the poison with
					   which the condemned
					   committed suicide
					royal bestowment of
					   poison as a death penalty
						사
						하사
						사사
						
						사약

賤 貝 8 1540	刀 貯 賤	月 賤 賤	貝 賤 賤	천할 賤待 賤人 賤薄	mean; cheap; despise treat with contempt man of humble origins shallow, superficial	천 천대 천인 천박
賣 貝 8 1541	士 壱 賣	吉 壽 賣	高 壽 賣	팔 賣買 競賣 賣店	sell; show off buy and sell; deal, trade sell at auction shop, retail outlet	매 매매 경매 매점
質 貝 8 1542	⺮ 竹 筲	竹 筲 質	竹 筲 質	바탕 質疑 質的 人質	nature, disposition; substance, matter question, interrogate qualitative a hostage	질 질의 질적 인질

趣 走 8 1543	土 起 趜	丰 赴 趣	走 走 趣	취미
				
				趣味
				趣旨
				
				趣向
					pleasure, delight; taste;
					   bias, tendency; meaning,
					   intent, purpose
					interest; hobby
					gist, substance;
					   objective, purpose
					taste, interest
						취
						
						취미
						취지
						
						취향

踏 足 8 1544	口 趼 跡	무 跊 踏	足 跁 踏	밟을 踏査 踏襲 踏步	tread, walk survey, explore the prospects follow, follow in the steps of marking time in place	답 답사 답습 답보

踐	口	呈	足	밟을 trample; tramp	천
	践	跬	践	實踐 execute, put into practice	실천
足 8 1545	踐	踐	踐		

輩	ㅋ	킈	非	무리 generation, age-group	배
	非	辈	辈	輩出 appear in succession	배출
				先輩 senior, one who preceded another (as in university)	선배
車 8 1546	辈	辈	輩	後輩 junior, one who followed another (as in university)	후배

輝	ㅄ	半	光	빛날 bright	휘
	光	焰	焰	光輝 brilliance, splendor	광휘
				輝煌燦爛 resplendent, brilliant	휘황찬란
車 8 1547	焰	輝	輝		

輪	二	百	車	바퀴 wheel; revolve, revolution	륜
	軒	軒	輪	輪廓 contours of the human body; an outline	윤곽
				輪轉機 rotary press	윤전기
車 8 1548	輪	輪	輪	輪番制 the system of working by shifts	윤번제

適	亠	产	商	맞을 to suit; pleasant, agreeable	적
	商	商	商	適當 suitable, appropriate	적당
				適合 suitable, compatible	적합
辶 11 1549	商	適	適	適切 appropriate	적절

遷	二	西	西	옮길 move, shift	천
	栗	栗	署	遷都 transfer the seat of government, move the capital	천도
辶 11 1550	遷	遷	遷	左遷 downgrade, demote	좌천

15 strokes

醉	西 西 西 酉 酉 酉 酉 酉 酉	취할	become intoxicated	취
酉 8 1551		醉中 醉氣 醉興	be drunk inebriation, intoxication joy of intoxication, fun of being drunk	취중 취기 취흥

銳	公 牟 金 釒 釒 釒 鉛 鉛 銳	날카로울	sharp, sharp-pointed, acute; zealous; valiant	예
金 7 1552		銳敏 銳利 銳氣	sharp, quick-witted sharp; keen vigor, dash, ardor	예민 예리 예기

隣	阝 阝 阝 阝 隣 隣 隣 隣 隣	이웃	neighbor; near to; connected	린
阜 12 1553		隣近 隣接 善隣	vicinity, neighborhood adjacent, contiguous good neighbors, friendly relationship	인근 인접 선린

養	丷 羊 羊 美 养 养 養 養 養	기를	rear, raise, care for, nourish; support, maintain	양
食 6 1554		養分 敎養 養成	nutrients; nutritional elements culture, refinement bring up, foster, train	양분 교양 양성

髮	下 트 長 髟 髟 髮 髮 髮 髮	터럭	hair; the human head	발
髟 5 1555		理髮 毛髮 散髮	haircut hair dishevelled hair	이발 모발 산발

齒	止 步 步 齿 齒 齒 齒 齒 齒	이	teeth; age; seniority	치
齒 0 1556		齒藥 蟲齒 齒牙	toothpaste caries, tooth decay tooth	치약 충치 치아

288

16 Strokes

儒 人 14 1557	亻	亻⁻	儒
	儒	儒	儒
	儒	儒	儒

선비 scholar, Confucian scholar, Confucianist; learned 유

儒教 Confucianism 유교
儒學 Confucianism 유학
儒生 Confucian scholar; student of Confucianism 유생

噫 口 13 1558	口	口⁻	口⁻
	吟	噫	噫
	噫	噫	噫

탄식할 sigh; titter 희
트림할 burp, belch 애

器 口 13 1559	口	叩	哭
	哭	器	器
	器	器	器

그릇 vessel, dish; implement; organ 기

食器 tableware 식기
器具 utensil, implement; fixture 기구
大器 a large vessel; a great talent 대기

壁 土 13 1560	尸	启	启`
	启⁻	启	辟
	辟	辟	壁

벽 wall; cliff; partition 벽

壁欌 wall closet, cupboard 벽장
壁畫 mural, fresco 벽화
壁紙 wall paper 벽지

墻 土 13 1561	土	圤	圤
	圤	坺	墻
	墻	墻	墻

담 wall, fence 장
墻壁 wall, fence; barrier 장벽

壇				제단	altar		단
				祭壇	altar		제단
				壇上	on the platform		단상
土 13 1562				文壇	literary world, literary circles		문단
奮				떨칠	rouse; spread the wings; impetuous; determined		분
				奮鬪	struggle, make strenuous efforts		분투
				奮發	exert oneself, put forth efforts		분발
大 13 1563				興奮	arouse, stimulate		흥분
學				배울	learning		학
				學校	school		학교
				學生	student, pupil		학생
子 13 1564				學術	learning, scholarship		학술
導				인도할	lead, guide		도
				引導	guide, lead		인도
				先導	precede, guide		선도
寸 13 1565				指導	instruction, direction		지도
憲				법	law; constitution		헌
				憲法	constitution; constitutional law		헌법
				憲章	constitution; charter		헌장
心 12 1566				憲兵	military police		헌병
憩				쉴	to rest		게
				休憩	recess, break, rest		휴게
心 12 1567				休憩室	lounge		휴게실

290

憶	忄	忄	忄	생각할	reflect upon; recall, remember	억
	愔	愔	憶	記憶	recall, remember	기억
心 13 1568	憶	憶	憶	追憶	reminisce, recollect	추억

戰	口	吅	門	싸움	war, battle; tremble	전
	甼	單	單	戰爭	war	전쟁
				戰鬪	combat, firefight	전투
戈 12 1569	戰	戰	戰	戰時	wartime	전시

擇	扌	扩	扪	가릴	select, choose	택
	押	押	擇	選擇	choose, select	선택
				揀擇	select; selection of a spouse for a king or crown prince	간택
手 13 1570	擇	擇	擇	採擇	adopt; pick	채택

操	扌	扩	扣	잡을	grasp; manage; restrain; exercise, drill	조
	押	揔	揔	操心	careful, cautious	조심
				操縱	steer, pilot; manipulate	조종
手 13 1571	撑	撑	操	操作	operate, manage, handle	조작

擔	扌	扩	扩	멜	carry	담
	抬	擔	擔	擔當	be in charge of	담당
				擔保	security, collateral	담보
手 13 1572	擔	擔	擔	擔任	take charge of	담임

據	扌	扩	护	의거할	depend on; take in the hands; occupy, take possession	거
	护	掳	掳	依據	depend on, based upon	의거
				根據	base, foundation	근거
手 13 1573	據	據	據	據點	base of operations	거점

整				정돈할	set in order, put right, repair, adjust; whole, in total	정
支 12 1574				整頓	put in order	정돈
				整理	arrange, adjust	정리
				整備	maintain, keep in order	정비

曉				새벽	dawn; understand	효
日 12 1575				曉星	morning star; a rarity	효성
				曉鐘	morning bells	효종

曆				책력	calculate; calendar	력
日 12 1576				陽曆	the solar calendar	양력
				陰曆	the lunar calendar	음력

樹				나무	tree; plant	수
木 12 1577				樹木	tree, trees	수목
				樹立	establish, found	수립
				街路樹	trees planted along streets	가로수

橋				다리	bridge	교
木 12 1578				鐵橋	railway bridge; iron bridge	철교
				架橋	bridge-building	가교
				陸橋	overpass; footbridge	육교

機				틀	loom; mechanism, machine; airplane; opportunity; secret	기
木 12 1579				機械	machine, machinery	기계
				機會	opportunity, chance	기회
				機動性	mobility	기동성

				가로	horizontal, crosswise, sidewise; perverse; unreasonable; unexpected	횡
横	才	扩	枏			
	棤	楷	横	横暴	arrogant, tyrannical	횡포
				横領	usurp; embezzle	횡령
木 12 1580	横	横	横	横書	write horizontally	횡서

				지날	pass through; in order; calendar; calculate	력
歷	厂	斤	麻			
	厤	厤	厤	歷史	history	역사
				歷代	successive; generation after generation	역대
止 12 1581	厤	歷	歷	履歷書	personal history statement	이력서

				못	pond; marsh; damp; enrich, fertilize; glossy	택
澤	氵	氵	沪			
	沤	澤	澤	光澤	luster, shine	광택
				惠澤	a favor, benevolence	혜택
水 13 1582	澤	澤	澤			

				흐릴	muddy	탁
濁	氵	氵	氵			
	沪	泗	渦	濁酒	coarse fermented rice wine, *makkŏlli*	탁주
				濁流	muddy stream, turbid water	탁류
水 13 1583	濁	濁	濁	混濁	muddy, turbid	혼탁

				과격할	violent; rouse; intimidate	격
激	氵	氵	泊			
	泊	激	激	過激	extreme, violent, radical	과격
				激勵	encourage, cheer on	격려
水 13 1584	激	激	激	激甚	severe, intense	격심

				짙을	dense; deep; dark; thick, strong	농
濃	氵	氵	曲			
	曲	濃	濃	濃厚	thick, dense	농후
				濃度	density; compactness	농도
水 13 1585	濃	濃	濃	濃霧	dense fog	농무

燃	小	火	炒	불탈 burn		연
	炒一	炒然	炒然	燃燒 burn, catch fire, ignite 燃料 fuel 可燃 combustible		연소 연료 가연
火 12 1586	燃	燃	燃			

燒	小	火+	火土	불사를 burn; heat; roast, bake; fever		소
	炸	火圭	烠	燒酒 a cheap distilled liquor 燒失 be destroyed by fire		소주 소실
火 12 1587	燒	燒	燒			

燈	小	炒	炒'	등불 lantern, lamp; light bulb		등
	燃	燈	燈	電燈 electric light 燈火 lamp light, light 燈臺 lighthouse; beacon		전등 등화 등대
火 12 1588	燈	燈	燈			

燕	廿	廿	苗	제비 a swallow		연
	苗	莊	燕	燕尾服 swallowtailed coat, evening coat		연미복
火 12 1589	燕	燕	燕			

獨	犭	狎	犸	홀로 alone; only; Germany		독
	狎	獨	獨	獨奏 solo, recital 獨裁 dictatorship; autocracy 獨身 celibacy; bachelorhood		독주 독재 독신
犬 13 1590	獨	獨	獨			

磨	广	庁	床	갈 grind, rub, sharpen		마
	麻	麻	麻	磨鍊 plan; prepare 研磨 drill, polish, improve 磨勘 deadline; close, conclude		마련 연마 마감
石 11 1591	磨	磨	磨			

294

積 千禾禾 秆積積 積積積 禾 11 1592	쌓을 store up, amass	적
	積立金 reserve fund, fixed reserve	적립금
	積極的 positive, constructive	적극적
	積載 load; carry	적재

篤 ⺮竹竹 竺笁筥 篤篤篤 竹 10 1593	두터울 true, sincere	독
	篤實 sincere, earnest	독실
	篤志 charity, benevolence; zeal, ardor	독지
	敦篤 sincere, simple and honest	돈독

築 ⺮竹竹 筑筑築 築築築 竹 10 1594	쌓을 build up, stack up; beat down earth	축
	築臺 built-up ground, an elevation	축대
	建築 construct, build	건축
	增築 build on, extend, enlarge	증축

糖 ⺉半米 粇粎粘 糖糖糖 米 10 1595	사탕 candy, sugar	당(탕)
	糖尿病 diabetes	당뇨병
	砂糖 candy, sweets	사탕
	雪糖 sugar	설탕

縣 日目旦 県県県 縣縣縣 糸 9 1596	고을 district, subprefecture	현

興 ⺀印印 冏冏冏 興興興 日 9 1597	일어날 arise; prosperous; enjoyment, fun	흥
	興味 enjoyable, interesting	흥미
	興奮 excite, arouse, stimulate	흥분
	復興 revival; resurgence	부흥

295

蔬 艸 12 1598	宀	艹	宀	나물	vegetables, food	소
	疋	蔬	蔬	蔬菜	vegetables, greens	소채
	蔬	蔬	蔬			
蔽 艸 12 1599	艹	艹	茐	가릴	conceal; shade, darken	폐
	蔽	蔽	蔽	掩蔽	concealment	엄폐
	蔽	蔽	蔽	遮蔽	cover, covering	차폐
螢 虫 10 1600	炒	炒	炊	반딧불	glowworm	형
	燚	燚	燈	螢光	fluorescent light	형광
	螢	螢	螢	螢光燈	a fluorescent lamp	형광등
				螢雪	glowworms and snow (source of light for indigent students), study diligently	형설
衛 行 10 1601	彳	行	佈	방위할	guard, protect; military station, military escort	위
	徍	衛	衛			
	衛	衛	衛	衛星	a satellite	위성
				衛生	sanitation, hygiene	위생
				守衛	a guard; a janitor	수위
親 見 9 1602	亠	立	辛	어버이	parents; intimate, close; related	친
	亲	新	親	親舊	friend	친구
	親	親	親	親切	kind, helpful	친절
				兩親	parents	양친
諸 言 9 1603	言	言	言	모두	all, every	제
	計	諸	諸	諸島	archipelago	제도
	諸	諸	諸	諸國	many countries, various countries	제국
				諸般	all, all kinds	제반

諾 言 9 1604	亠 言 諕 諕	言 言 諾 諾	言 諆 諾 諾	허락할 permit; respond; promise 許諾 permit, approve 承諾 agree, assent 快諾 hearty consent, 　　　ready permission	락 (낙) 허락 승낙 쾌락
謀 言 9 1605	亠 計 諆	言 諆 謀	言 諆 謀	꾀할 scheme, plot; devise, 　　　contrive 謀略 stratagem, scheme 謀叛 revolt, rebel; plot, conspire 謀利輩 a profiteer	모 모략 모반 모리배
謁 言 9 1606	亠 訂 謁	言 謁 謁	言 謁 謁	뵐 visit a superior 拜謁 audience with a superior 謁見 audience with a king	알 배알 알현
謂 言 9 1607	亠 訂 謂	言 謂 謂	言 謂 謂	이를 speak of, say, called, 　　　styled 所謂 so-called 可謂 as can truly be said; 　　　so to speak, as it were	위 소위 가위
豫 豕 9 1608	豸 豵 豫	豵 豵 豫	豵 豫 豫	미리 beforehand, prior; prepare 豫備 reserve; spare; preparation 豫告 advance notice 豫防 prevent, preventive	예 예비 예고 예방
賴 貝 9 1609	曰 軇 軇	束 軇 軇	軇 軇 賴	의지할 trust, rely on; 　　　repudiate; shameless 依賴 rely on, depend on; 　　　entrust 信賴 trust, put faith in 無賴漢 hoodlum, rowdy	뢰 의뢰 신뢰 무뢰한

輪 車 9 1610	曰 軷 輪	亘 軡 輪	車 軡 輸	보낼 輸出 輸入 輸送	send, transport, introduce; pay tribute; offering; lose; be beaten, exhausted export import; introduce transport	수 수출 수입 수송
辨 辛 9 1611	亠 剃 剃	立 剃 剃	辛 剃 辨	분별할 辨明 辨償 辨濟	distinguish between, discriminate vindicate, exculpate compensation; reparation repay	변 변명 변상 변제
遲 辵 12 1612	尸 屖 犀	尺 屋 遲	屖 犀 遲	더딜 遲滯 遲刻 遲遲不進	slow; tardy, late defer, delay late, behind time progress at a snail's pace	지 지체 지각 지지부진
選 辵 12 1613	巳 맭 巽	맫 巽 選	맫 巽 選	가릴 選擧 選手 當選	select, choose; choice election, elect member of an athletic team, a player be elected; be selected	선 선거 선수 당선
遵 辵 12 1614	丷 酋 尊	产 尊 遵	酋 尊 遵	좇을 遵守 遵法 遵行	follow, obey; honor observe, comply with abide by law follow rules, follow orders	준 준수 준법 준행
遺 辵 12 1615	中 青 貴	虫 貴 遺	貴 遺 遺	끼칠 遺物 遺傳 遺書	bequeath, hand down; forget, neglect; loose relics, remains heredity; inheritance posthumous writings, work left by a dead author	유 유물 유전 유서

298

錄 金 8 1616	스 全 金 釒 釒 釸 釸 錄 錄	기록할 to record, make an entry; choose 記録 to record, a record 録音 tape record, record sounds 會議録 minutes, proceedings	록 기록 녹음 회의록
鋼 金 8 1617	스 全 金 釒 鋼 鋼 鋼 鋼 鋼	강철 steel; strong, hard; diamond 鋼鐵 steel	강 강철
錯 金 8 1618	스 全 余 釒 釗 錯 錯 錯 錯	그르칠 wrong, mistaken 錯誤 error, mistake 錯覺 hallucination, optical illusion 錯雜 confused; complicated, involved	착 착오 착각 착잡
錢 金 8 1619	스 全 余 釒 錢 錢 錢 錢 錢	돈 money, coppers, coins 金錢 cash, money; gold coins 銅錢 copper coins 口錢 fee, commission	전 금전 동전 구전
錦 金 8 1620	스 全 余 釒 釘 鉑 鉑 鎬 錦	비단 thin silk brocade 錦繡 brocades and embroidery; rich scenary 錦衣 silk brocade clothing 錦繡江山 land of embroidered rivers and mountains; beautiful Korea	금 금수 금의 금수강산
險 阜 13 1621	阝 阝 阽 阽 險 險 險 險 險	험할 rugged, dangerous; narrow pass 險惡 rough, rugged; serious, grave 險談 slander, calumny 險難 difficulty, danger	험 험악 험담 험난

隨	阝	阝ナ	阝ナ		따를	follow, accord with; accompany, together; forthwith, instantly; subsequently	수
	阝ナ	隋	隋		隨筆家	essayist	수필가
阜 13 1622	隋	隋	隨		隨時	as occasion arises; any time	수시
					隨行	accompany on a trip	수행

靜	‡	丰	青		고요	quiet, peaceful	정
	青	靜	靜		動靜	movements; development; state of things	동정
青 8 1623	靜	靜	靜		靜肅	silent, quiet	정숙
					安靜	tranquil, quiet	안정

頭	口	豆	豆		머리	head; first, top	두
	豆	頭	頭		頭目	leader, prime mover	두목
					先頭	the head; the lead, the van	선두
頁 7 1624	頭	頭	頭		頭痛	headache	두통

頻	止	꾸	步		자주	frequent; repeated; incessant; urgent, hurried	빈
	步	頻	頻		頻繁	repeated; incessant	빈번
					頻發	occur frequently, be frequent	빈발
頁 7 1625	頻	頻	頻		頻度數	frequency of occurrence	빈도수

餘	人	今	食		남을	remainder, balance, excess; over, plus; the last	여
	食	食	飠		餘裕	extra space, extra time, extra capability	여유
					餘暇	spare time, leisure	여가
食 7 1626	餘	餘	餘		餘念	irrelevant thoughts, wandering mind	여념

餓	人	今	食		주릴	hungry, starved	아
	食	飠	飠		餓鬼	hungry ghost, starving spirit; person of voracious appetite	아귀
					餓死	die of starvation	아사
食 7 1627	餓	餓	餓		飢餓	hunger, starvation	기아

默	罒	回	甲	말없을 silent; dark; secret	묵
	里	黑	黑	默默 히 silently, mutely; tacitly 默認 tacitly approve; tolerate, overlook	묵묵 묵인
黑 4 1628	默	默	默	默過 overlook	묵과

龍	亠	立	咅	용 dragon	룡
	咅	咅	龍	龍王 the dragon king (god of rain and water) 龍宮 dragon palace; palace of the dragon king	용왕 용궁
龍 0 1629	龍	龍	龍	龍顔 the royal countenance	용안

17 Strokes

償	亻	亻	償	갚을 repay; make restitution, indemnify; fulfill	상
	償	償	償	償還 repay; amortize 賠償 compensate, indemnify 報償 compensate, remunerate	상환 배상 보상
人 15 1630	償	償	償		

優	亻	亻	佰	넉넉할 plenty, abundant, enough; satisfactory; excellent; actor	우
	佰	偱	憂	優勢 ascendant, superior 優秀 superior, excellent 優先 precedence, priority	우세 우수 우선
人 15 1631	優	優	優		

勵	厂	厈	严	힘쓸 urge, encourage, incite	려
	厗	厲	厲	激勵 encourage, cheer on 督勵 encourage, stimulate 奬勵 encouragement	격려 독려 장려
力 15 1632	厲	厲丁	勵		

壓	厂	戶	厈	누를	press down; oppress; crush; keep in order; urge		압
	屑	屑	厭	壓力	pressure, stress	압력
土 14 1633	厭	壓	壓	壓迫	oppression, tyranny	압박
				壓縮	compress, constrict	압축
嶺	山	岁	岑	고개	high mountain pass; mountain range		령
	岒	嶺	嶺	嶺東	eastern provinces of Korea	영동
山 14 1634	嶺	嶺	嶺	嶺南	southern provinces of Korea	영남
				峻嶺	steep mountain pass	준령
懇	夕	豸	豸	간절할	earnest; supplicate, beseech		간
	豺	狠	狠	懇切	earnest, sincere	간절
心 13 1635	懇	懇	懇	懇請	entreat, solicit	간청
				懇曲	warm, cordial	간곡
應	广	疒	疛	응할	reply; correspond to; ought		응
	疟	疟	雁	應用	apply, put into practice	응용
心 13 1636	雁	應	應	應當	without fail, for sure	응당
				應答	answer, reply	응답
戲	占	虍	虐	희롱할	joke; play		희
	虍	虐	虛	戲弄	joke, jest; mock	희롱
戈 13 1637	戲	戲	戲	戲曲	drama, play	희곡
				遊戲	play, play at a game	유희
擊	戸	亘	車	칠	strike; attack; rout		격
	車	轂	轂	擊破	defeat, smash	격파
手 13 1638	轂	轂	擊	擊退	repulse, repel	격퇴
				擊墜	shoot down an aircraft	격추

擧 手 13 1639				들	raise, lift, hold up; entire	거
				擧行	celebrate a rite; carry out, observe	거행
				擧動	behavior, conduct	거동
				擧手	raise one's hand	거수
檀 木 13 1640				박달나무 sandalwood		단
				檀君	legendary founder and first king of Korea	단군
				檀紀	era with years numbered from the time Tangun founded Korea in 2333 B.C.	단기
檢 木 13 1641				검사할 inspect, examine, check; restrict, restrain; arrange		검
				檢査	inspection, examination	검사
				檢定	official approval, authorization	검정
				檢討	review, examine	검토
濕 水 14 1642				습할	damp, moist, wet	습
				濕氣	humidity, dampness, moisture	습기
				濕度	humidity level	습도
				濕疹	eczema	습진
濫 水 14 1643				넘칠	overflow; excess	람
				濫用	misuse, misappropriation	남용
				氾濫	overflow, flooding; presumption	범람
				濫發	overissue, excessive distribution	남발
濯 水 14 1644				씻을	wash	탁
				洗濯	wash, launder	세탁
				洗濯所	a laundry	세탁소
				洗濯物	laundry, clothes to be washed	세탁물

				구제할	aid, relieve; cross a stream; to complete	제
濟				救濟	save, redeem	구제
				辨濟	repay, pay back	변제
水 14 1645				共濟	help each other, aid each other	공제
燥				마를	parched, scorched	조
				乾燥	dry; arid	건조
				燥渴	thirst	조갈
火 13 1646						
燭				촛불	candle	촉
				燭光	candlelight; candlepower	촉광
				燭數	candlepower	촉수
火 13 1647				燭臺	candlestick, candle holder	촉대
營				진영	camp, encampment; regulate; found; plan; define	영
				營業	engage in business, operate a business	영업
火 13 1648				營利	earn money, make profits	영리
				營農	engage in agriculture, farm	영농
獲				얻을	take, seize	획
				獲得	acquire, obtain	획득
				漁獲	catch fish; a catch of fish	어획
犬 14 1649				捕獲	capture, seize	포획
環				고리	ring	환
				環境	environment, surroundings	환경
				指環	a ring	지환
玉 13 1650				花環	a wreath	화환

瞬 目 12 1651	月 目 目´ 目ズ 睜 睟 瞬 瞬 瞬	잠깐 blink, wink; glance; instant 瞬間 instant, second, moment 一瞬 an instant, a moment 瞬息間 brief instant, in the twinkling of an eye	순 순간 일순 순식간
矯 矢 12 1652	二 矢 矢´ 妖 矯 矯 矯 矯 矯	바로잡을 straighten, bend straight, rectify; raise the head; forceful; feign 矯正 remedy, set right 矯導所 penitentiary	교 교정 교도소
禪 示 12 1653	礻 礻 礻 礻 礻 禑 禑 禮 禪	사양할 yield, abdicate; Buddhist; meditation; Zen 禪道 Zen, the way of Zen 參禪 meditation; practice of Zen 座禪 sit in meditation	선 선도 참선 좌선
縱 糸 11 1654	幺 糸 糸 糸 絆 絲 絲 縱 縱	세로 lengthwise, perpendicular, vertical; to relax, let go; to loose; indulgent 操縱 pilot, steer 放縱 self-indulgent, dissolute 縱橫 length and breadth	종 조종 방종 종횡
縮 糸 11 1655	幺 糸 糸 糸 縮 縮 縮 縮 縮	줄 shrink, draw in, draw back, recoil 縮小 reduce, curtail; dwindle, shrink 縮圖 miniature drawing; condensed edition 緊縮 curtail, cut down	축 축소 축도 긴축
績 糸 11 1656	幺 糸 糸 糸 績 績 績 績 績	길쌈 weave, spin thread; an affair; to complete; result, effect; merit 成績 grades, record 功績 achievements, merits 業績 contributions, achievements	적 성적 공적 업적

					거느릴 manage, supervise; all, overall; summarize	총
總						
					總理 control, superintend, oversee	총리
					總計 sum total, whole amount	총계
糸 11 1657					總數 total number, aggregate number	총수

					번성할 abundant, luxuriant; prolific; exuberant	번
繁						
					繁昌 flourish; prosper	번창
					繁榮 prosper, thrive	번영
糸 11 1658					繁殖 multiply, increase	번식

					날개 wing; flank of an army; assist; shelter	익
翼						
					左翼 the left wing; left flank	좌익
					右翼 the right wing; right flank	우익
羽 11 1659						

					이을 connect; joint; unite; associated	연
聯						
					聯盟 league, federation	연맹
					聯立 allied, combined	연립
耳 11 1660					聯關 connected with, related to	연관

					총명할 clever, quick to understand	총
聰						
					聰明 intelligent, wise; have a retentive memory	총명
					聰氣 intelligence, perspicacity	총기
耳 11 1661						

					소리 sound, voice, tone, music; fame, reputation; to voice, state, make known	성
聲						
					聲樂 vocal music	성악
					名聲 fame, renown	명성
耳 11 1662					銃聲 sound of gunfire	총성

臨 臣 11 1663	臣 臨 臨	臣 臨 臨	臥 臨 臨	임할 臨時 臨迫 臨席	descend, come to; near to, on the point of; imitate temporary; acting; provisional approaching, impending attend, be present at	림 임시 임박 임석
薄 艸 13 1664	艹 菏 薄	艹 蒲 薄	艹 蓮 薄	엷을 薄弱 薄荷 薄俸	thin, slight, pale, poor; stingy; careless; reach to infirm, weak peppermint, mint **meager salary, low wages**	박 박약 박하 박봉
薦 艸 13 1665	艹 芦 薦	艹 薦 薦	芦 薦 薦	천거할 薦擧 推薦	recommend, introduce; offer; worship; fodder recommend a person recommend, sponsor	천 천거 추천
謠 言 10 1666	亠 訡 譯	言 診 謠	言 謠 謠	노래 歌謠 民謠 童謠	song; sing; rumor song, ballad folk song children's song, nursery rhyme	요 가요 민요 동요
講 言 10 1667	亠 諎 講	言 諎 講	言 諎 講	익힐 講究 講演 講義	lecture, discuss, speak, expound, preach deliberate, consider lecture, address a lecture	강 강구 강연 강의
謝 言 10 1668	亠 訂 謝	言 訃 謝	言 謝 謝	사례할 謝禮 謝絶 謝過	gratitude; decline; fade; hand over; confess faults gratitude; remuneration, gratuity refuse, decline apology	사 사례 사절 사과

謙			겸손할 humble, modest		겸
			謙遜	humility, modesty	겸손
			謙虛	modest, retiring	겸허
			謙讓	humility, diffidence	겸양
言 10 1669					

輿			수레 palanquin; many		여
			輿論	public opinion, popular sentiment	여론
			輿望	esteem, confidence, trust	여망
車 10 1670			喪輿	funeral bier	상여

還			돌아올 return		환
			送還	send back, return	송환
			歸還	return	귀환
			還國	return to one's country; repatriate	환국
辵 13 1671					

避			피할 shun; avoid; flee		피
			避亂	flee from war, seek refuge	피란
			避身	escape secretly, hide oneself	피신
			回避	avoid, eschew; escape, evade	회피
辵 13 1672					

醜			더러울 vile; ugly		추
			醜態	scandalous conduct; ugly scene	추태
			醜雜	indecent, filthy	추잡
			醜惡	vile, repulsive	추악
酉 10 1673					

鍊			단련할 smelt, refine; discipline		련
			鍛鍊	forge, anneal; train, discipline	단련
			鍊磨	practice, drill, cultivate	연마
金 9 1674					

隱 阜 14 1675	阝 阝 阞 阞 陷 隱 隱 隱 隱	숨을 隱隱 隱遁 隱退	hidden, mysterious, secret; conceal; small; painful dim, vague, faint renounce the world, retire from society retire, withdraw from active life	은 은은 은둔 은퇴
雖 隹 9 1676	口 吕 吊 虽 蚤 蚤 雖 雖 雖	비록	though, although, however	수
霜 雨 9 1677	一 雨 雨 雪 雪 雪 霜 霜 霜	서리 霜降 霜雪 風霜	frost frost fall, 18th of the 24 seasonal divisions frost and snow wind and frost; hardships	상 상강 상설 풍상
韓 韋 8 1678	宀 古 直 草 草 韓 韓 韓 韓	나라 韓國 韓服 韓人	Korea Korea (abbreviation for Republic of Korea) Korean clothes; traditional female costume a Korean person	한 한국 한복 한인
館 食 8 1679	𠆢 今 食 食 食 節 館 館 館	집 館長 學館	building, house, hall director (as of a library) academy, private institute	관 관장 학관
鮮 魚 6 1680	夕 多 鱼 魚 魚 魚 鮮 鮮 鮮	고을 朝鮮 生鮮 新鮮	calm; fresh, new; delicious; rare; fish; Korea Korea, Land of Morning Calm, name of the Yi Dynasty fresh fish freshness	선 조선 생선 신선

鴻 鳥 6 1681	氵 沪 鴻 鴻 氵 汋 鴻 氵 江 鴻	큰기러기 wild goose 鴻恩　great favor, benevolence	홍 홍은
點 黑 5 1682	四 黑 黙 罒 黑 點 甲 黒 點	점　point, spot, dot; a bit, a little; check off 點心　lunch, luncheon 點數　grades, marks; score, points 點檢　inspect, examine	점 점심 점수 점검

18 Strokes

擴 手 15 1683	扌 抻 擴 扩 掉 擴 疒 擔 擴	넓힐 expand 擴大　enlarge, expand 擴充　expand, amplify 擴張　expand, extend	확 확대 확충 확장
斷 斤 14 1684	幺 絲 斷 絲 斷 斷 絲 斷 斷	끊을　cut; decision, judgment; resolution, resolve 決斷　decide; determine to; resolve to 斷交　sever relations 斷絶　cut off, amputate	단 결단 단교 단절
歸 止 14 1685	白 皀 皀 皀 皀 皀 皀 歸 歸	돌아올 return 歸國　return to one's country; repatriate 歸還　revert to, restore to 復歸　revert to former condition	귀 귀국 귀환 복귀

爵				벼슬	degree of nobility	작
				公爵	prince; duke	공작
				子爵	viscount	자작
爪 14 1686				爵位	peerage, title and rank of nobility	작위

礎				주춧돌	stone used as a base of a pillar	초
				柱礎	stone used as a base of a pillar, foundation stone	주초
				礎石	cornerstone, foundation stone	초석
石 13 1687				基礎	foundation	기초

禮				예도	propriety, good manners; politeness; ceremony; worship	례
				禮拜堂	a church (building)	예배당
				禮儀	etiquette; decorum; propriety	예의
示 13 1688				禮式	rite, ceremony	예식

簡				편지	letter; slip of bamboo for taking notes; documents; abridge; simple	간
				簡單	simple, short, easy	간단
				簡便	convenient, easy	간편
竹 12 1689				簡素	simplicity, simplify	간소

糧				양식	provisions, grain, food, rations	량
				糧食	provisions, food supplies	양식
				糧穀	grains, cereals	양곡
米 12 1690				軍糧	military rations	군량

織				짤	weave	직
				紡織	spin and weave	방직
				織造	weaving	직조
糸 12 1691				織物	woven goods, textiles	직물

職	⺊	耳	耳	직분	office, post, position; govern, manage, direct, oversee	직
	耳	耶	聆	職員	staff, personnel	**직**원
				職工	worker, factory worker	직공
耳 12 1692	暗	職	職	職場	job, occupation, place of work	직장

舊	⺾	⺾	艹	예	old, ancient, not new	구
	花	雈	萑	親舊	friend, companion	친구
				舊式	old style, old methods	구식
臼 12 1693	舊	舊	舊	復舊	restore	복구

藏	⺾	⺾	芌	감출	store, hoard; hide; Tibet	장
	扗	萨	萨	貯藏	store, storage	저장
				藏書	collect books, build a library	장서
艸 14 1694	藏	藏	藏	所藏	possess	소장

藍	⺾	⺾	艹	푸를	blue, indigo	람
	萨	萨	蓝	藍色	indigo, dark blue	남색
				伽藍	Buddhist temple; cathedral	가람
艸 14 1695	藍	藍	藍			

蟲	口	虫	虫	벌레	insects; bugs; vermin	충
	虫	虫	虫	蟲齒	tooth decay, caries	충치
				害蟲	harmful insects; vermin; blight	해충
虫 12 1696	蚰	蟲	蟲	寄生蟲	parasite, parasitic insect	기생충

謹	言	言	言	삼갈	careful, cautious; respectful	근
	訐	訔	謹	謹愼	prudence, discretion	근신
				謹嚴	sober; stern	근엄
言 11 1697	謹	謹	謹	謹賀	respectful congratulations	근하

豐	三 / 丰 / 非 / 非 / 幽 / 豊	豊 / 豊 / 豊	풍년	fruitful year; good crop	풍
豆 11 1698			豐年	year of plenty, fruitful year	풍년
			豐富	plentiful, abundant	풍부
			豐盛	rich, abundant	풍성

蹟	口 / 무 / 足 / 足 / 跬 / 蹟 / 蹟 / 蹟 / 蹟		사적	traces, footsteps; follow up	적
足 11 1699			史蹟	historical relics; place of historical interest	사적
			古蹟	historic remains, ruins	고적
			奇蹟	miracle; mystery, wonder	기적

轉	口 / 白 / 車 / 輒 / 車輔 / 輾 / 轉 / 轉 / 轉		구를	turn, transfer, transmit	전
車 11 1700			轉換	convert, switch over to	전환
			轉落	fall low, sink in the world	전락
			轉勤	transfer to another office	전근

醫	二 / 天 / 医 / 医几 / 殴 / 殹 / 醫 / 醫 / 醫		의원	medical science, medicine; physician	의
酉 11 1701			醫師	physician	의사
			醫學	medical science, medicine	의학
			醫療	treatment, medical care	의료

鎭	人 / 午 / 牟 / 金 / 釷 / 鎖 / 鎖 / 鎭 / 鎭		진압할	press down; guard; ward off evil influences; brigade; market town	진
金 10 1702			鎭壓	suppress, repress, quell	진압
			鎭靜	quiet, allay, pacify	진정
			鎭痛	alleviate pain	진통

鎖	人 / 午 / 牟 / 金 / 釗 / 鎖 / 鎖 / 鎖 / 鎖		막을	lock, fetters, chains	쇄
金 10 1703			鎖國	close a country to foreigners	쇄국
			連鎖	a chain; a series; connection	연쇄
			連鎖店	a chain store	연쇄점

雜	亠	方	产	섞일	varied, miscellaneous; rough, coarse; mixed, impure; loose, lax, immoral; idle, useless	잡
	杂	牵	新			
隹 10 1704	新	雜	雜	雜誌 magazine, journal 雜草 weeds 雜談 small talk, chat		잡지 잡초 잡담

雙	亻	仁	佳	둘	two, double; pair, couple; both	쌍
	佳′	伊	俳	雙方 both parties, both sides 雙生兒 twins 雙曲線 a hyperbola		쌍방 쌍생아 쌍곡선
隹 10 1705	俳	雙	雙			

題	日	旦	是	제목	title, heading; subject; theme; proposition	제
	是	是	題	題目 subject, theme, title 問題 problem, question; subject; issue		제목 문제
頁 9 1706	題	題	題	宿題 homework		숙제

顔	亠	立	彦	얼굴	face, countenance; complexion; pigmentation; color	안
	彦	彦	顔	顔面 the face; acquaintance 顔目 sense of discrimination		안면 안목
頁 9 1707	彦	顔	顔	顔色 complexion, color of the face		안색

額	宀	夾	客	이마	forehead; fixed number, quantity	액
	客	客	額	額數 sum, amount 額面 par value, face value		액수 액면
頁 9 1708	額	額	額	總額 total amount		총액

騎	F	耳	馬	말탈	ride a horse, ride; stride	기
	馬	馬	馬	騎馬 riding a horse 騎兵 cavalryman; the cavalry		기마 기병
馬 8 1709	騎	騎	騎	騎手 rider, jockey		기수

龜				거북 tortoise, turtle 본뜰 pattern, model 갈라질 chapped	귀 구 균
龜 0 1710				龜鑑 pattern, model 龜裂 chapped; cracked; fail	귀감 균열

19 Strokes

壞				부술 destroy	괴
土 16 1711				破壞 destroy, demolish 壞血病 scurvy 壞滅 destroy, demolish	파괴 괴혈병 괴멸

懲				징계할 punishment, warning	징
心 15 1712				懲戒 discipline, reprimand 懲役 be in prison, serve time 懲罰 discipline, punish	징계 징역 징벌

懷				품을 clasp to the bosom	회
心 16 1713				懷中 inside one's heart; in 　　 one's pocket 懷疑 doubt, be skeptical about 懷抱 innermost thoughts	회중 회의 회포

爆				터질 explode	폭
火 15 1714				爆彈 artillery shell, explosive 　　 shell 爆擊 bombing attack, to bomb 爆發 explode	폭탄 폭격 폭발

獸 犬 15 1715	吅	吅	吵 畄	畕	嘼 獸	길짐승 wild animals, beasts 猛獸 beast of prey, fierce animal 獸醫 veterinarian 獸心 bestial mind, brutal heart	수 맹수 수의 수심

獸 犬 15 1715	吅 / 吅 / 吵 / 畄 / 畕 / 嘼 / 獸 / 獸	길짐승 wild animals, beasts	수
		猛獸 beast of prey, fierce animal	맹수
		獸醫 veterinarian	수의
		獸心 bestial mind, brutal heart	수심

穫 禾 14 1716	才 / 禾 / 秒 / 秒 / 秼 / 稚 / 稚 / 穫 / 穫	거둘 reap, harvest	확
		收穫 harvest, reap	수확

簿 竹 13 1717	竹 / 竹 / 竹 / 笆 / 笟 / 笥 / 薄 / 薄 / 簿	장부 account book, blank book, memorandum book; register	부
		簿記 bookkeeping	부기
		名簿 register, roster	명부
		家計簿 domestic account book, family account book	가계부

羅 网 14 1718	罒 / 罒 / 罗 / 罗 / 罗 / 罘 / 羅 / 羅 / 羅	비단 thin silk; gauze; netting; arrange, spread out	라
		羅列 arrange in a row; display statistics	나열
		羅針盤 compass	나침반
		羅紗 woolen cloth	나사

藝 艸 15 1719	艹 / 艹 / 艺 / 芸 / 莕 / 藝 / 蓺 / 藝 / 藝	재주 skill; art	예
		藝術 art, the arts	예술
		工藝 handicrafts; industrial arts	공예
		演藝 a performance; dramatical or musical entertainment	연예

藥 艸 15 1720	艹 / 艹 / 首 / 苩 / 茁 / 蕗 / 蕬 / 藥 / 藥	약 medicine, drugs	약
		藥品 medicine, drugs	약품
		藥房 pharmacy, drugstore	약방
		漢藥 herbal remedies, Chinese medicine	한약

證	言 言 訂 訒 諮 證	증거	evidence, proof	증
言 12 1721	證 證 證	證據 證券 證明	evidence, proof certificate; bond; stock proof, corroboration	증거 증권 증명

識	言 言 言 訁 諳 諳	알	recognize, know, distinguish	식
		기록할	to record	지
言 12 1722	諳 識 識	認識 常識 標識	recognize, realize common sense mark, sign, signal	인식 상식 표지

譜	言 言 言 訁 訵 譜	계보	genealogical table; list, chart, register; musical score; treatise	보
言 12 1723	諳 譜 譜	系譜 族譜	genealogical table; genealogy clan register, genealogical table	계보 족보

贈	月 貝 貝 貯 貯 貯	줄	give, bestow, confer	증
貝 12 1724	贈 贈 贈	贈呈 贈與 寄贈	proffer, present donate, confer donate, contribute	증정 증여 기증

贊	生 先 先 先生 兟 贊	도울	help, assist; praise	찬
貝 12 1725	贊 贊 贊	贊成 贊同 贊助	approve; favor, support approve, support endorse, advocate; sponsor	찬성 찬동 찬조

辭	爫 爫 爫 爲 爲 爲	말씀	words, speech; sentence; message, instructions; statement; resign	사
辛 12 1726	爲 辭 辭	辭表 祝辭 辭典	letter of resignation message of congratulation dictionary, lexicon	사표 축사 사전

邊 辵 15 1727	彳	自	皀	가	bank, side, edge, border, margin	변
	臱	臱	臱	江邊 邊利 周邊	riverside, river bank interest on money surrounding area; perimeter	강변 변리 주변
	皁	邊	邊			

鏡 金 11 1728	仝	余	金	거울	mirror, speculum	경
	釒	鈞	鈶	眼鏡 鏡臺 破鏡	glasses, spectacles dressing table broken mirror; divorce, separation	안경 경대 파경
	鐏	鐛	鏡			

關 門 11 1729	尸	門	門	빗장	frontier pass, frontier gate, customhouse; shut, close; bolt	관
	閂	閼	關	關係 關心 關稅	relationship, connection interest, concern customs, custom duties	관계 관심 관세
	關	關	關			

離 隹 11 1730	文	卤	卤	떠날	leave; retire; separate; distant from, apart from	리
	离	离	离	離別	part, separate; bid farewell to	이별
	離	離	離	離脫 離婚	secede, break away from divorce; annulment	이탈 이혼

難 隹 11 1731	廿	苫	苫	어려울	trouble, difficulty	난
	菓	菓	菓	難點	fault, weakness; difficult point	난점
	難	難	難	難關 難處	grave obstacle; a deadlock difficult to deal with, sensitive	난관 난처

霧 雨 11 1732	雨	雨	雨	안개	fog, mist, vapor	무
	雫	零	雺	噴霧器	sprayer, vaporizer, atomizer	분무기
	霧	霧	霧	濃霧 霧散	dense fog dissipate, disperse	농무 무산

| 韻 音 10 1733 | | | | 운 | rhyme; harmony; expression | 운 |
| | | | | 韻致 餘韻 | artistic effect, elegance / trailing note; lingering effect; reverberation | 운치 여운 |

| 願 頁 10 1734 | | | | 원할 | desire; desirous, willing; vow | 원 |
| | | | | 所願 願書 祈願 | desire, wish / application form / supplicate, petition, pray | 소원 원서 기원 |

| 類 頁 10 1735 | | | | 무리 | class, species, kind | 류 |
| | | | | 分類 類似 種類 | classify, divide into groups / be similar, resemble / kind, type; class; species | 분류 유사 종류 |

| 麗 鹿 8 1736 | | | | 고울 | elegant, beautiful | 려 |
| | | | | 華麗 高麗 秀麗 | splendid, magnificent / ancient Korean state, 918-1392 / graceful, beautiful | 화려 고려 수려 |

20 Strokes

| 勸 力 18 1737 | | | | 권할 | encourage; exhort; persuade | 권 |
| | | | | 勸告 勸誘 勸獎 | counsel, advice / solicit, induce / encourage; promote | 권고 권유 권장 |

嚴	叩叩	罒罒	严	엄할	stern, strict, majestic, dignified; private; severely, extremely	엄
	严	严	崖			
口 17 1738	腎	嚴	嚴	嚴肅 嚴重 嚴冬	solemn, grave majesty, stately severe winter	엄숙 엄중 엄동

壞	圹	圹	坮	흙덩이	soil, earth, clod; place, region; rich soil	양
	坮	壇	壞	土壤 天壤之差	soil extreme difference, be poles apart	토양 천양지차
土 17 1739	壞	壞	壞			

寶	宀	宝	㝬	보배	treasure; valuable, precious	보
	㝬	寙	寶	寶貝 國寶 寶石	a treasure a national treasure jewel, precious gem	보배 국보 보석
宀 17 1740	寶	寶	寶			

懸	目	旦	県	달	hang, suspend	현
	県	県	縣	懸賞 懸案	offer a prize, offer a reward pending bill; outstanding question	현상 현안
心 16 1741	縣	懸	懸	懸賞金	a prize, prize money	현상금

爐	火	灼	炉	화로	brazier, stove, fireplace	로
	爐	爐	爐	火爐 煖爐 風爐	brazier a stove; a fireplace vented cooking brazier	화로 난로 풍로
火 16 1742	爐	爐	爐			

獻	卢	虍	虍	드릴	humbly give; present, offer	헌
	虍	虍	鬳	獻金 獻身 獻納	offering, contribution devotion, self-sacrifice donate, contribute	헌금 헌신 헌납
犬 16 1743	獻	獻	獻			

籍 竹 14 1744	호적	register, record, list	적
	戶籍	family register, census register	호적
	國籍	nationality, citizenship	국적
	學籍	school register, educational record	학적

競 立 15 1745	다툴	quarrel, wrangle; vie; compete; contest	경
	競技	match, contest, sporting event	경기
	競爭	compete with, vie with	경쟁
	競馬	horse race, horse racing	경마

繼 糸 14 1746	이을	connect; continue; follow; adopt	계
	繼續	continue	계속
	繼承	inherit; succeed to	계승
	引繼	transfer duties; assume duties	인계

蘇 艸 16 1747	소생할	revive; relieve; cheerful; plentiful; Russia	소
	蘇生	revive, resuscitate; come back to life	소생
	蘇聯	the Soviet Union	소련
	耶蘇	Jesus	야소

觸 角 13 1748	닿을	touch; stimulate; offend; butt, gore	촉
	觸覺	sense of touch	촉각
	感觸	touch, feel, perceive through the senses	감촉

覺 見 13 1749	깨달을	perceive; aware, conscious	각
	覺書	protocol, note	각서
	覺悟	ready; resolved; perceive; understand	각오
	錯覺	illusion, hallucination	착각

警 言 13 1750	艹 苟ʲ 警	芍 敬 警	苟 敬 警	경계할 警戒 警察官 警告	warn, caution warning, caution; guard policeman, police officer warning, admonition	경 경계 경찰관 경고
譯 言 13 1751	言 訂 譯	言 評 譯	訂 譯 譯	번역할 通譯 誤譯 譯書	translate; interpret; explain interpret, interpreter mistranslate, erroneous interpretation a translation	역 통역 오역 역서
議 言 13 1752	言 諚 議	言 諪 議	言 諆 議	의논할 議論 議員 討議	discuss; consult; criticism; agreement discuss, deliberate; to dispute National Assemblyman, congressman discuss, debate	의 의논 의원 토의
譽 言 13 1753	臼 與 擧	肖 與 譽	卽 與 譽	명예 名譽 榮譽	eulogize, praise; flatter; fame glory, honor; fame; dignity, prestige honor; distinction	예 명예 영예
釋 采 13 1754	千 采ʲ 釋	禾 釋 釋	利 釋 釋	놓을 解釋 釋放 註釋	release, unloose; explain; Sakyamuni, the historic Buddha explicate, explain release from confinement, set free annotate, comment on	석 해석 석방 주석
鐘 金 12 1755	全 鈶 鐘	余 鈶 鐘	金 鋕 鐘	종 警鐘 鐘閣 晩鐘	bell; clock alarm bell; a warning bell house; belfry evening bells; vesper bells (Also written 鍾 .)	종 경종 종각 만종

21 strokes

騷	耳	馬	馬	소란할 stir up; agitate; annoy; grieved; moved	소
馬 10 1756	馹	馭	馭	騷亂 turmoil, tumult, disturbance 騷動 raise a disturbance, stir up trouble	소란 소동
	騄	騷	騷	騷音 noise; cacophony	소음

鬪	王	王二	王王	싸울 fight, quarrel	투
鬥 10 1757	王王	馬王	鬥	鬪爭 struggle, fight 鬪士 a fighter, a champion 鬪志 fighting spirit, militant spirit	투쟁 투사 투지
	鬪	鬪	鬪		

黨	尚	当	尚	무리 clique, gang; party	당
黑 8 1758	當	黨	黨	黨派 faction, clique, party 黨員 party member 黨爭 party strife; factionalism	당파 당원 당쟁
	黨	黨	黨		

21 Strokes

懼	忄冂	忄目	忄刖	두려울 fear; carefulness	구
心 18 1759	忄刖	忄罪	忄瞿	悚懼 fearful, afraid; ill at ease 疑懼 doubt, suspect	송구 의구
	忄瞿	懼	懼		

欄	木	枦	枦門	난간 railing, balustrade; column in a newspaper	란
木 17 1760	枦門	棍門	楣門	欄干 railing, handrail 空欄 vacant column on a page, empty space, margin	난간 공란
	欄	欄	欄		

323

				빛날	bright, glistening; rotten; overripe; smashed; ragged	란
爛	炉	炉	炉			
	炉	炉	炉	燦爛	brilliant, resplendent	찬란
				爛漫	be in full bloom	난만
火 17 1761	燭	燭	爛	爛熟	overripe; fully matured	난숙
續	糸	綝	絏	이을	connect, join; add to; sequel, continuation	속
	結	綪	績	繼續	continue	계속
				連續	occur in succession, follow one after another	연속
糸 15 1762	績	績	續	續出	appear in succession, crop up successively	속출
蘭	艹	芦	芦	난초	orchid; epidendrum; fragrant, elegant, refined; Holland	란
	芦	蕑	蕳			
				蘭草	orchid; iris	난초
艸 17 1763	蘭	蘭	蘭	蘭香	fragrance of the orchid	난향
覽	臣	臣丶	医丶	볼	look at, inspect; perceive	람
	贬	臨	臂	展覽	exhibition, showing	전람
				閱覽	read, peruse	열람
				觀覽	view, inspect	관람
見 14 1764	臂	覽	覽			
護	言	言	言丶	보호할 guard		호
	詳	誁	諽	護衛	escort, guard, convoy	호위
				護國	defense of the fatherland	호국
				護送	send under guard, escort	호송
言 14 1765	諅	護	護			
屬	尸	屏	屈	붙을	connected with; subject to; belong to; depending upon; class, kind	속
	屬	屬	屬	附屬	attached; affiliated; part	부속
				屬國	tributary state, subject state	속국
尸 18 1766	屬	屬	屬	歸屬	revert, return, be restored	귀속

辯 辛 14 1767	立 辛 䇂 䇂 䇂	立 辛 䇂 辯	䇂 䇂 䇂 辯	말씀 argue, dispute; discuss; explain 辯論 discuss; argue 辯護士 attorney, lawyer 口辯 speech, eloquence	변 변론 변호사 구변
鐵 金 13 1768	全 鈝 鐘	金 銔 鐵	針 鐘 鐵	쇠 iron; firm 鐵道 railroad, railway 鐵絲 wire 鐵板 an iron or steel plate	철 철도 철사 철판
露 雨 13 1769	雨 霏 霰	霏 霏 露	霗 霳 露	이슬 dew; expose, disclose 露骨的 frankly, candidly 露天 the open air, the open 露店 street stall, roadside stand	로 노골적 노천 노점
顧 頁 12 1770	户 雇 雇	户 雇 雇	戶 雇 顧	돌아볼 look after, care for; regard; turn the head around to look 顧問 adviser, advise 顧客 client, customer 回顧 recall, recollect	고 고문 고객 회고
翻 飛 12 1771	平 番 翻	釆 番 翻	番 番 翻	뒤집을 upset, overturn; come back; reopen 翻譯 translate; render, put into 翻覆 reverse; capsize, turn upside down 翻意 reverse oneself, reconsider	번 번역 번복 번의
驅 馬 11 1772	馬 馬 騙	馬 馬 騙	馬 騙 驅	몰 expel, drive away 驅除 exterminate, destroy 驅迫 mistreat, treat harshly 驅使 order about; use freely, have a command of	구 구제 구박 구사

325

鷄 鳥 10 1773	鷄	鷄	鷄	닭	chicken	계
				鷄卵	egg (of a chicken)	계란
				養鷄	poultry farming	양계
				鷄鳴	crowing of a rooster	계명

鶴 鳥 10 1774	鶴	鶴	鶴	학	a crane (bird)	학
				白鶴	á crane	백학
				鶴首苦待	eagerly await, wait with neck craned	학수고대

22 Strokes

權 木 18 1775	權	權	權	권세	authority, power	권
				權勢	power, influence, authority	권세
				權利	right, prerogative	권리
				權力	power, influence	권력

歡 欠 18 1776	歡	歡	歡	기쁠	joyful	환
				歡迎	welcome	환영
				歡喜	delight, gladness	환희
				歡聲	cheer, shout of joy	환성

聽 耳 16 1777	聽	聽	聽	들을	listen, hear; understand; acknowledge, comply with	청
				聽覺	sense of hearing, auditory sense	청각
				視聽	see and hear	시청
				聽衆	audience, crowd, auditors	청중

臟	月	肚	脏	오장	viscera, the Five Vital Organs	장
	脏	臟	臟	内臟	internal organs, the viscera	내장
				五臟	the Five Vital Organs (heart, liver, spleen, lungs, kidneys)	오장
肉 18 1778	臟	臟	臟	心臟	the heart	심장

襲	立	音	竜	엄습할	raid; lining; double; hereditary	습
	龍	龍	龍	襲擊	surprise attack	습격
				奇襲	surprise attack	기습
衣 16 1779	龒	襲	襲	因襲	convention, long-established custom	인습

讀	言	言	言	읽을	read; study	독
	讀	讀	讀	讀者	reader; subscriber	독자
				讀書	reading	독서
言 15 1780	讀	讀	讀	熟讀	peruse	숙독

鑑	牟	余	鈢	거울	mirror; metal; examine, criticize, appreciate	감
	鈢	鉅	鑑	鑑賞	appreciation	감상
				鑑定	judge, appraise; expert evidence	감정
金 14 1781	鑑	鑑	鑑	鑑識	discernment, discrimination	감식

響	夕	組	狼	소리	noise; echo	향
	鄉	鄉	鄉	影響	influence, effect	영향
				響應	entertain, treat to	향응
音 13 1782	響	響	響	響板	sounding board	향판

鷗	口	品	區	갈매기	sea gull; tern	구
	鷗	鷗	鷗	白鷗	sea gull	백구
				海鷗	sea gull	해구
鳥 11 1783	鷗	鷗	鷗			

23 Strokes

巖 山 20 1784	岩 岸 岸	岩 崖 巖	岸 崖 巖	바위 cliff, rock; grotto 巖石 a boulder 巖盤 solid foundation; rock floor 巖窟 cave; grotto	암 암석 암반 암굴
戀 心 19 1785	言 縞 綜	信 絲 戀	結 戀 戀	사모할 dote on, be fond of, love 戀愛 romantic love 戀情 tenderness, love; passion 戀人 lover, sweetheart	연 연애 연정 연인
變 言 16 1786	言 絲 綜	信 絲 攣	管 戀 變	변할 change, transform; incident; rebellion 變化 change, transform; inflection 變動 change 變更 change, alter	변 변화 변동 변경
鑛 金 15 1787	牟 鈩 鑛	金 鏈 鑛	釘 鑛 鑛	광물 ore; mining; mine 鑛山 a mine 鑛業 mining, the mining industry 鑛夫 miner	광 광산 광업 광부
顯 頁·14 1788	目 晃 晃	显 晃 顯	晃 晃 顯	나타날 appear, manifest; illustrious 顯微鏡 microscope 顯著 marked, conspicuous, striking	현 현미경 현저

驗 馬 13 1789	실험할 examine, test	험
	實驗 experiment, test, laboratory work	실험
	試驗 examination, test	시험
	經驗 experience	경험

驚 馬 13 1790	놀랄 startle, frighten	경
	驚異 wonder; a wonder, a miracle	경이
	驚歎 admire, marvel at	경탄
	驚愕 surprise, astonishment	경악

驛 馬 13 1791	역 government post; station	역
	驛前 in front of the station	역전
	驛馬車 stagecoach	역마차
	驛長 stationmaster	역장

體 骨 13 1792	몸 body; substance; style; real	체
	體面 honor, prestige, face	체면
	體溫 body temperature	체온
	體育 physical education; athletics	체육

24 Strokes

蠶 虫 18 1793	누에 silkworms	잠
	蠶絲 silk thread	잠사
	蠶食 encroach, make inroads into, eat into	잠식
	養蠶 sericulture	양잠

讓	言 言 讓 / 讓 讓 讓 / 言 17 / 1794 · 讓 讓 讓	사양할 / 辭讓 / 讓步 / 讓渡	yield, submit, resign; cede, relinquish; polite / decline courteously; hesitate / yield; concede, compromise / cede, transfer	양 / 사양 / 양보 / 양도
靈	雨 16 / 1795	신령 / 靈魂 / 神靈 / 靈柩車	spirit; spiritual, divine; supernatural; efficacious; ingenious, smart / the soul, the spirit / spirit, god, deity; spirits of the dead / hearse, funeral carriage	령 / 영혼 / 신령 / 영구차
鹽	鹵 13 / 1796	소금 / 鹽酸 / 鹽素 / 鹽分	salt; brine / hydrochloric acid / chlorine / salinity, salt content	염 / 염산 / 염소 / 염분

25 Strokes

廳	广 22 / 1797	마루 / 大廳 / 官廳 / 廳舍	hall, court; sub-prefecture / hall, main room / government office, official building / government buildings	청 / 대청 / 관청 / 청사
蠻	虫 19 / 1798	오랑캐 / 野蠻 / 蠻行 / 蠻勇	barbarian, savage; uncivilized; fierce / barbaric, savage / atrocity, barbaric act, outrage / daring; foolhardiness, recklessness	만 / 야만 / 만행 / 만용

觀	荃	荘	荘	볼	see, behold; aspect, view	관
	茻	蒲	蕹ﾉ	觀念	idea, conception; sense	관념
見 18	雚目	雚目	觀見	觀點	point of view	관점
1799				觀光	tourism, sightseeing	관광

26 Strokes

讚	言	言	言	칭찬할 praise; admire	찬
	讚ﾉ	讚	讚	稱讚 praise, laud	칭찬
言 19	讚門	讚貝	讚	讚頌歌 hymn, psalm	찬송가
1800				讚揚 praise, laud	찬양

26 Smokes

APPENDICES

KOREAN SURNAMES

The surnames are listed in order of frequency of usage. The chart reads from left to right.

李이	金김	朴박	鄭정	尹윤	崔최	柳유	洪홍	申신	權권	趙조	韓한	吳오
姜강	沈심	安안	許허	張장	閔민	任임	林임	南남	徐서	具구	成성	宋송
俞유	元원	黃황	曹조	呂여	梁양	禹우	羅라	孫손	盧노	魚어	睦목	蔡채
丁정	裵배	孟맹	郭곽	卞변	邊변	愼신	慶경	白백	全전	康강	嚴엄	高고
田전	玄현	文문	尙상	河하	蘇소	池지	奇기	陳진	庾유	琴금	吉길	延연
朱주	周주	廉염	房방	方방	潘반	孔공	王왕	偰설	劉유	秦진	卓탁	咸함
楊양	薛설	奉봉	太태	馬마	表표	殷은	余여	卜복	芮예	牟모	魯노	玉옥
丘구	宣선	都도	蔣장	魏위	車차	邢형	韋위	唐당	仇구	邕옹	明명	莊장
葉섭	皮피	甘감	鞠국	承승	公공	石석	印인	昔석	龔공	杜두	賓빈	門문
于우	秋추	桓환	胡호	雙쌍	伊이	榮영	思사	邵소	貢공	史사	異이	陶도
龐방	溫온	陰음	龍룡	諸제	夫부	景경	强강	扈호	錢전	桂계	簡간	段단
彭팽	苑범	千천	片편	葛갈	頓돈	乃내	間간	路로	平평	馮풍	翁옹	童동
鐘종	鄷풍	宗종	江강	蒙몽	董동	陽양	揚양	章장	桑상	葰장	程정	荊형
耿경	敬경	甯영	京경	荀순	井정	原원	袁원	萬만	班반	員원	堅견	蹇건
燕연	時시	傳전	瞿구	稽혜	米미	艾애	梅매	雷뇌	柴시	聶섭	包포	和화
賀하	花화	華화	賈가	夏하	麻마	牛우	僧승	候후	曲곡	栢백	翟적	畢필
谷곡	弓궁	種종	邦방	凉량	良양	芳방	卿경	刑형	永영	乘승	登등	昇승
勝승	信신	順순	俊준	藩번	端단	鮮선	芊천	牙아	水수	彌미	吾오	珠주
斧부	甫보	部부	素소	凡범	固고	台태	才재	對대	標표	肖초	那나	瓜과
化화	壽수	祐우	價가	尋심	森삼	占점	汎범	克극	郁욱	翊익	宅택	直직
則칙	澤택	綠록	赫혁	冊책	濯탁	骨골	燭촉	律율	物물	別별	實실	弼필
合합	也야	西서	南宮남궁	皇甫황보	鮮于선우	石抹석말	扶餘부여	獨孤독고	令狐영호	東方동방	司馬사마	司空공

335

EASILY CONFUSED CHARACTERS

人 (인)…入 (입)	矢 (시)…失 (실)	若 (약)…苦 (고)	刀 (도)…刃 (인)
于 (우)…干 (간)	互 (호)…瓦 (와)	虛 (허)…虐 (학)	嗚 (오)…鳴 (명)
又 (우)…叉 (차)	亦 (역)…赤 (적)	胃 (위)…胄 (주)	微 (미)…徵 (징)
土 (토)…士 (사)	早 (조)…旱 (한)	候 (후)…侯 (후)	傳 (전)…傅 (부)
分 (분)…兮 (혜)	亨 (형)…享 (향)	哲 (철)…暫 (잠)	兢 (긍)…競 (경)
丸 (환)…九 (구)	兵 (병)…丘 (구)	師 (사)…帥 (수)	穀 (곡)…殼 (각)
予 (여)…矛 (모)	免 (면)…兔 (토)	徒 (도)…徙 (사)	遺 (유)…遣 (견)
友 (우)…反 (반)	天 (천)…夫 (부)	根 (근)…垠 (은)	衝 (충)…衡 (형)
王 (왕)…玉 (옥)	手 (수)…毛 (모)	栽 (재)…裁 (재)	億 (억)…憶 (억)
日 (일)…曰 (왈)	貝 (패)…具 (구)	栗 (률)…粟 (속)	歷 (력)…曆 (력)
牛 (우)…午 (오)	折 (절)…析 (석)	烏 (오)…鳥 (조)	綱 (강)…網 (망)
巨 (거)…臣 (신)	抗 (항)…坑 (갱)	短 (단)…矩 (구)	辯 (변)…辨 (변)
代 (대)…伐 (벌)	技 (기)…枝 (지)	密 (밀)…蜜 (밀)	獲 (획)…穫 (확)
且 (차)…旦 (단)	雨 (우)…兩 (량)	孤 (고)…弧 (호)	壞 (괴)…壤 (양)
功 (공)…巧 (교)	侍 (시)…待 (대)	貧 (빈)…貪 (탐)	簿 (부)…薄 (박)
句 (구)…旬 (순)	卷 (권)…券 (권)	逐 (축)…遂 (수)	籍 (적)…藉 (자)
古 (고)…占 (점)	往 (왕)…住 (주)	頃 (경)…項 (항)	籃 (람)…藍 (남)
字 (자)…宇 (우)	忽 (홀)…悤 (총)	惑 (혹)…感 (감)	大 (대)…太 (태)…犬 (견)
未 (미)…末 (말)	明 (명)…朋 (붕)	班 (반)…斑 (반)	巳 (사)…已 (이)…己 (기)
水 (수)…氷 (빙)	宣 (선)…宜 (의)	幼 (유)…幻 (환)	比 (비)…北 (북)…此 (차)
甲 (갑)…申 (신)	暑 (서)…署 (서)	瓜 (과)…爪 (조)	囚 (수)…因 (인)…困 (곤)
名 (명)…各 (각)	枯 (고)…姑 (고)	不 (불)…丕 (비)	戊 (무)…戌 (수)…戌 (술)

COMMONLY ABBREVIATED CHARACTERS

〔가〕假—仮	讀—読	〔쌍〕雙—双	〔위〕圍—囲	〔체〕體—体
價—価	〔래〕來—来	〔서〕敍—叙	〔응〕應—応	〔촉〕觸—触
〔거〕擧—挙	〔량〕兩—両	〔석〕釋—釈	〔의〕醫—医	〔충〕蟲—虫
〔경〕經—経	〔련〕戀—恋	〔성〕聲—声	〔이〕貳—弐	衝—冲
輕—軽	〔례〕禮—礼	〔속〕屬—属	〔일〕壹—壱	〔취〕醉—酔
〔계〕繼—継	〔로〕勞—労	續—続	〔잔〕殘—残	〔치〕齒—歯
〔관〕館—舘	〔룡〕龍—竜	〔수〕收—収	〔잠〕蠶—蚕	恥—耻
關—関	〔루〕樓—楼	壽—寿	〔잡〕雜—雑	〔칭〕稱—称
〔광〕廣—広	〔만〕蠻—蛮	數—数	〔전〕戰—戦	〔택〕擇—択
〔구〕區—区	萬—万	〔숙〕肅—粛	轉—転	澤—沢
舊—旧	〔매〕賣—売	〔실〕實—実	〔점〕點—点	〔폐〕廢—廃
龜—亀	〔맥〕麥—麦	〔아〕亞—亜	〔제〕齊—斉	〔풍〕豐—豊
驅—駆	〔발〕發—発	兒—児	濟—済	〔학〕學—学
〔국〕國—国	〔배〕拜—拝	〔악〕惡—悪	〔주〕晝—昼	〔해〕解—觧
〔기〕氣—気	〔변〕變—変	〔암〕巖—岩	〔증〕證—証	〔허〕虛—虚
〔단〕團—団	辨—弁	〔압〕壓—圧	〔진〕眞—真	〔헌〕獻—献
斷—断	辯—弁	〔여〕與—与	盡—尽	〔호〕號—号
〔담〕擔—担	邊—辺	〔역〕驛—駅	〔찬〕贊—賛	〔화〕畫—画
〔당〕當—当	〔병〕竝—並	譯—訳	讚—讃	〔확〕擴—拡
黨—党	〔보〕寶—宝	〔염〕鹽—塩	〔책〕冊—册	〔환〕歡—歓
〔대〕對—対	〔불〕拂—払	〔영〕榮—栄	〔처〕處—処	〔회〕會—会
臺—台	佛—仏	〔예〕豫—予	〔철〕鐵—鉄	〔획〕劃—画
〔도〕圖—図	〔사〕寫—写	藝—芸	〔청〕靑—青	〔후〕後—后
〔독〕獨—独	辭—辞	〔원〕圓—円	廳—庁	〔효〕效—効

CHARACTERS WITH MULTIPLE READINGS

降	내릴 항복할	강 항	復	회복할 다시	복 부	識	알 기록할	식 지
更	다시 고칠	갱 경	否	아닐 막힐	부 비	惡	악할 미워할	악 오
車	수레	거 차	北	북녘 달아날	북 배	易	바꿀 쉬울	역 이
見	볼 드러날	견 현	狀	형상 문서	상 장	切	끊을 온통	절 체
金	쇠금 성	금 김	殺	죽일 감할	살 쇄	參	참여할 석	참 삼
茶	차	다 차	塞	변방 막을	새 색	則	법칙 곧	칙 즉
度	법 헤아릴	도 탁	索	찾을 쓸쓸할	색 삭	暴	사나울	폭 포
讀	읽을 귀절	독 두	省	살필 덜	성 생	便	편할 오줌	편 변
洞	마을 통할	동 통	數	수 자주	수 삭	行	갈 항렬	행 항
率	비 거느릴	률 솔	拾	주울 열	습 십	畫	그림 꾀할	화 획
樂	즐길 풍류 좋아할	락 악 요	說	말씀 달랠 기쁠	설 세 열	龜	본뜰 거북 갈라질	구 귀 균

THE 900 MIDDLE SCHOOL CHARACTERS IN TEXTBOOK ORDER

The list reads down from the left.

一	1	四	147	枝	516	字	238	多	232	族	956	雨	565	農	1320
日	95	東	510	仙	121	十	14	少	81	父	105	露	1769	業	1258
月	97	明	500	味	437	百	269	高	883	母	171	雪	1051	田	183
山	38	相	665	和	440	千	28	低	296	祖	824	喜	1071	路	1317
川	39	困	321	功	154	萬	1296	長	561	孫	740	怒	613	開	1200
火	104	林	512	歌	1372	億	1454	短	1143	兄	125	哀	409	設	1021
水	103	休	207	放	498	兆	209	強	1089	弟	339	樂	1497	耕	841
木	98	加	130	七	4	壹	1080	弱	756	姉	449	善	1070	作	301
土	30	好	237	庭	755	貳	1182	輕	1428	妹	450	惡	1094	穀	1510
二	8	五	54	園	1227	參	896	重	702	夫	78	是	632	秋	671
耳	277	孝	328	宇	242	拾	621	遠	1431	婦	910	非	567	收	252
目	189	友	75	花	552	方	94	深	977	子	35	自	280	種	1391
手	89	男	375	霜	1677	位	293	淺	978	女	34	然	1128	改	358
足	392	安	243	房	484	西	147	身	393	天	77	樹	1577	良	383
人	9	見	384	想	1237	南	584	體	1792	文	91	於	499	所	485
口	29	炎	531	忠	478	北	133	鼻	1449	地	231	松	511	得	929
心	86	習	1008	近	558	左	153	齒	1556	陰	1047	巖	1784	增	1458
力	13	武	517	賞	1537	右	145	皮	188	陽	1202	石	192	植	1118
三	17	兵	304	案	791	内	60	骨	882	星	628	草	851	造	1038
上	18	里	402	聞	1404	外	149	血	285	辰	396	海	800	有	256
中	49	六	62	八	11	前	581	肉	278	風	707	洋	646	實	1357
下	20	江	264	竹	270	後	612	首	710	雲	1209	河	519	原	729
本	169	村	365	九	6	大	33	尾	331	寒	1083	湖	1125	始	452
末	168	注	529	數	1489	小	37	家	744	暑	1252	秀	377	病	817

世 113	現 986	夜 443	貧 1025	利 309	生 181	誠 1420	蟲 1696
代 122	視 1174	讀 1780	貞 695	經 1282	產 988	信 577	害 743
春 633	鄉 1330	等 1151	淑 975	決 368	技 356	義 1287	防 403
細 1003	太 79	受 435	純 833	算 1394	料 775	臣 279	止 99
青 566	極 1259	惠 1095	潔 1503	要 692	製 1415	烈 809	伐 206
白 187	無 1129	均 322	言 386	給 1160	工 40	士 31	採 943
夕 32	建 609	完 329	論 1535	消 806	施 627	爲 1130	禁 1279
煙 1268	理 987	備 1061	由 184	約 675	基 906	國 902	綠 1397
靜 1623	念 480	終 1005	說 1424	活 652	立 196	節 1514	化 68
晚 960	韓 1678	如 235	記 858	素 838	授 941	商 900	保 576
鐘 1755	歷 1581	老 274	者 678	發 1139	學 1564	品 590	氣 796
城 734	史 143	思 714	事 406	度 608	登 1138	價 1451	盛 1141
滿 1373	主 116	之 51	取 433	成 347	校 782	賣 1541	夏 736
爭 532	意 1240	恩 764	材 363	用 182	席 752	買 1184	暴 1490
富 1082	識 1722	朋 506	報 1077	厚 586	呼 438	入 10	嚴 1738
興 1597	課 1530	結 1158	號 1301	民 172	歸 1685	支 90	冬 127
亡 25	片 106	馬 881	送 867	福 1390	卒 430	出 128	波 527
吉 222	丹 50	己 41	共 213	尊 1085	故 626	易 501	溫 1266
凶 64	守 241	莫 1015	鳴 1448	敬 1249	知 541	都 1194	聖 1288
勝 1065	運 1324	逆 869	書 778	賢 1538	新 1250	散 1105	君 315
敗 953	動 893	交 197	特 810	貴 1183	修 714	市 156	德 1473
過 1325	未 167	居 465	筆 1150	正 170	治 521	場 1079	行 286
失 151	年 247	危 218	柔 638	直 540	平 158	道 1329	美 677
益 819	獨 1590	殺 795	虛 1167	親 1602	先 210	揚 1099	勇 582
減 1124	歲 1260	仁 57	傳 1218	愛 1241	公 61	投 353	將 917
反 74	布 157	救 952	畫 958	清 981	私 378	分 65	名 224

每 367	常 922	宿 913	令 123	使 410	申 186	進 1193	可 144
去 137	坐 323	佛 300	絲 1162	命 439	請 1534	就 1086	否 316
因 228	臥 550	寺 244	敢 1103	榮 1370	再 214	歡 1776	曲 255
果 515	起 862	走 391	比 100	協 431	質 1542	悅 767	問 901
永 174	判 307	往 475	官 459	同 223	應 1636	幸 469	眞 820
久 22	初 1786	鳥 1056	養 1554	神 826	答 1153	泰 797	探 944
恒 618	變 481	舉 1639	打 164	扶 350	表 556	斗 92	究 379
驚 1790	性 346	勸 1737	追 865	助 310	半 134	效 774	調 1532
異 991	快 208	野 1043	間 1197	崇 920	彼 476	情 934	考 275
移 996	充 560	菜 1165	願 1734	尚 464	此 260	限 703	察 1354
集 1207	金 672	栽 785	顏 1707	郎 871	兩 419	關 1729	證 1721
朝 1115	科 177	貯 1181	面 704	以 124	古 138	責 1030	向 227
暮 1491	玉 597	落 1297	洗 647	戰 1569	典 422	形 340	欲 969
遇 1321	威 597	米 271	浴 804	退 866	遺 1615	通 1034	速 1035
頂 1052	街 1169	茂 690	室 600	英 691	訓 857	聽 1777	不 47
門 562	頭 1624	豐 1698	傷 1221	雄 1205	音 706	電 1334	達 1326
針 876	妙 325	墨 1457	處 1016	匹 69	香 711	話 1310	界 657
唯 897	續 1762	黑 258	復 1090	刀 12	漢 1377	紙 834	來 412
乾 885	定 463	朱 1693	舊 1693	對 1358	元 59	便 571	計 694
坤 442	試 1306	赤 390	練 1517	敵 1488	食 709	至 281	希 333
篇 1516	競 1745	虎 555	觀 1799	壯 324	端 1393	急 617	望 962
律 611	畫 1135	死 261	光 211	最 1112	午 108	回 229	渴 1121
苦 689	展 747	留 814	旅 776	統 1157	教 950	仰 200	志 344
迎 557	示 193	悟 769	奉 446	軍 698	育 546	眾 1168	堅 1078
服 507	也 23	感 1243	仕 119	陸 1045	章 998	會 1255	固 441
熱 1506	從 931	泣 526	貨 1027	空 544	的 538	議 1752	精 1396

與	1295	順	1212	着	1142	鷄	1773	慶	1477	暖	1253	別	308	壽	1349
看	666	哉	591	脫	1011	卵	313	祝	825	期	1114	幼	159	醫	1701
物	534	誰	1529	淨	973	乘	712	杯	509	到	423	客	598	藥	1720
戶	88	何	299	飯	1338	除	880	賀	1188	降	877	船	1012	眼	992
堂	907	根	786	麥	1058	徒	759	招	497	伏	204	停	887	免	303
句	140	指	624	混	976	絕	1159	訪	1022	昌	503	車	394	許	1023
色	284	而	276	飲	1337	烏	808	拜	620	容	745	序	335	廣	1467
又	16	合	221	宅	240	飛	708	禮	1688	冷	305	列	216	告	320
景	1110	財	861	瓦	179	角	385	謝	1668	甚	656	王	110	持	622
燈	1588	稅	1147	屋	602	圓	1228	祭	995	溪	1263	鮮	1680	讓	1794
黃	1213	銀	1434	致	847	線	1520	酒	875	谷	287	法	525	步	366
楓	1257	店	473	誤	1423	式	248	他	118	浪	803	政	625	連	1037
紅	674	油	520	愁	1238	京	409	犬	109	吹	317	權	1775	量	1195
葉	1299	羊	272	惜	936	各	220	勞	1066	氷	173	務	894	部	1042
佳	411	毛	101	喪	1073	郡	872	破	822	解	1305	求	369	笑	830
接	947	貝	389	怨	616	邑	397	勢	1224	泉	645	刑	215	亦	199
更	361	錢	1619	恨	619	洞	649	漁	1379	尤	82	領	1443	單	1074
猶	1131	借	719	罪	1285	鐵	1768	聲	1662	餘	1626	島	749	但	294
盡	1386	執	904	慈	1236	橋	1578	語	1421	師	751	勿	67	只	139
難	1731	個	716	悲	1092	豆	388	印	219	皆	662	凡	26	須	1210
及	73	能	843	必	162	憂	1481	胸	842	且	112	例	717	則	580
時	777	省	668	若	686	患	932	全	212	余	298	或	483	著	1300
當	1272	忍	343	牛	108	尺	83	密	916	曰	96	適	1549	暗	1254
勉	583	衣	287	井	55	童	1149	閉	1044	汝	266	巨	155	宙	462
待	610	住	297	我	348	華	1166	眠	821	乎	117	腳	1009	射	746
勤	1225	既	957	引	85	婚	908	季	362	倫	723	其	420	姓	453

番	1134	庚	472	講	1667	俗	575	抱	487	凉	727	逢	1039	宗	461
窓	997	辛	395	圖	1345	談	1531	偉	883	流	798	妻	451	甘	180
諸	1603	壬	76	研	669	選	1613	皇	663	吟	314	假	886	冊	126
云	52	癸	661	推	948	卷	432	帝	605	晴	1109	存	239	乃	5
幾	1088	丑	48	憶	1568	寸	36	今	56	浮	801	已	42	雖	1676
千	44	寅	914	認	1417	卽	585	昔	505	舞	1407	忘	345	矣	376
甲	185	卯	136	題	1706	早	253	弓	45	在	230	魚	1055	吾	319
乙	2	巳	43	硯	1145	昨	631	忙	249	遊	1323	舍	551		
丙	115	酉	401	藝	1719	曾	1111	閑	1199	叔	434	依	416		
丁	3	戌	250	承	486	才	46	詩	1307	氏	102	兒	418		
戊	163	亥	198	于	24	第	1000	柳	641	次	259	唱	898		

INDEX

HOW TO USE A CHARACTER DICTIONARY INDEX

Access to the characters in a *hanja* dictionary is possible through a phonetic index, a stroke-count index or a radical index. Each of these is explained below. Beginning students may find the use of a radical arrangement difficult until they have mastered basic characters.

Phonetic Index. Characters are listed in this type of index in *hangŭl* alphabetical order. This order appears as the first column of the Syllable Practice Chart at the inside back cover. A phonetic index is simple to use but suffers from limited utility because a character can be located only if its reading is already known.

Stroke-count Index. Characters are listed in this type of index according to the number of separate strokes used to write them. There is no need for such an index in this book because the 1,800 Basic *Hanja* in the main section are already arranged in stroke-count order. To find a character in a stroke-count arrangement, simply count its strokes, turn to the section in which *hanja* of that stroke count are grouped and locate the target graph. Characters are listed in radical order within each section. It is not uncommon to miscount strokes, so if a character is not in one stroke-count section, peruse the two adjacent sections.

Radical Index. Character dictionaries are divided into 214 sections. Each section is headed by a radical, or "section head," which appears as a common element in every character within its section. The order of the 214 radicals is firmly fixed according to ascending stroke count.

To find a character in a radical arrangement, it is first necessary to estimate which part of the target character serves as its radical. Familiarity with the radicals will facilitate this task, and it is generally the case that the left-hand or topmost component of a character serves as its radical. After settling on the radical, count its strokes and pick it out of the index from among other radicals with the same stroke count. The index will indicate the page of the dictionary proper where the desired radical section begins. Next, determine the stroke count of the non-radical portion of the target graph. Characters are listed in each radical section according to the stroke count of their non-radical portions, so it is a simple matter to locate a target graph among characters within a section which share a like stroke count.

Let's assume we want to find the character, 明, in a dictionary. By inspection, we take 日 as the radical because it is the left-hand element. We see that our radical is composed of four strokes, so we locate it among other four-stroke radicals in the index and turn from there to the page in the dictionary proper where the 日 radical section begins. The non-radical portion of 明 is 月 and also has four strokes. It is not difficult to locate 明 among the characters listed in the 日 radical section which have four strokes in their non-radical portions.

Commonly-Abbreviated Radicals

Abbreviated radicals appear below in stroke-count order. The original form of a radical is listed to the right of each abbreviation and is followed by its stroke count (where different) to facilitate use of the following radical index.

1 stroke		扌	手 (4)	⺥	爪	⺲	网 (6)
乚	乙 (1)	氵	水 (4)	牜	牛	衤	衣 (6)
2 strokes		犭	犬 (4)	王	玉 (5)	**6 strokes**	
亻	人	阝 (right)	邑 (7)	礻	示 (5)	羊	羊
刂	刀	阝 (left)	阜 (8)	罒	网 (6)	**7 strokes**	
㔾	卩	⺊	艸 (6)	耂	老 (6)	𧾷	足
3 strokes		**4 strokes**		月	肉 (6)	長	長 (8)
兀	尢	忄	心	⺿	艸 (6)	**9 strokes**	
川	巛	攵	攴	辶	辵 (7)	𩙿	食
彑	彐	旡	无	**5 strokes**			
忄	心 (4)	灬	火	⺫	目		

RADICAL INDEX

Radicals are listed in this index only under their original forms. Refer to the chart on the preceding page to determine the original form of an abbreviated radical.

1 Stroke	了 7	住 297	佐 295	元 59	凍 726	功 131
一	予 111	但 294	伯 290	兄 125	几	加 130
一 1	**2 Strokes**	低 296	伸 291	充 208	凡 26	勇 582
丁 3	二	余 298	供 414	兆 209	凵	助 310
七 4	二 8	何 299	侍 415	光 211	凶 64	勉 583
三 17	于 24	位 293	侵 569	先 210	出 128	動 893
下 20	五 54	作 301	係 572	免 303	刀(刂)	務 894
上 18	井 55	佛 300	俊 573	兒 418	刀 12	勞 1066
不 47	云 52	來 412	促 574	兔 417	分 65	勝 1065
丑 48	互 53	例 413	侯 570	克 302	刑 215	勤 1225
丙 115	亞 407	依 416	倍 718	入	列 216	勢 1224
世 113	亠	佳 411	倒 717	入 10	初 306	勸 1737
丘 114	亡 25	使 410	候 721	内 60	判 307	劣 217
丈 19	亦 199	俗 575	俱 713	全 212	別 308	努 311
且 112	亥 198	保 576	值 722	兩 419	利 309	募 1223
丨	交 197	便 571	倉 715	八	到 423	勵 1632
中 49	京 409	信 577	做 720	八 11	前 581	勹
丶	亨 289	倫 723	健 889	公 61	則 580	勿 67
丹 50	享 408	借 719	側 890	六 62	刃 27	包 132
主 116	亭 568	修 714	偶 891	共 213	切 66	匕
丸 21	人(亻)	個 716	傑 1062	兵 304	刊 129	化 68
丿	人 9	偉 888	傍 1060	典 422	券 426	北 133
乃 5	仁 57	停 887	催 1216	其 420	制 424	匚
久 22	今 56	假 886	僅 1220	兮 63	刷 425	匹 69
之 51	仙 121	備 1061	傾 1222	具 421	削 579	區 895
乎 117	以 124	傳 1218	債 1219	兼 724	刺 427	十
乘 712	仕 119	傷 1221	傲 1217	冂	剛 728	十 14
乙(乚)	令 123	億 1454	像 1340	冊 126	副 892	千 28
乙 2	他 118	價 1451	僞 1342	再 214	創 1064	午 71
九 6	代 122	介 58	僧 1341	冖	割 1063	半 134
乾 885	伏 204	付 120	儉 1453	冠 578	劇 1455	卒 430
也 23	伐 206	仲 201	儀 1452	冥 725	劍 1456	協 431
乳 405	休 207	件 202	儒 1557	冫	刻 428	南 584
亂 121	仰 200	企 203	優 1631	冬 127	劃 1343	升 70
亅		任 205	償 1630	冷 305	力	卑 429
事 406		似 292	儿	涼 727	力 13	博 1067

卜		名	224	善	1070	奉	446	壁	1560	執	911	小	
卜	15	各	220	喉	1072	央	150	壓	1633	學	1564	小	37
占	135	同	223	啓	899	夷	233	壞	1711	孔	80	少	81
卩(㔾)		向	227	嘗	1344	奈	445	壤	1739	孟	456	尚	464
卯	136	吉	222	鳴	1226	奇	444	女		孤	458	尖	245
危	218	合	221	器	1559	奔	447	女	34	宀		尢(兀)	
印	219	吾	319	噫	1558	契	592	好	237	宇	242	尤	82
卵	313	君	315	囗		奚	737	如	235	宅	240	就	1086
卷	432	告	320	四	147	獎	1351	妙	325	安	243	尸	
即	585	否	316	回	229	奪	1352	妻	451	守	241	尺	83
卻	312	吹	317	因	228	奮	1563	妾	448	完	329	尾	331
卿	1068	吟	314	困	321	土		姓	453	官	459	居	465
厂		味	437	固	441	土	30	姊	449	宙	462	屋	602
厚	586	和	440	國	902	地	231	始	452	定	463	展	747
原	729	命	439	圓	1228	在	230	妹	450	宗	461	局	330
厄	72	呼	438	園	1227	坐	323	威	597	室	600	屈	466
厥	1069	哀	588	圖	1345	坤	442	婦	910	宣	599	屏	603
又		品	590	囚	148	均	322	婚	908	客	598	屢	1359
又	16	問	901	圍	1075	城	734	奴	152	害	743	層	1464
反	74	商	900	團	1346	基	906	妄	236	家	744	履	1465
友	75	唯	897	士		執	904	妃	234	容	745	屬	1766
及	73	唱	898	士	31	培	905	妨	326	密	916	寸	
叔	434	喜	1071	壯	324	堅	1078	妥	327	宿	913	寸	36
取	433	喪	1073	壬	76	堂	907	姑	454	寅	914	寺	244
受	435	單	1074	壹	1080	場	1079	姪	596	寒	1083	射	746
叛	587	嚴	1738	壽	1349	報	1077	姻	593	富	1082	將	917
厶		召	142	夕		增	1458	姦	594	實	1357	尊	1085
去	137	司	146	夕	32	墨	1457	姿	595	察	1354	對	1358
參	896	叫	141	外	149	埋	735	娘	738	宜	460	封	601
		吐	226	多	232	域	903	娛	739	宴	742	尋	1084
3 Strokes		吏	225	夢	1350	堤	1076	婢	909	宮	741	專	918
		周	436	夜	443	塞	1231	媒	1081	寄	915	導	1565
口		咸	589	夂		塔	1229	委	455	寂	912	山	
口	29	含	404	夏	736	塊	1230	子		寧	1356	山	38
古	138	吸	318	大		境	1348	子	35	寡	1355	島	749
可	144	哉	591	大	33	墓	1347	存	239	寢	1353	崇	920
右	145	員	732	天	77	墮	1459	字	238	審	1462	巖	1784
史	143	哭	731	太	79	墳	1460	孝	328	寬	1461	岳	468
只	139	哲	730	夫	78	壇	1562	季	457	寫	1463	岸	467
句	140	唐	733	失	151	墙	1561	孫	740	寶	1740	峯	748

崩	919	幣	1466	張	927	怒	613	惟	937	戒	349	拔	494
嶺	1634	广		彈	1471	怨	616	愚	1242	威	938	拳	770
巛(川)		序	335	彡		急	617	愈	1239	戲	1637	挑	623
川	39	店	473	形	340	性	481	惱	1096	支		振	773
州	246	庚	472	彩	928	恩	764	慎	1245	支	90	捉	772
巡	332	度	608	影	1472	恨	619	愧	1244	手(扌)		捕	771
工		庭	755	彳		恆	618	態	1361	手	89	掛	945
工	40	廣	1467	往	475	悅	767	慕	1476	才	46	掃	939
左	153	床	334	彼	476	患	932	慧	1478	打	164	捨	940
巨	155	底	470	待	610	悟	769	慢	1363	承	486	掌	1097
巧	154	府	471	後	612	惜	936	慨	1365	投	353	掠	946
差	750	庫	754	律	611	情	934	慣	1366	技	356	排	942
幺		座	753	徒	759	悲	1092	慘	1364	扶	350	換	1101
幼	159	庸	924	得	929	惡	1094	慾	1480	抱	487	揮	1100
幾	1088	庶	925	從	931	惠	1095	慚	1362	拜	620	援	1102
幽	607	康	926	復	1090	意	1240	慮	1479	招	497	提	1098
干		廊	1233	德	1473	愛	1241	憲	1566	持	622	攜	1248
干	44	廉	1234	役	341	愁	1238	憎	1483	拾	621	損	1247
平	158	廟	1468	征	477	想	1237	慰	1482	指	624	搖	1246
年	247	廢	1469	徑	758	感	1243	憤	1486	採	943	摘	1367
幸	469	廳	1797	徐	757	慈	1236	憫	1485	探	944	播	1487
幹	1232	廴		御	930	憂	1481	憐	1484	接	947	操	1571
己		建	609	循	1091	慶	1477	懇	1635	授	941	擇	1570
己	41	延	337	微	1235	憩	1567	懲	1712	推	948	據	1573
巳	43	廷	336	徵	1475	應	1636	懸	1741	揚	1099	擴	1683
已	42	廾		徹	1474	憶	1568	懷	1713	舉	1639	擔	1572
巷	604	弄	338			忌	342	懼	1759	托	251	擊	1638
巾		弊	1470	**4 Strokes**		忽	479	戀	1785	批	351	支(攵)	
布	157	弋		心(忄,⺗)		怠	615	戶		抑	354	收	252
市	156	式	248	心	86	怪	482	戶	88	折	357	改	358
希	333	弓		必	162	恣	761	所	485	抄	352	政	625
帝	605	弓	45	忍	343	耻	763	房	484	抗	355	放	498
席	752	引	85	志	344	恐	762	戈		拒	491	故	626
師	751	弟	339	忙	249	恭	765	戊	163	拘	495	效	774
常	922	弱	756	忘	345	恕	760	戍	250	拓	493	敗	953
帥	606	強	1089	忠	478	息	766	我	348	拍	492	救	952
帶	923	弔	84	念	480	悠	933	成	347	抽	489	教	950
帳	921	弘	160	快	346	悔	768	或	483	拂	490	敢	1103
幅	1087	弗	161	忠	478	悽	935	戰	1569	抵	488	散	1105
幕	1360	弦	474	思	614	惑	1093	戈	87	拙	496		

潮 1504
潛 1500
濃 1585
澤 1582
激 1584
濁 1583
濫 1643
濯 1644
濕 1642
濟 1645
波 527

火 (灬)
火 104
炎 531
烏 808
烈 809
無 1129
然 1128
煙 1268
熱 1506
燈 1588
灰 268
災 374
炭 654
焉 982
熙 1269
煩 1271
照 1270
熟 1505
燒 1587
燕 1589
燃 1586
燥 1646
營 1648
燭 1647
爐 1742
爆 1714
爛 1761

爪 (爫)
爭 532

爲 1130
爵 1686
父
父 105
片
片 106
版 533
牙
牙 107
牛 (牜)
牛 108
物 534
特 810
牧 535
犬 (犭)
犬 109
獨 1590
犯 175
狀 536
狗 537
猛 983
猶 1131
獄 1385
獲 1649
獸 1715
獻 1743

5 Strokes

玉 (王)
王 110
玉 177
理 987
現 986
珍 655
班 812
球 985
琴 1133
琢 1132
環 1650

玄
玄 176
玆 811
率 984
瓜
瓜 178
瓦
瓦 179
甘
甘 180
甚 656
生
生 181
產 988
用
用 182
田
田 183
甲 185
申 186
由 184
男 375
界 657
留 814
異 991
畫 1135
番 1134
當 1272
畏 659
奮 658
畜 813
略 990
畢 989
畿 1507
疋
疏 1136
疑 1384
疒
病 817
疫 660

疲 816
疾 815
症 818
痛 1137
癶
癸 661
登 1138
發 1139
白
白 187
百 269
的 538
皆 662
皇 663
皮
皮 188
皿
益 819
盛 1141
盜 1140
盟 1273
盡 1386
監 1387
盤 1508
目 (罒)
目 189
省 668
直 540
盾 664
相 665
看 666
眠 821
眞 820
眼 992
着 1142
盲 539
眉 667
睦 1275
督 1276
睡 1274

瞬 1651
矛
矛 190
矢
矢 191
知 541
短 1143
矣 376
矯 1652
石
石 192
研 669
破 822
硯 1145
硬 1144
碑 1277
碧 1388
確 1509
磨 1591
礎 1687
示
示 193
神 826
祖 824
祝 825
祭 995
禁 1279
福 1390
禮 1688
社 543
祀 542
祈 670
秘 823
票 993
祥 994
祿 1278
禍 1389
禪 1653
内
禽 1280

禾
禾 194
秀 377
秋 671
科 672
移 996
稅 1147
種 1391
穀 1510
私 378
秩 828
租 827
稀 1146
程 1148
稚 1281
稱 1392
稻 1512
稿 1511
積 1592
穫 1716
穴
穴 195
究 379
空 544
窓 997
突 673
窮 1513
立
立 196
章 998
童 1149
端 1393
競 1745
竝 829
竟 999

6 Strokes

缶
缺 839

网 (罒)
罔 545
罪 1285
置 1284
署 1403
罰 1402
罷 1524
羅 1718
羊
羊 272
美 677
義 1287
群 1286
羽
羽 273
習 1008
翁 840
翼 1659
老
老 274
考 275
者 678
而
而 276
耐 679
耒
耕 841
耳
耳 277
聖 1288
聞 1404
聲 1662
聽 1777
耶 680
聘 1289
聰 1661
聯 1660
職 1692
聿
肅 1290

353

肉(月)	興 1597	莊 1013	第 1000	絃 1006	裏 1303	語 1421
肉 278	舊 1693	菊 1163	答 1153	結 1158	裝 1304	說 1424
育 546	舌	菌 1164	等 1151	給 1160	裳 1414	誤 1423
能 843	舌 282	葬 1298	策 1152	絡 1161	複 1416	認 1417
胸 842	舍 551	蒙 1408	筆 1150	絲 1162	襲 1779	誠 1420
脚 1009	舛	蓋 1412	管 1395	絕 1159	行	論 1535
脫 1011	舞 1407	蒼 1410	算 1394	統 1157	行 286	談 1531
肖 381	舟	蒸 1409	範 1515	絹 1283	街 1169	課 1530
肝 382	舟 283	蓄 1411	節 1514	經 1282	衝 1528	誰 1529
肥 547	船 1012	蔬 1598	篇 1516	綱 1398	衛 1601	請 1534
肺 684	般 849	蓮 1526	篤 1593	緊 1401	術 1018	調 1532
肩 548	航 848	蔽 1599	築 1594	綠 1397	襾	諸 1603
胃 681	艮	薦 1665	簡 1689	綿 1400	西 288	謝 1668
肯 549	良 383	薄 1664	簿 1717	維 1399	要 692	講 1667
胡 682	色	藏 1694	籍 1744	練 1517		證 1721
背 683	色 284	藍 1695	米	緒 1518	**7 Strokes**	識 1722
胞 685	艸(艹)	蘇 1747	米 271	緯 1522	見	議 1752
脅 844	花 552	蘭 1763	粉 831	編 1523	見 384	讀 1780
脈 845	苦 689	虍	粟 781	縣 1596	視 1174	變 1786
屑 1010	若 686	虎 555	粧 1154	繁 1658	親 1602	讓 1794
腐 1405	英 691	處 1016	精 1396	績 1656	觀 1799	訂 693
腦 1291	茂 690	虛 1167	糖 1595	縱 1654	覺 1749	討 856
腰 1292	草 851	號 1301	糧 1690	總 1657	覽 1764	訟 1020
腸 1294	莫 1015	虫	糸	縮 1655	角	評 1177
腹 1293	華 1166	蟲 1696	系 380	織 1691	角 385	詞 1178
膚 1525	菜 1165	蛇 1017	紀 676	繼 1746	解 1305	訴 1175
臟 1778	著 1300	蜂 1302	約 675	續 1762	觸 1748	詐 1176
臣	萬 1296	蜜 1413	紅 674	線 1520	言	詠 1179
臣 279	葉 1299	蝶 1527	級 835	緣 1519	言 386	詳 1309
臥 550	落 1297	營 1600	納 832	緩 1521	計 694	該 1308
臨 1663	藝 1719	蠱 1793	紛 837	衣(衤)	記 858	誇 1311
自	藥 1720	蠻 1798	索 836	衣 287	訓 857	誦 1422
自 280	芽 553	血	素 838	表 556	許 1023	誌 1418
臭 846	芳 554	血 285	純 833	製 1415	訪 1022	誘 1419
至	苟 688	衆 1168	紙 834	衰 854	設 1021	諒 1533
至 281	苗 687	竹	累 1004	被 855	詩 1307	謂 1607
致 847	茶 852	竹 270	細 1003	裂 1171	話 1310	謁 1606
臺 1406	茫 850	笑 830	紫 1156	裁 1170	試 1306	諾 1604
白	荒 853	符 1002	組 1007	補 1173		謀 1605
與 1295	荷 1014	笛 1001	終 1005	裕 1172		謠 1666

謙 1669	販 1029	軟 1031	返 559	酸 1432	閉 1044	雌 1332
謹 1697	貪 1026	較 1318	述 700	醜 1673	間 1197	雜 1704
譜 1723	貿 1187	載 1319	迫 699	醉 1551	閑 1199	雙 1705
警 1750	費 1186	輝 1547	迷 870	**采**	開 1200	離 1730
譯 1751	貸 1185	輪 1548	逃 868	釋 1754	關 1729	**雨**
護 1765	資 1314	輩 1546	途 1032	**里**	閏 1198	雨 565
譽 1753	賊 1312	輸 1610	逐 1036	里 402	閣 1438	雲 1209
讚 1800	賃 1313	輿 1670	透 1033	重 702	閨 1437	雪 1051
谷	賓 1427	轉 1700	遂 1322	野 1043	**阜(⻖)**	電 1334
谷 387	賦 1536	**辛**	逸 1192	量 1195	防 403	霜 1677
豆	賜 1539	辛 395	遍 1327		限 703	露 1769
豆 388	賤 1540	辨 1611	違 1328	**8 Strokes**	降 877	雷 1335
豐 1698	贊 1725	辯 1767	過 1325	**金**	除 880	零 1333
豈 859	賴 1609	辭 1726	遙 1429	金 560	陰 1047	需 1441
豕	贈 1724	**辰**	遣 1430	針 876	陸 1045	霧 1732
象 1180	**赤**	辰 396	遲 1612	銀 1434	陽 1202	靈 1795
豚 1024	赤 390	農 1320	遷 1550	錢 1619	阿 564	**青**
豪 1425	**走**	辱 864	邊 1614	鐘 1755	附 563	青 566
豫 1608	走 396	**辵(辶)**	避 1672	鐵 1768	陣 879	靜 1623
豸	起 862	近 558	還 1671	鉛 1331	院 878	**非**
貌 1426	赴 697	迎 557	邊 1727	鈍 1196	陵 1049	非 567
貝	超 1189	送 867	**邑(⻏)**	銅 1436	陶 1048	
貝 389	越 1190	追 865	邑 397	銘 1435	陳 1050	**9 Strokes**
貞 695	趣 1543	退 866	郎 871	銃 1433	陷 1046	
財 861	**足(⻊)**	逆 869	郡 872	銳 1552	隊 1203	**面**
責 1030	足 392	通 1034	鄉 1330	鎖 1703	隆 1201	面 704
貨 1027	路 1317	逢 1039	部 1042	錦 1620	階 1204	**革**
貧 1025	距 1191	連 1037	都 1194	錯 1618	際 1439	革 705
貯 1181	跳 1316	速 1035	邦 399	錄 1616	障 1440	**韋**
貴 1183	跡 1315	造 1038	那 400	鋼 1617	鄰 1553	韓 1678
買 1184	踐 1545	進 1193	邪 398	鍊 1674	隨 1622	**頁**
貳 1182	踏 1544	道 1329	郊 701	鎮 1702	險 1621	頂 1052
賀 1188	蹟 1699	遇 1321	郭 1041	鏡 1728	隱 1675	順 1212
賣 1541	**身**	運 1324	郵 1040	鑛 1787	**隹**	須 1210
質 1542	身 393	遊 1323	**酉**	鑑 1781	集 1207	領 1443
賢 1538	**車**	達 1326	酉 401	**長(镸)**	雄 1205	頭 1624
賞 1537	車 394	遠 1431	酒 875	長 561	雁 1208	顏 1707
負 696	軍 698	適 1549	醫 1701	**門**	雉 1676	題 1706
貢 860	輕 1428	選 1613	配 873	門 562	難 1731	願 1734
貫 1028	軒 863	遺 1615	酌 874		雅 1206	頃 1053

PHONETIC INDEX

Hangŭl alphabetical order: ㄱ, ㄴ, ㄷ, ㄹ, ㅁ, ㅂ, ㅅ, ㅇ(아, 어, 오, 우, 으, 이), ㅈ, ㅊ, ㅋ, ㅌ, ㅍ, ㅎ

【ㄱ】

〔가〕
家 744
佳 411
街 1169
可 144
歌 1372
加 130
價 1451
假 886
架 635
暇 1251

〔각〕
各 220
角 385
脚 1009
閣 1438
却 312
覺 1749
刻 428

〔간〕
干 44
間 1197
看 666
刊 129
肝 382
幹 1232
簡 1689
姦 594
懇 1635

〔갈〕
渴 1121

〔감〕
甘 180
減 1124
感 1243
敢 1103
監 1387
鑑 1781

〔갑〕
甲 185

〔강〕
江 264
降 877
講 1667
強 1089
康 926
剛 728
鋼 1617
綱 1398

〔개〕
豈 859
改 358
皆 662
個 716
開 1200
介 58
慨 1365
概 1494
蓋 1412

〔객〕
客 598

〔갱〕
更 361

〔거〕
去 137
巨 155
居 465
車 394
擧 1639
距 1191
拒 491
據 1573

〔건〕
建 609
乾 885
件 202
健 889

〔걸〕
傑 1062

〔검〕
儉 1453
劍 1456
檢 1641

〔게〕
憩 1567

〔격〕
格 788
擊 1638
激 1584

〔견〕
犬 109
見 384
堅 1078
肩 548
絹 1283
遣 1430

〔결〕
決 368
結 1158
潔 1503
缺 839

〔겸〕
兼 724
謙 1669

〔경〕
京 409
景 1110
輕 1428
經 1282
庚 472
耕 841
敬 1249
驚 1790
慶 1477
競 1745
竟 999
鏡 1728
頃 1053
境 1348
更 361
傾 1222
硬 1144
警 1750
徑 758
卿 1068

〔계〕
癸 661
季 457
界 657
計 694
溪 1263
鷄 1773
系 380
戒 349
械 968
繼 1746
契 592
桂 787
啓 899
階 1204
係 572

〔고〕
古 138
故 626
固 441
考 275
高 883
告 320
苦 689
姑 454
庫 754
孤 458
稿 1511
顧 1770
枯 634
鼓 1339

〔곡〕
谷 387
曲 255
穀 1510
哭 731

〔곤〕
困 321
坤 442

〔골〕
骨 882

〔공〕
工 40
功 131
空 544
共 213
公 61
孔 80
供 414
恭 765
攻 359
恐 762
貢 860

〔과〕
果 515
課 1530
科 672
過 1325
戈 87
瓜 178
誇 1311
寡 1355

〔곽〕
郭 1041

〔관〕
觀 1799
關 1729
官 459
館 1679
管 1395
貫 1028
慣 1366
冠 578
寬 1461

〔광〕
光 211
廣 1467
鑛 1787

〔괘〕
掛 945

〔괴〕
塊 1230
愧 1244
怪 482
壞 1711

〔교〕
交 197
校 782
橋 1578
教 950
郊 701
較 1318
巧 154
矯 1652

〔구〕
九 6
口 29
求 369
救 952
究 379
久 22
句 140
舊 1693
構 1371
具 421
俱 713
區 895
驅 1772
鷗 1783
苟 688
拘 495
狗 537
丘 114
懼 1759
龜 1710
球 985

〔국〕
國 902
菊 1163
局 330

〔군〕
君 315
郡 872
軍 698
群 1286

〔굴〕
屈 466

〔궁〕
弓 45
宮 741
窮 1513

〔권〕	〔급〕	【ㄴ】	〔능〕	大 33	敦 1104	欄 1760
卷 432	及 73		能 843	代 122	〔돌〕	爛 1761
權 1775	給 1160	〔나〕	〔니〕	待 610	突 673	〔람〕
勸 1737	急 617	那 400	泥 528	對 1358	〔동〕	覽 1764
券 426	級 835	奈 445		帶 923	洞 649	藍 1695
拳 770	〔궁〕	〔낙〕	【ㄷ】	臺 1406	同 223	濫 1643
〔궐〕	肯 549	諾 1604		貸 1185	童 1149	〔랑〕
厥 1069	〔기〕	〔난〕	〔다〕	隊 1203	冬 127	浪 803
〔귀〕	己 41	暖 1253	多 232	〔댁〕	東 510	郎 871
貴 1183	記 858	難 1731	茶 852	宅 240	動 893	朗 961
歸 1685	起 862	〔남〕	〔단〕	〔덕〕	銅 1436	廊 1233
鬼 884	其 420	南 584	丹 50	德 1473	桐 790	〔래〕
句 140	期 1114	男 375	但 294	〔도〕	凍 726	來 412
龜 1710	基 906	〔납〕	單 1074	刀 12	〔두〕	〔랭〕
〔규〕	氣 796	納 832	短 1143	到 423	斗 92	冷 305
叫 141	技 356	〔낭〕	端 1393	度 608	豆 388	〔략〕
規 1019	幾 1088	娘 738	旦 166	道 1329	頭 1624	略 990
閨 1437	旣 957	〔내〕	段 644	島 749	讀 1780	掠 946
〔균〕	紀 676	內 60	檀 1640	徒 759	〔둔〕	〔량〕
均 322	忌 342	乃 5	壇 1562	都 1194	鈍 1196	良 383
菌 1164	旗 1368	奈 445	斷 1684	圖 1345	〔득〕	兩 419
龜 1710	欺 1119	耐 679	團 1346	倒 717	得 929	量 1195
〔극〕	奇 444	〔녀〕	〔달〕	挑 623	〔등〕	凉 727
極 1259	騎 1709	女 34	達 1326	桃 789	等 1151	梁 963
克 302	豈 859	〔년〕	〔담〕	跳 1316	登 1138	糧 1690
劇 1455	寄 915	年 247	談 1531	逃 868	燈 1588	諒 1533
〔근〕	棄 1116	〔념〕	淡 974	渡 1123		〔려〕
近 558	祈 670	念 480	潭 1502	陶 1048	【ㄹ】	旅 776
勤 1225	企 203	〔녕〕	擔 1572	途 1032		麗 1736
根 786	畿 1507	寧 1356	〔답〕	稻 1512	〔라〕	慮 1479
斤 93	飢 1054	〔노〕	答 1153	導 1565	羅 1718	勵 1632
僅 1220	機 1579	怒 613	畓 658	盜 1140	〔락〕	〔력〕
謹 1697	器 1559	奴 152	踏 1544	〔독〕	落 1297	力 13
〔금〕	〔긴〕	努 311	〔당〕	讀 1780	樂 1497	歷 1581
金 560	緊 1401	〔농〕	堂 907	獨 1590	洛 648	曆 1576
今 56	〔길〕	農 1320	當 1272	毒 518	絡 1161	〔련〕
禁 1279	吉 222	濃 1585	唐 733	督 1276	〔란〕	連 1037
錦 1620	〔김〕	〔뇌〕	糖 1595	篤 1593	卵 313	練 1517
禽 1280	金 560	腦 1291	黨 1758	〔돈〕	亂 1215	鍊 1674
琴 1133		惱 1096	〔대〕	豚 1024	蘭 1763	憐 1484

358

SELECTED BIBLIOGRAPHY

Chang, Sam-sik, ed. *Comprehensive Chinese-Korean Dictionary* (tae han han sachŏn). Seoul: Sŏngmun Company, 1965.

DeFrancis, John. *Beginning Chinese Reader*, Part I. New Haven: Yale University Press, 1965.

High School Classical Korean Education Research Society, ed. *High School Classical Korean for Liberal Arts High Schools* (inmunkye kotŭng hakkyo: kotŭng hanmun). Seoul: Kongsin Publishing Company, 1973.

Kwŏn, Chung-ku. *General Principles of Classical Korean* (hanmun taekang). Seoul: Inu Printing Company, 1971.

Martin, Samuel E., ed. *New Korean-English Dictionary*. Seoul: Minjungseogwan, 1977.

Middle School Classical Korean Research Society, ed. *Middle School Classical Korean* (chunghak hanmun). Seoul: Minjungseogwan, 1972.

Min, Chae-sik, ed. *The New World Comprehensive Korean-English Dictionary* (nyu wŏld hanyŏng taesachŏn). Seoul: The Si-sa-yong-o Publishers, 1979.

Ministry of Education, Republic of Korea. *Middle School Classical Korean*, Volumes I, II and III (chunghak hanmun). Seoul: National Textbook Company, 1979.

Ministry of Education, Republic of Korea. *Study of Word Frequency in the Korean Language* (urimal malsu sayong'ŭi chatki chosa). Seoul: T'aesŏng Printing Company, 1956.

Nam, Kwang-u. *A Study of the Basic Characters for Educational Use Selected by the Ministry of Education* (munkyopu sŏnchŏng kyoyukyong kich'o hanja yŏnku). Seoul: Republic of Korea Textbook Company, 1972.

Song, Chong-man. *A New Explication of Sino-Korean Characters* (sinhae hanja). Seoul:Namhyang Munhwa Company, 1970.

Yi, Ka-wŏn. *New Lectures on Classical Korean* (hanmun sinkang). Seoul: Sinku Munhwa Company, 1973.

HANGŬL WRITING MODELS

Perpendicular strokes are written from top to bottom; horizontals from left to right. Strokes are not interrupted by a change of direction. (Read these charts left and down.)

ㄱ	ㄱ			ㅋ	ㄱㅋ		아	ㅇ ㅇ 아	의	ㅇ ㅡ 의
k				k'			a		ŭi	
ㄴ	ㄴ			ㅌ	ㅡ ㅌ ㅌ		어	ㅇ ㅇ 어	야	ㅇ ㅇ 아 / 야
n				t'			ŏ		ya	
ㄷ	ㄱ ㄷ			ㅍ	ㅡ ㅍ ㅍ		오	ㅇ ㅇ 오	여	ㅇ ㅇ ㅕ / 여
t				p'			o		yŏ	
ㄹ	ㄱ ㄱ ㄹ			ㅎ	ᐟ ㅡ ㅎ		우	ㅇ ㅇ 우	요	ㅇ ㅇ ㅛ / 요
r, l				h			u		yo	
ㅁ	ㅣ ㅁ ㅁ			ㄲ	ㄱ ㄲ		으	ㅇ ㅡ	유	ㅇ ㅡ 우 / 유
m				gg			ŭ		yu	
ㅂ	ㅣ ㅐ ㅐ / ㅐ			ㄸ	ㅡ ㄷ ㄷ / ㄸ		이	ㅇ ㅇ 이	와	ㅇ ㅇ 오 / 외 와
p				dd			i		wa	
ㅅ	ㅣ ㅅ			ㅃ	ㅣ ㅐ ㅐ / ㅂ ㅂㅣ ㅐ / ㅐ ㅃ		애	ㅇ ㅇ 아 아 / 애	왜	ㅇ ㅇ 오 / 외 와 왜
s				bb			ae		wae	
ㅇ	ㅇ			ㅆ	ㅣ ㅅ ㅅ / ㅆ		에	ㅇ ㅇ 어 / 에	워	ㅇ ㅡ 우 / 우 워
-ng				ss			e		wo	
ㅈ	ㄱ ㅈ			ㅉ	ㄱ ㅈ ㅈ / ㅉ		외	ㅇ ㅇ 오 / 외		
ch				jj			oe			
ㅊ	ᐟ ㅈ ㅊ						위	ㅇ ㅡ 우 / 위		
ch'							ui			